POWER IN THE BLOOD

RICHARD PORTER

POWER IN THE BLOOD

Biology as Key to Joining Philosophy, Faith and Science

iUniverse, Inc.
New York Bloomington

POWER IN THE BLOOD

Biology as Key to Joining Philosophy, Faith and Science

iUniverse books may be ordered through booksellers or by contacting:
iUniverse
1663 Liberty Drive
Bloomington, IN 47403
www.iuniverse.com
1-800-Authors (1-800-288-4677)

ISBN: 978-1-4502-2951-7 (pbk)
ISBN: 978-1-4502-2952-4 (ebk)
ISBN: 978-1-4502-2953-1 (hbk)

Printed in the United States of America
iUniverse rev. date: 5/3/10

Chapters

Preface

The intent and motivating purpose of this book is manifold, in accordance with the complicated issues it tries to explore. In part that purpose is to address the question of biological evolution from three angles, scientific, spiritual, and philosophical, and thereby illuminate a view of Nature and human nature contingent not upon causal constraints within the space-time continuum but defined by existential parameters, or axioms, that are endlessly true in metaphysical regions accessible to the mind, within whose landscape the Infinite can assume unlimited forms and aspects. The reality of that landscape, imbued with potentials that in Nature and human life can manifest, is what, in a manner mainly beyond our understanding, enables not only physical consciousness but organic life, and of the latter many strange and puzzling examples are presented by way of showing their relevance to the vision of a living Universe whose true proportions are immeasurable by any system of knowledge. That perspective grants humanity an expanded role in the Cosmos, by contrast with what we become in a virtually dead Universe where life and consciousness could in theory yield their secrets, and where all meaning evaporates in face of the spiritual void evoked by, in the name of reason, banishing the supernatural and trans-physical Infinite.

"Power in the Blood" is a metaphor representing the wondrous aspects of living Nature especially exemplified by numerous examples presented in the following pages, facts enlisted to help counter pseudo-objective "mismeasures of Man" that disdain all notions of psyche and spirit. For in fact no scientific truths are at odds with subjective and metaphysical parameters of faith that are germane to human nature and destiny. Moreover, those parameters are axioms that science, itself a subjectively-driven endeavor, cannot deny because its journey is open-ended, however often lured into oases of apparent certainty where the ceaseless call of a wilderness where exploration shall never end may briefly be ignored.

Among those facts most defiant of scientific solution, many are found in biology whose riddles are ubiquitous though rarely publicized. These curious realities, however, are quite relevant to belief that our existence has more than self-invented meaning, a supposition that deserves support for the sake not only of truth, but its practical resonance as well. For bleak visions of a Cosmos that is but the accidentally assembled stage for a "walking shadow" whose wishful pretence of consciousness fleetingly flutters above oblivion, hardly favor values such as reverence for life that can help a self-endangered species struggle to preserve its planetary home while not neglecting higher aspirations. Instead, a living Universe where faith and reason share in mutual interests, is one whose proportions are reflected in a saying of Heraclitus—"you could not find out the boundaries of the soul, not if you followed every path, so deep a measure does it have." And the view those words might recommend is close to that offered in the following chapters. For the mystic powers that imbue and flow through Nature and evolution are also intrinsic to human nature, and accepting that truth will attenuate the specter of impending ecological desolation while furthering social justice and a sustainable society that can successfully confront an imperative that is both Darwinian and moral. And that same realization also conforms to a conception of Life, whose profound enigmas beggar human intellect that floats upon its surface, as inseparable from psyche and spirit and consequently holding not only deeper fascination for the mind, but also brighter prospects both for body and soul.

1. Talking Points

In a vast land extending from the gray, forbidding seas of quantum physics and relativity towards lofty ranges of the psycho-spiritual enigma of consciousness, there dwells biology and its "key organizing principle" that is called evolution, and that opens broader and more colorful vistas on the world and human nature than any other science. For what philosophical resonance might be sought in physics is muted by the bafflement of questions as to the ultimate nature of substance and of time and space, that present the daunting austerity of a virtual nothing that is something or vice-versa* And all explanatory pursuit of consciousness is fated to be caught by the gravity of a lonely star that revolves around its axis of the Vedic riddle, "how can the knower be known?" But the issue of how and from what beginnings the kingdoms of Life have risen like a serpent uncoiling from obscurest depths of geologic time, affords an intimidating yet instructive challenge that cannot rightly be dismissed on religious grounds, nor trivialized by simplistically reductive theories without committing intellectual dishonesty—a form of avoidance which makes perfect psychological sense in the face of overwhelming odds.

*Although not only is interstellar and all of space not really empty because it contains both energy and every property required to support the visible reality of stars, planets, and the biosphere, but the "no-thing-ness" that is called in Sanskrit sunyatta or in Tibetan, tongpanyid[3] is rather than just a bleakly alienating vacuum, an inviting region where the personal self and all its fussy concerns can be laid aside

For those unfavorable chances are that the same challenge cannot be accepted with any better hope of gaining full comprehension of the subject or even what it actually constitutes than in quantum physics, where scientists are still struggling to answer "key questions for assessing the true nature of quantum reality."[1] Nonetheless, those issues, both small and large, that obsess biology and evolution have a manifold philosophical significance whose balanced assessment can only end by expanding, not diminishing, our view of human nature and its place in the Universe, despite that scrutiny may lead to lesser certainty and greater bafflement than before. Hence, whatever truth may endow the Socratic saying that "the unexamined life is not worth living" the more we examine Life itself and its worlds within worlds that are also within ourselves, the more of power, magic, and glory it seems to contain, and thereby render nearly moot any debating over what significance may or may not attach to that larger stream of collective lives wherein there tremulously subsists our own self-endangered species. For every scrap of melody in the enormous choir of changes that resounds within the curving horn of Time, encrypts no secret any plainer than what overarching mystery imbues the mighty "river out of Eden" that ever bears us onward.

For example, when the cub of a South American anteater rides on its mother's back, a stripe on its coat matches up with another on the mother's fur so as to form the appearance of a continuous band, as if the two creatures were one. And as the small passenger grows and changes position accordingly so as to keep the best distribution of weight, the mother's marking also moves in order to maintain the illusion of a single unbroken stripe. Thus the pair's casual resemblance to just one larger animal tends to discourage any predator who else might think to snatch the baby before its parent—whose digging claws can be lethally powerful weapons—could respond to prevent the abduction[2]. How did the suite of requisite mutations arise and, unless by extraordinary serendipity or then was clearly useful enough to be retained in subsequent generations? But simply claiming this phenomenon was "selected" as indeed it must have been, provides no better explanation than to say that bubble gum or the Beatles achieved success because they were likewise chosen by the favor of popular opinion. Nor does ascribing the various mutations presumably involved in producing the anteater's camouflage either to chance, or to a Supreme Being's having written the entire sequence of genetic changes into the overall scheme of how Life was meant to evolve, provide any real information or understanding.

Thus any possible solutions for evolutionary enigmas that involve various forms of the "irreducible complexity" most notably attributed to the "black box" of intracellular biology—wherein protein molecules are somehow endowed with the knowledge of how to fulfill their tasks of maintaining cellular metabolism and of assisting in cell division—cannot escape the fact of biology being inherently more difficult than physics, so that the system of a cell belongs to a higher rational order than the system of a star. Nor can the issues presented by living Nature be clarified either by mantras like "intelligent design" or by saying that vital forces drive the physiology of living organisms to carry out activities whose underlying pattern might only be explicable in a language even harder to interpret than the genetic code. The single celled parasite Toxoplasma is able to reproduce only in cats—a restriction whose evolutionary logic could scarcely be surmised, although perhaps appropriate to the small world these creatures have. Therefore when finding itself in the body of a rat, the parasite somehow modifies the rodent's psychology, making it hyperactive and fearless enough to erase its normally instinctive fear of cats.[4] On the other hand there is no shortage of ideas prepared to rhetorically substitute for whatever any so-called "real" answers could be. For example, one might remark that our ignorance concerning how thought is accomplished is logically equivalent to similar ignorance of how a parasite like Toxoplasma manages to alter the behavior of its host. And those same ideas are often relevant to myriad issues where the word "answer" is most unfortunate and misleading. For within the subjective context of human thought, that has long directed part of its efforts towards trying to grasp the existential riddle of which evolution constitutes a significant portion, any apparent vulnerability of the Magnum Mysterium to rational conquest often proves to be merely the deceptive allure of a mutable veil, whose removal simply exposes thornier obstacles that were heretofore concealed. Accordingly, amidst the fluid immensity of illusory Maya that reason and language ever strive to negotiate, there drifts a flimsy lattice of loosely connected talking points whose associations and meanings are open to pursuit within the relativistic mental palace of whoever desires to thus be occupied.

Hence, a vast variety of said talking points can be inspired in contemplating the staggering proportions of life upon our planet, whose sweeping multiplicity that beggars metaphor is combined with temporal extension back into abyssal geologic Time and its origin from tiny seeds of molecular magic already imbued, as it were, with all subsequent powers of transformation. And in every epoch of that history unfolding between the planet-wide disasters that have normally marked the beginning and end of each grand evolutionary era, Life has burst kaleidoscopically into a galaxy of wondrous creatures for most of which, like the once ubiquitous trilobites whose eyes uncannily utilized crystals of calcite to form lenses, that in some cases also included "a lower half of chitin" that served "to correct for optical aberration" in a manner "identical to that proposed… by Descartes and Huyghens half a billion years later" and in so doing "solved an elegant physical problem" involving "Fermat's principle, Abbe's sine law, Snell's laws of refraction, and the optics of birifringent crystals" with no clue as to "by what mechanism did these 'primitive' creatures' discover how to incorporate calcite crystals, align them precisely, and protect them with a cornea?"[5]—their time has come and gone. Yet continuous between the old and new, those durable species and orders fundamental to every ecological system following their advent, such as plankton, grasses and pollinating bees, have ever since endured as underpinnings of the whole scheme of Life now represented by the 26 basic body plans or phyla that first emerged in the Cambrian seas of several hundred million years ago[6]—not long before the trilobites themselves—and shall doubtless remain till in the throes of a dying Sun shall perish all terrestrial life.

But whether our species keeps its privileged place at the growth tip of a process that in humans has achieved the social and cultural vehicles for growing self-awareness, depends not just on natural but on moral law as well. For the flower of human consciousness having crowned all prior evolution, yet must prove its worth not simply by instituting a global vision for survival, whose need for abjuring any further ecological harm invokes the critical value of reverence for life, but through reforming all brutish existence of the poor and working classes while putting aside symbolic survival equivalents such as mindless and bloody conflicts involving national and religious identities.. In the post-Darwinian world of psychological, social and spiritual evolution wherein issues of knowledge and destiny, and of the human dignity demanding life and liberty are now unfolding, there is cause to examine what relevance to those issues is borne by the nature of Life throughout its entire prehistoric and pre-human past, not only scientifically, but spiritually and philosophically as well. And in consequence of that examination can emerge a whole realm of ideas ranging across all fields of understanding and reaching every corner of the mind, and finding ourselves in that world, whether simply gazing on its vistas or exploring their far horizons, we can better appreciate our place and meaning in a Cosmos that is not merely outward and external but of inward psycho-spiritual time and space.

Accordingly, just one of these talking points can address the nature and scope of knowledge itself, in tandem with psychology of the subjective human observer. As part of science, evolution, like the fact of Earth revolving around the Sun which in turn travels around the hub of our Galaxy, has been virtually established to the high degree of probability inherent in the kind of assertions on which evolving knowledge is grounded no less than any progressive society depends on moral truths that "are held to be self-evident." But precisely how it happened is far less obvious than what factors were likely involved in forming the Solar System or Earth itself, a question that only surfaced in the wake of the true astronomical pattern of the stars and planets having replaced the mediaeval concept of our planet as center of the Universe—although if the Universe has a center, Earth remains as good a candidate as any other world whose inhabitants might thus regard themselves. But continued debate on issues revolving around the general theory of evolution have obscured any closer examination of many curious features of the living world that are often so immensely problematic that they would seem to illuminate, more than any other questions in science, where the limits of our understanding the external world—including the brain itself and its role in creating or enabling physical awareness—may reside. And these limits themselves, whose true extent can but be roughly drawn upon the face of the vast unknown beyond them, may in turn reflect upon the nature and extent of the inward and subjective kingdoms of human consciousness, where the quality, value and purpose of knowledge itself is ultimately decided.

In other words, endless discussion and debate can be generated along the many paths that can pursue the topics of biology and evolution. And that is especially true concerning the relevance of these subjects to human nature and self-awareness, a connection which may be ignored by mortal minds seeking to take measure of timeless truths, but cannot be rationally denied. Thus, whoever embarks upon this network of pathways should not expect to ever reach a conclusive destination. For the origins and the multifarious character of consciousness in all its degrees and kinds, along with many other so-called eternal questions, are no less inseparably bonded with evolution per se than organic life with non-living matter-energy, just as the latter can hardly derive from any other source than what is ultimately our own as well. And all of these issues can converge in a kaleidoscopic splendor like that of Nature itself, in regarding how the wonder of Life's mercurial multiplicity is magnified by its interwoven context of a bottomless complexity, whose challenge to facile reductionism and simplistic dogma plainly underscores that any philosophical concerns regarding human nature or that of the Cosmos must bow to no lesser mystery. That is because issues as to whether we have, or are, a soul or spirit that abides when the body falls away, or whether the whole Universe is just as alive as those who talk about it and thus pervaded with vital awareness, cannot be detached from questions regarding the core dynamics of Life and its history. For the same Gestalt whereof all terrestrial or alien biology are part and parcel, must also be the ultimate ground of our own spiritual essence and provenance if these are anything better than rhetorical flourish or metaphor. Yet either way, whatever kind of light could truly illumine the subject might well, like that of Blake's "Tiger, tiger, burning bright" blind our vision more severely than intricate shadows of Nature's magic already baffle and obscure it "In the forests of the night."

2. Bio-Existentialism

For while Life can be said to have instinctively ascended by twists and turns from complex chemicals to the interactive proteins of single cells and thence to human self-aware intelligence now dwelling in folds of Earth's ecological garment that evolution has happily for us provided—a view whose possible validity, as opposed to that of saying that the stirring and shaking of molecules by physical forces has jiggled them ever upwards from rung to rung of the ladder of biological complexity until at last they have combined into the dreamy glow of consciousness, may seem to be supported more by rhetoric than reason—it has done so within a larger existential context no less exalted and arcane than what envelops the Universe itself, whose earliest beginning is of comparable obscurity to that of biology upon our own and likely many other worlds. That context is called "existential" because it is one of beingness, or the potential for all we regard as being, in all its varied degrees and kinds of freedom and activity. Moreover, that same context, hypothetically, also has room for a Deity (to which or to Whom it might in that case correspond) and for spiritual existence including what human beings may realize in some transcendent state from whence we came and shall someday return when our Earthly experience has run its course. That is not to insist that such a state exists, for in cold rational objectivity such metaphysical parameters as a spiritual cosmic consciousness may or may not obtain. However, in reality such issues were decided long before becoming the topic of endless disputations whose full significance is but incidental, amid the starry savannahs of a Cosmos that while including the subjective aspect of human awareness remains not only "queerer than we suppose, but queerer than we can suppose."[1]

However, if such a metaphysical condition does belong to any true description of the world, then it certainly cannot be separated from physical phenomena including those of biology and of the neurology underlying human thought. Thus, for example, in asking how a parasite such as a "lancet fluke" could have evolved the ability to program the behavior of its host, as the fluke is able to do by guiding an ant to the tip of a blade of grass to be eaten by a sheep in whose body the fluke will then continue its life-cycle[2] the answer could be that while genetic mutation may have fashioned this clever parasite from an earlier and cruder animal, the change was not random but instead, brought about by some talent of Life of which we neither have nor could possess the slightest conception. And that same facility, despite being hard or impossible to scientifically demonstrate should then have resonance with yet greater domains of spirit—the "many mansions" wherein resides a fuller interpreting of human psychology and purpose, and the nature of human awareness and its destiny upon this Earth or in worlds to come, than could be derived from scientific knowledge of a biological kingdom viewed as lacking any spiritual or trans-finite factors which already are presumed as non-existent anyway—a presumption tending to impoverish all consequent explanation.

The spiritual or metaphysical account, however, does not compel our believing that the Darwinian scheme of evolutionary theory is wrong. Instead, in a context already untellably vast even without the dimension attached by faith, these kinds of explanation are the only ones possible. Both mutation and natural selection are clearly true and cannot be otherwise. Without mutation of the genes, no change would ever happen and without natural selection could not be progressive. Furthermore, to the rough Darwinian outline there is no alternative except direct creation of new species, whether by Divine or angelic hands or by those species somehow precipitating into matter from some ethereal domain. Moreover one could say, in reference to natural selection, that the principle of order which is absolutely basic to the existence of anything, having once been established in some degree like that expressed by molecules whether of DNA or so-called inert matter, can hardly backslide but is bound to advance toward higher levels of the ladder of complexity. For whatever rational cause provoked any kind of order to arise in the first place is not going to disappear, but is apt to bring about further change in the direction of deeper ordering and profounder complexity—otherwise there would have to be some preferred point for order to begin to fade away and life start devolving towards the primordial slime or further, given that production of literal slime as by bacteria who exude it when they coalesce into a single collective called a "slime mold" is already a biological marvel. But there is no point in Life's history where that reversal could logically be more anticipated, since every step achieved thus far has been equally improbable, whether from fish to lizards or from the small, shrew-like mammals of the Cretaceous (and somewhat larger ones as well, according to recent discoveries) to creatures as diverse as bats and whales that took only around ten million years to evolve after the unleashing of mammal evolution by the cometary cataclysm in 65 million B.C. that apparently consigned all dinosaurs, but inexplicably not most members of other animal groups to oblivion. Even that seemingly straightforward event, however, is shadowed by the riddle as to why even small dinosaurs, unlike reptiles, mammals and birds, could not survive the harsh conditions that must have prevailed for decades or centuries after the comet had fallen, thus raising for example a question as to whether the impact alone was responsible for the dinosaurs' terminal obliteration.

3. Fate and Responsibility

There is no clear and simple way to describe, much less explain, how and why all the wondrous adaptations of living Nature have happened to arise, and thus now distinguish Earth as exceptional, perhaps even uniquely beautiful in the entire universe. Countless biologically active planets may indeed abound in the Milky Way and other galaxies, but of these the great majority might be ecologically barren and austere compared to Earth—even, in fact, the natural homes for what are called extremophiles that on our world, inhabit those dauntingly harsh environments where until recent discoveries the existence of any viable organism would have been deemed impossible. And continuing degradation of the natural world by a feckless human species could also convert our planet into such a place, a grim transformation that could happen swiftly, if as in words of a Hopi prophecy Earth could "belong to the ants" after the "gourd of ashes" that Western civilization has created, nuclear fission and fusion weapons, was shattered to release an apocalyptic ending of the human experiment.

Indeed. similar tragedy may have played out time and again throughout the Cosmos, as one civilization after another failed the moral test imposed by high technology, while but few managed to advance the evolutionary principle into the broader than merely biological dimensions represented by brotherhood, creativity and social justice. (These broader dimensions, however, while not strictly biological are of Darwinian significance since attaining them globally is key to continued human survival). Then again, those who became the chosen and whose planetary homes remained unspoiled could be few only as compared to the vastly greater number of civilizations who by their own misguided hand were consigned to perdition. Thus the absolute number of fully successful and sustainable societies in the Cosmos that grew from primitive beginnings by the same natural process that led from single–celled animals to the primates that became ourselves could be large though also eclipsed by vaster ranks of intelligent species who had no sooner attained some shape of civilization than they perished like baby turtles, many of whom after hatching out from eggs laid in the sand of ocean beaches are seized by voracious birds before they can scramble into the waves, where of course piscine predators will gobble many more. And it remains to be seen if humanity shall securely join that lucky minority, assuming it exists, because the kind of choices that could open the gates to earthly happiness that is our only alternative to either extinction or what at best, amidst ecological ruin, could amount to a mongrel subsistence, have as yet been simply put forward in the marketplace of ideas but not by every government acknowledged or confirmed. The business of the world is still a sorry business that keeps unraveling the ecological web whose irreplaceable wealth far surpasses any man-made artifact or technological invention. Thus proper appreciation of that wealth, a "reverence for life" which clearly must also embrace the lives of hungry children and other wretched of the Earth, is vital not only to sheer human survival in Darwinian terms, but to realizing the vision once expressed by novelist William Faulkner in saying that "Man will not only survive—he will prevail."[1] And significant towards furthering that sort of appreciation is to fully grasp the overwhelming scope and the sheer depth in both complexity and abyssal time of organic evolution, whose temporal dimension of progressive change is no less enigmatic than the nature of Time itself as fourth dimension of the space-time continuum. For if truth is beauty, then that truth is found supremely in the realms of Nature—of course including human nature—that to cherish and protect is essential towards whatever kind of truth can be attained in our mortal human existence

4. Ch-Ch-Changes

Then again, to comprehend the evolutionary process and fathom its workings may surpass all powers of intellect beyond the rhetorical power to seize on "talking points" and argue them endlessly, for the simple reason that biology is incalculably more involved than other sciences, where the hardest riddles like that of so-called "dark matter," whose currently undetectable mass is thought to somehow account for the improbably rapid rotation of the galaxies, remain unsolved. In fact, Darwin himself seemingly allowed as much in confessing his bafflement regarding how "macro-evolution" could have bridged the major gaps that separate fish from their amphibian descendants, or mammals from the cold blooded reptile lineage that evolved into whatever warm blooded ancestors we descended from even as dinosaurs were likely dining on the slower and less wary of those diminutive creatures. In grappling with the method of these grand transitions, Darwin described himself as feeling helpless as an ape pondering on a book of Euclidean geometry.[1] Yet his great discovery was primarily that evolution has generated the whole panorama of life, rather than any precise formula to explain how the evolutionary process has applied in specific cases. For those cases, of which such miracles as eyes and feathers are not the most problematic, have mainly scientific implications whereas the discovery of evolution per se bears social, philosophical and religious relevance as well, that is more significant than any particular theory which could be demonstrated by hard evidence of how some species turned into a radically different creature as in the case of scurrying insectivores becoming bats or dull marine invertebrates transforming into clever octopi. Even with the aid of a time machine, this kind of proof could be hard to obtain, for while it has been possible to discover the fossils of walking lungfish whose subsequent lineage presumably acquired features, like better lungs and longer legs, that led to the emergence of mammals, live examples in the sequence still might fail to disclose exactly why any genetic changes that had to have occurred had actually done so.

After all, to say that these mutations were random leaves open the possibility that they happened for some inscrutable reason whose function of biological ordering eludes the investigative capacities of science. Thus the actual theory remains little more than the obvious principles of mutation and natural selection which are clearly inescapable as concluding that a crater inside a ring of ejected material indicates that a meteorite has fallen from the sky. As an aspect of Change itself, genetic changes are bound to happen, and in so doing are bent by selective pressures in favor of the increasingly well-ordered complexity whose acme is the human brain. Otherwise, without the "ratchet effect" of natural selection, evolution could just as easily go sideways or backwards and so lacking any preferred direction, would never occur. These nearly self-evident and general truths can be stated again and again in endless variations, but the vitally particular essence of how Life and evolution really operate still evades human understanding no less than any grasp of the great Gestalt enfolding them, whose quintessential truth dwells largely beyond the conceptual horizon of any creed, religion, or philosophy, excepting insofar as pre-Christian philosophers like Heraclitus or the Vedic sages did perceive that kind of truth as flowing through every fiber of Creation.[2] The price for recognition of what amounts to the virtually infinite complexities accessed by science has been to lose sight of the great equation of the All, whereof all lesser lives are ever partaking

5. Made to Order

Of course, the principle of order expressed in living Nature, and ramified in Life's winding journey towards what in humans, and perhaps alien minds on other worlds, has become self-awareness is present in so-called non-living matter-energy as well. And "present" means inseparably co-existent because the idea of substance without form, a pure chaos from which the material universe might have arisen by injection of order into a formless but substantial void is scarcely conceivable—the primal, undivided unity of a "god-particle" whose explosion may have initiated our space-time universe would constitute minimum entropy and thus maximum order, rather than chaos in the figurative sense of rampant randomness or total confusion. Even energy, radiation, all by itself has an invisible pattern because it is made of standardized particles or quanta called photons, not to mention the as yet undetected gravitons that hypothetically transmit the force of gravity and the so-called "virtual" photons that are said to carry the force of magnetism,[1] (a force that unlike heat and light is clearly not carried by detectable photons) and that seemingly must inhabit some hyper-spatial region from whence perhaps there sprang the space-time continuum and its inherent laws that engendered the visible Cosmos, if that continuum has not always existed. And if not, and space-time itself thus had a beginning from some unknowable state of pre-existence—a beginning of but not in Time itself, which could then only be regarded as having precipitated from an indescribable Eternity—then its laws and their implicit order also began to manifest from that point of origin, bearing in mind that in physics, the patterns of Nature also represent an increase in entropy, or disorder, as compared to the hypothetical state of undifferentiated Being that may have obtained when Time began and Space first started expanding.[2]

These laws, however can be and are both real and abstract, the former shaping the "real" reality and the latter only approximating whatever features of that shape may be apparent within the far lesser existential field of corporeal minds who, if the glass is half-full, are more gifted with knowledge and understanding than ever in recorded history, and if half-empty have on an endless path of discovery only covered a fragmentary portion of what remains an infinite distance between them and some ultimate Truth that may itself be infinite and thus unknowable in any rational or finite sense. Then again, the half-full glass can seem half-empty if we happen to reflect that modern scientific knowledge has brought us to a place of peril just as much as opportunity, where to practice the art of living may face difficulties even greater than confronted many ancient peoples. And the half-empty glass looks considerably fuller upon considering that if the journey were finitely destined to attain some core cosmic secret to be thenceforth forever enshrined and admired by the human race, to have reached that ending would conclude all meaningful existence—unless it were then decided that mere scientific knowledge was not so important after all and life really about something else altogether. But if Time is not the highest dimension, it may also not suffice for the truest measure of a more essential pathway leading on some uncharted course beyond the place our species has gained thus far in pursuing its temporal career of organic and social evolution.

6. Dimensions, Boundaries and Laws

Thus the philosophical dimension of evolution, from whose process our mental capacities have emerged as a function of survival that now also demands social and moral survival calling for harmonious co-existence with Nature, and for self-understanding that can ultimately yield the vision of an ideal homeland for humanity in realms whose higher existence is reflected in the microcosm of the soul (or may be nothing other than the soul whose journey has become the path itself) does not exclude there being metaphysical parameters for Nature and human nature in addition to the harshly "Darwinian" quality of laws whose punitive effects continued eco-delinquency well might bring upon ourselves For the retributive power of those laws, caring nought for our "dreams of reason" could conceivably grow to dominate, as in the distant past, the whole of human experience should our species decline to pursue its brightest promise and instead, succumb to the worst instincts and weakest thinking of the godless animal that a monotonal philosophy, largely derived from biology and evolutionary science, has deemed us to be. Thus, indeed, the biologically logical view of life that bars from it any spiritual factor or connection also provides important metaphors that portray the grim abyss of constant struggle whence our failure to be fully human, and thus worthy of distinction even in stark evolutionary terms, could force us to return. And in that survivalist chasm wherein any notion of God could be hard to maintain let alone entertain, we then at last might perish from the Earth as utterly as many less noble creatures have left the fossil evidence of having done.

However, it is neither the facts nor unflinching analysis which can render that philosophical dimension difficult to interpret as providing room for any spiritual essence permeating the Cosmos. Many facts of biology, combined with analysis of how they could have possibly evolved, are wondrous and strange in the utmost degree. Moreover, honest logic tells us that the foundations of biology have to be at least coeval and congruent with and therefore not more obvious than those of other science. And the latter does indeed suggest a likelihood of transcendent proportions for the Universe in the form of more than merely the four familiar space-time dimensions being required to explain quantum phenomena. Thus to rule out any relation between biology and such hidden regions—whether the same or different than called for in physics—as constituting the ground of some ineffable meta-causality, of informational content shaping genetic change, or of some deep, instinctive intelligence at the heart of Nature ever striving for expression in a rising sequence that has finally culminated in higher animals including ourselves, is quite preposterous. For those hyper-spatial regions whose reality seems inescapable—in providing the domain of the aforementioned "virtual photons" for example—are not trivial or incidental. They are an indispensable though virtually trans-physical indicator of the nature of physical existence including life—"trans-physical" because the laws or modes of being they incorporate may well surpass the highest understanding of Nature that is humanly possible. But that same understanding which has probed into the depths of both the atom and the Cosmos, has largely bypassed the most difficult questions in biology and for good reason: living organisms express a higher degree of freedom than the nonliving entities approached by physics, and are correspondingly harder to explain. If theoretical models for quantum and for astronomical phenomena, in other words, have not as yet approached completion or shed uncertainty, how much more so in the case of biology and especially its vast evolutionary dimension, above whose temporal abyss now flits the sprite of human consciousness.

And if that consciousness somehow reflects, channels or focuses what is in fact a "res ipsa" or thing in itself of no weaker claim to objective identity than, for instance, electricity—in other words, not merely a random side-effect, emergent property or logical consequence of more solidly existent physical laws, then its role becomes just as germane to living Nature and the ascent of Man as the quantum framework of space-time itself. And in that case, our individual awareness is in some sense coeval and coexistent with an all-pervading metaphysical thread woven through every fold of the Universe, though anchored beyond constraints of temporal causality. And if so, then it is that same ingredient or potential of awareness that provides the reservoir of organic and cerebral organization, while lending inner fire to Life's advancement through a self-improving series of vital forms for what constitutes, or corresponds to, the existential content of the human mind and spirit.

None of the above however need obviate or interfere with so-called "Darwinian" evolution, but instead, merely grants more dignity to a theory thus removed from a mechanistic bondage, and from the kind of constraint imposed by abhorrence of "vitalism" and its threat to rational pre-eminence of one little species in a Universe that God forbid should be regarded as alive. For in the spiritual view of Nature and human nature that is vital towards realizing the latter's highest possibilities, natural selection becomes not simply some harsh conditional of unforgiving Nature but an aspect of a virtually mathematical principle of order so fundamental that reality itself cannot be conceived in its absence. For in fact, order emerges with existence itself. As soon as there is any thing or entity, the latter by definition must be bounded and thus retains inherent order which cannot be lost through multiplicity as for example in the multiplicity of particles of energy and matter that sprang into being when the Universe first began expanding, either from a singularity or quantum glitch that leapt from a virtual void of eternal pre-existence, or from a primal fireball wherein all force and substance had been melted down to unity through collapse of a prior universe as part of the endless cycle described in Hindu scriptures. Clearly, that common origin for all particles of matter-energy, and their respective fields, calls for strict uniformity for all members of a certain class such as electrons, photons, or quarks, whose nature must also conform to logical rules of association with all other classes and their members of the "particle zoo" that invisibly substands and populates the world of external appearances, passions and strife. But that same logic is so deeply hidden that science cannot begin to guess why, for example, the ratio of the mass of an electron to that of a proton is what it is, approximately 1 to 1800, or why the structure and laws of this particular Universe have chanced to manifest instead of some totally other kind whose actual quality and character, assuming it could even exist, can hardly be surmised.

7. Cry of the Blood

Therefore, given that despite its wild display of loose ends (like the still hypothetical "string" particles) that keep blowing about in the wind, physics remains inherently simpler than biology, the rhyme and reason of Life and how its mercurial order burst from a chemical seed and then expanded into the broad panorama of ecological diversity ever changing through the ages is more deeply hidden still. However, it is possible to consider how change accelerates as a surging complexity burgeons in the ranks of living creatures. For just as matter-energy, once having attained its present shape from the sub-atomic to galactic scale has scarcely altered—although titanic explosions keep forging new stars and the raw material for planets able to foster life—so have species forming the substrate of the biosphere, namely bacteria, single-celled animals like plankton and invertebrates such as nematodes, ants and spiders, scarcely deviated from their ancient forms whereas modern mammals and homo sapiens evolved from a cruder ancestry in but the last several million years. No creature today is nearly so ungainly as the huge herbivorous marsupial Protodon that may have been hunted to extinction by Australian aborigines as recently as 30,000 BC. And in society and culture, as befits their pride of place at the forefront of progress that began with emergence of the first living cell, the same principle of accelerating change applies yet more strongly. As social complexity increases, global transformation matches that increase by quickening its pace, while even at its lowest ebb a substrate of civilized order has ever been maintained, as in the murky transitions from the Pax Romana to the Holy Roman Empire and Byzantium and subsequently to modern Europe and Western democracy. But as new waves of change keep cresting in the wake of the old under impetus of factors like global media and galloping technology, their grimmer troughs—the inventoried arsenals of death and toothless desolation rows, the battered jungles and fouled waters, barren boulevards of commerce and embittered alleys of ignorance—have spread to the point of menacing not only civilization but arguably human life itself. (And what the fate of souls no longer able to incarnate on a sickly planet from which humankind and perhaps all higher animals had perished?) Hence "the voice of the blood" is crying urgently from depths of the collective unconscious, that we must reconnect to the natural realm whose preservation means no less for human survival than reverence for Life, including the lives of animals currently raised for food in conditions of revolting squalor, for any hope of humanity's achieving the moral dignity of true civilization.

8. So Many Reasons Why

In any case, the principle of evolving order that, along with the self-regulating autonomy of organisms distinguishes life from the steady state and fixed order of non-living matter-energy, could hardly obtain without natural selection. But the latter, whose discovery revealed the key idea behind why evolution happens, is merely what Aristotle called a "formal cause," rather than an effective cause or "mechanism," as selection has often unthinkingly been called. Gravity, for example, is a "formal cause" that is necessary for rainfall, but the effective causes of rain are found in the processes of evaporation and condensation and in shifting weather patterns that determine where moisture drawn into the atmosphere by solar energy will fall back to the Earth's surface. And solar energy itself could be described as both a formal and effective cause of the evaporation, but is a formal cause of the patterns shaped by winds whose energy comes from the Sun. However, natural selection cannot explain why, for example, some parasites have learned to program the behavior of their hosts though clearly the pernicious life-style of the former has indeed been "selected" as a highly successful adaptation whose origin remains one of the great mysteries of biology. And as to how and why such adaptations arose, genetic change provides but a partial explanation. It is hard to imagine that the mutations required for the parasite to produce a chemical agent that can alter the behavior of a host (like the luckless ant which accommodates the needs of a "lancet fluke" it has ingested by climbing a blade of grass to await being grazed by a sheep in whose body the fluke's life cycle will continue [1]) through somehow targeting its nervous system—and the question of exactly how the command for changed behavior is conveyed to the host's nervous system, or the knowledge of how and when to send it was encoded in the parasite's genes, is utterly confounding—could have arisen by a building sequence of random rearrangements of genetic material that finally conferred upon the lancet fluke its utterly weird ability..

Hence the only answer possible is not strictly scientific, yet does emerge through comparison with what could be regarded as the "virtual intelligence" of intra-cellular activity. Molecules within the cell somehow know how to do their jobs, for example repairing damaged DNA or transporting metabolic waste to a place of disposal.[2] Given the fact that we do not really know how the mind works in carrying out presumably intelligent activity such as solving an equation, composing a sonnet, or finding the right melodic theme for a symphonic movement—feats whose enabling increments operate in profound concealment from personal awareness within the folds and crannies of cerebral tissue—it is hard to deny that equally purposeful molecular activity within the cell is no less intelligent, whereas to claim these molecules lack "awareness" and are thus not intelligent is scientifically meaningless, given that awareness cannot be measured by scientific instruments. And that is especially true if we discount any notion of a non-physical or ethereal "mind" inhabiting the body, for in that case there is nothing left to identify as human intelligence in and of itself—except, of course, for the plain observation that humans can willfully alter their behavior, sometimes against their own best interests whereas cells clearly cannot deviate from the pre-ordained pattern of their life cycle. (unless they become cancerous in which case, unlike repentant humans, reformation is not possible).Therefore, it becomes quite simple to conceive that mutations may in some sense be directed and purposeful, and in some inscrutable fashion seemingly guided by an inherent power of mind or consciousness abiding everywhere in the natural world And in that case, human intelligence is simply a higher expression, through a far more elaborate mechanism than that of cells or even of mammals and birds whose repertoire appears to include emotion, of that same universal consciousness whose character of a "formal cause" subsuming all activities of Life can scarcely be suggested by a highly rhetorical term like "intelligent design."

In fact that phrase, which seems to posit a Divine mind precipitating or calling forth into physical being the whole panorama of Nature in one fell swoop, after having first conceived it entire in the realm of ideas, may have deserved the scorn of scientists who abhor metaphysical pseudo-explanations of natural phenomena. For why would that God have chosen to create a world so alien to human beings that the latter would be foolish to dream they can even begin, through the study of Nature, to understand how God's mind actually works and yet allow them to keep imagining that the Divine intelligence is not inscrutable? For instance, if the so-called Darwinian process can in fact provide an adequate account for the evolutionary origin of such wonders as mites that cling like slippers to the feet of certain species of ants[3] then would God not have chosen that same process as the means to forge the whole system of organic life whose progress S/He then left entirely to chance guided only by the ordering powers of natural selection and of the DNA which the Deity foreknew was bound to arise through whatever chemical wizardry helped form the first cellular prototypes?

Then again, placing a Deity of boundless potency—of light, love and life as in the Hindu trinity—at the core of existence, opens the possibility, for example, of living and conscious power proceeding from that core into the depths of a primal abyss whose virtual chaos contains only a crudely elemental existence and then shaping those elements into the mutable rungs of an evolutionary ladder that builds itself through the power of Life, whose instinctual intelligence reflects a Divine origin. Thus from the humblest quantum particles—themselves already members of an exquisitely ordered matrix—can come about the crowning awareness of creatures able to perceive the metaphysical truth of their origin and so doing begin to constitute a bridge between Earth and Heaven. And in this kind of scheme, whose immensity and glory are scarcely suggested by words like "intelligent design"—whose casual usage also begs the question of what "intelligence" means—there is room for countless and largely unknowable influences affecting organic life throughout its profound history, and not restricted to such factors as transmission of genetic material between species by viruses[4], that can or could be identified.

However, the hypothesis of "intelligent design" is clearly more rhetorical than scientific, since it tries to account for what is called "irreducible complexity" by disguising the indisputable observation that the entire issue is an unsolved mystery by attributing the origin of molecular mechanisms in living cells that seem incapable to have arisen from the Darwinian update of simpler structures, to an "intelligent designer," namely God or some angelic intermediary. Clearly, such examples as the molecular motor which drives the rotary motion of the flagella in certain bacteria are hard to conceive as deriving from a more basic form that itself was useful enough to be selected. Nothing simpler than the flagellum, as a preceding step on the evolutionary ladder, would work in any useful manner according to the argument which thus proposes what is called "intelligent design," a rather curious way to cover a gap that human intelligence is unable to bridge by any real understanding of how structures like the flagellum could have evolved. An analogy provided by those who have identified this type of evolutionary puzzle—repeated in many other intracellular mechanisms that do not appear capable of having arisen from less complicated structures that could have served no useful purpose—is a simple man-made device like a mousetrap, which would be worthless if any of the parts, like the spring or the trigger, were missing[5]—although it has been suggested that the flagella were once independent organisms that attached themselves to the outer wall of larger bacteria as just one example of the symbiotic relationships that are found throughout Nature, such as the symbiosis of yeast and fungi that constitutes the organism used to brew Kombucha tea. Moreover, recent discoveries of bacterial mechanisms analogous to the flagellum and utilizing some of the same protein molecules cast further doubt on the idea of some intelligent agency having forged the entire cell in one fell swoop as a finished unit.[6] For that quite nebulous idea would imply a similar explanation for every step in the evolutionary process which requires a coordinated series or array of interlocking genetic changes. Just one example would be the alteration of the toed foot of a primitive horse like Eohippus into a modern hoof, a transition requiring parallel changes in the lower leg and its bone, muscles and ligaments as well. In all such cases, the holistic sweep of change maintained vital integrity in each new creature in the temporal chain of evolving forms, just as the body maintains integrity from day to day in the process of all its seamlessly interdependent functions.

9. The Cosmos: Conjured or Conjuring?

Hence it would seem disingenuous to suggest that a Deity or Divine agency simply conjured each separate species in the progressive lineage of horses from the aether and then planted them on the Earth to replace the former and inferior kinds, which then, in accordance with Darwinian principle died out or were "de-selected." But while primitive bacteria lacking the rotary flagella may have left no fossils, the basic character of biological change that began with the first living cell can hardly have been altered or superceded in the later evolutionary path of multicellular organisms, despite how adequately any further intermediate steps along that path can be described. It hardly makes sense, in other words, to imagine that up to a point the earliest unicellular creatures were Divinely fashioned out of whole cloth and then left to evolve thenceforth by the more "normal" method that the fossil record appears to demonstrate. On the other hand, it can seem disingenuous to maintain that the relentless advance of organic complexity can have occurred without there being at the very least, some innately willful tropism of Life itself—perhaps akin to the "virtual intelligence" of a human body performing its minute-to-minute metabolic tasks—that like the methods of a human magician, remains deeply hidden from intellects already sorely tested by strictly inorganic science. But referring this tropism to the nebulous agency of "intelligent design" also demands a parallel supposition, namely that development of a human body from an embryo, or an oak from an acorn, must likewise be guided by some conscious yet immaterial agent –presumably not God, but an angel informed by the will of God to carry out the tasks of creation.

In other words—words that effectively fail in trying to explain how Life does what it does unless we disregard the deeper enigmas of evolution—it is at least possible to say that sometime in the distant past, Nature produced nucleated, single-celled animals or Eukaryotes, with all their staggeringly intricate molecular machinery, from more primitive bacteria or Prokaryotes by no other than whatever inherent power also drove each subsequent step in the process of evolution. Moreover, though outside the strictures of science, it is equally possible to claim that the intrinsic capabilities of Life could be regarded as intelligent, since "intelligence" is no better defined than what is meant by the "randomness" typically cited as the ultimate cause for genetic mutations, including those whose survival value allowed their continuance through succeeding generations—say, a mutation causing the skin of a toad to exude poison, thus protecting the creature and its progeny from predators who likewise evolve the wisdom to avoid trying to eat this deadly amphibian. Nor can it be denied that many useful mutations could have arisen for no obvious or less than accidental reason, such as the impact of a cosmic ray. Yet even these have to be integrated into a larger genetic whole that in turn is coordinated with the working of the entire organism, and the means of that integration would seem to fit the definition of intelligence at least as well as the functioning of human societies and the often serendipitous process of scientific discoveries on which those societies largely depend. Furthermore, the genetic machinery is also self-correcting. Hence bad mutations occurring "randomly" are apt to be weeded out, with equal appearance of purposeful and thus quasi-intelligent behavior as in the case of the immune system, if we are lucky, purging entire cells which themselves have succumbed to genetic errors that turn them cancerous.

But this kind of intelligence or whatever it may be called instead if semantics are an issue, is clearly other than the full awareness of, a higher mind that might in similar sense as a human architect or engineer, have imagined or designed the whole of Life, including insect vampires that lure ants from their trails with a sweet narcotic syrup these tiny monsters exude, so as to drain at leisure the vital juices of their besotted victim.[1] In fact, in the shifty sort of context where the meaning of words like "randomness"—whose most accurate usage is found in mathematics where the definition of a random number is still not easy to explain—can greatly affect the gist of what is being said, it is hard to seize upon definitive arguments for making one's case. Hence the great clouds of rhetoric swirling round the topic of evolution, whose depth of psychological associations—the psychology behind religiously or scientismically tilted opinion, for example—easily exceeds what attaches to any other science. Scarcely anyone feels compelled to argue that the wonder and beauty of the Cosmos, whether at the astronomical or quantum scale, does or does not urge the necessity of spiritual belief, because the facts themselves are sufficiently stunning to embrace both agnostic and religious views. But the facts of biology that are if anything more wondrous still, do not preoccupy the human imagination so much as verbal battles over their provenance and philosophical implications, which indeed might seem reducible to the question of whether any spiritual dimension as may exist—for if it does not, the whole issue evaporates—could also have any conceivable or perhaps inscrutable connection to the workings of Nature. Nonetheless, crystals of calcite were incorporated into the complicated eyes of trilobites,[2] by some profound innate wisdom of an organism that effectively knew how and why to draw this mineral from the environment. Parrots, with their tiny brains, can understand and talk human language in a manner that qualifies them as having "minds." The wings of certain butterflies when folded at rest display a coherent design (known as Oudemann's phenomenon) where the separate markings on each individual wing join together in a continuous pattern that serves no purpose of camouflage that could have caused the genes responsible to have been selected.[3] The long litany of facts like these speaks for itself convincingly enough to beggar all attempts to domesticate their meaning.

10. Matters of Interpretation

The sciences of physics and chemistry have undoubtedly served not only human social and cultural evolution through helping to provide the material underpinnings of progress, but have also helped our species gain a deeper vision of the Cosmos that in turn reflects upon our inward psycho-spiritual being. For what Bertrand Russell called "the awful power of non-human things," and the alien dimensions of vastness and smallness those things possess at their Cosmic and sub-atomic levels of magnitude, simply illuminate how utterly other are the truths of human nature from those of Nature herself, within whose mighty framework those former truths reside. And life science has likewise furthered the goals of society, as in the human biology of medicine. But evolution per se as "the key organizing principle" of biology is also vitally important in a philosophical context that goes far beyond knowing, for example, that natural selection can force the development of bacterial resistance to drugs that must then be replaced with new pharmaceutical inventions, or that the human cerebral cortex may have evolved in response to the need for greater intelligence on the part of hominid creatures impelled by climate change to venture from jungles onto the open African savannah. For the awesome fact of humanity's place in the ever-unfolding evolutionary panorama is of equal significance to our vision of a Cosmos where new vistas of meaning can as readily as new species arise to repudiate stultified views of a barren landscape where our self-endangered race, convinced by gloomy reasoning of its lacking any better than a figurative soul, might cringe before the harsh Darwinian prospect of being deleted from the book of organic Life, by some caprice of the same kind of laws that can work through a combination of chance and genetic wizardry to preserve noxious pests from the assault of poisons designed to destroy them.

Thus, to cite an example that can but hugely complicate any honest view of living Nature and thereby of human nature as well, no rational powers can explain the strange ability of some bacteria to transfer a copy of a part of their genetic material providing drug resistance, to a different bacterial species. For the quasi-intentional character of this act is shown by the fact that these genes are not simply released into the environment to be randomly scavenged, but instead are transferred through a tube of protoplasm in a manner that resembles the midair refueling of an airplane from a tanker aircraft.[1] There just isn't any logical or theoretical formula able to describe how such microbial magic is accomplished. Of course whatever genetic mutations are involved in granting this exotic ability must have occurred, and must certainly be retained by natural selection for their evident survival value, although when benefits are conferred to another species than that of the donor, whatever Darwinian advantage the latter has gained is hard to perceive. Yet for the sake of preserving a theory whose sketchy wisdom may comfort those who in it have heavily invested their psychic capital, such riddles are typically ignored. But to do so however is needless. There is no real cause to dismiss the most puzzling and curious wonders of biology for even while admitting them openly, the Darwinian scheme as a "good general approximation"[2] remains secure. For however inadequate should that model appear, no better nor for that matter sweepingly metaphorical, version could conceivably subsist within the scope of a human intellect more seriously challenged by Life than in all other sectors of knowledge.

Therefore, any qualms about the truth of so-called neo-Darwinian theory—natural selection plus genetics—have strayed into a thicket of conflicting interpretations, such as what "natural selection," sometimes criticized as equivalent to "survivors survive," really means, not to mention other imponderables such as the why and how of mutation. For what remains immune to doubt is the core of the theory, namely that the flow of genetic change has clearly continued from the very dawn of Life and has at least ever been restrained from slipping backwards from men to monkeys or from worms to germs by the "ratchet effect" of natural selection—things change, and in doing so tend to preserve whatever degree of order and complexity has been attained. Hence the problem becomes one of how that pair of concepts, change and selection, are interpreted, and to do so reductively only tends to make them less robust and more open to attack. Calling mutations "random," for example, simply means that the genetic factors involved in any particular change such as weeds becoming resistant to herbicides or gills turning into or being replaced with lungs, remain ineluctably obscure. And to dispute the role of natural selection obscures the greater truth that Life itself exemplifies, which is that the key dynamic of the Universe is one of progressive change, which on our planet has recently shifted into the arena of human society, art and science—and should that entire Universe as in the case of every living thing, succumb to death and dissolution, nonetheless in what may be countless others, the pageant shall continue and new banners be unfurled.

11. Wise Blood

However, when words like "chance" and "randomness" are seen as explanatory wraiths rather than pillars in terms of accounting for the complexly coordinated multiple mutations required for every transitional stage of evolving Life, a more deeply metaphysical expression can seem just as fitting in the same explanatory role—namely, the wisdom or "wise blood" of Nature herself. For the latter agency, however conceived, is clearly responsible for the day-to-day workings of our own brains and bodies, where as no scientific experiment could either dismiss or demonstrate, the manner of that agency is hardly "random" but plainly an integral power which is greater than the sum of whatever of its derivative parts, such as chemical signals from cell to cell, can be identified. Moreover, to label that agent as "intelligent design," with clear reference to a God whose specific manner of intervention or management (perhaps by angelic emissaries) is not and could not be specified, does not serve the cause of understanding any better than determinedly non-metaphysical words like "randomness." Hence what remains aside from whatever strange facts the ongoing study of Nature may reveal, is that acolytes of either science or religion will keep looking for assurance that their beliefs and understanding are justified, however slight any reason to suppose that the most perplexing riddles of science, as in cosmology where resides the fate of the Universe, will ever be resolved—or even might have been by some older and wiser civilization orbiting a distant star. Yet evolution per se keeps enhancing our consciousness towards concerns beyond mere comfort or survival, despite whatever scientific or religious certainty can or cannot be achieved in the face of human temporal insecurity. Therefore, there shall at least, in the intensely psychological arenas of intellect and academia, continue being generated an endless stream of discourse with regard to vastly trans-human arcana like evolution, whereof any mystical and/or rational mainsprings may ever stay beyond the farthest frontiers of knowledge. Darwinian principles may be true, yet their role in helping to bring about or foster the most profound puzzles in biology, like parasites that program the behavior of their hosts, cannot be shown to be more than the formal causes of variation and selection that are clearly indispensable. And any spiritual or metaphysical factors that have furthered the cause of Life—and these certainly exist unless we live in a dead Universe, do not have souls and are merely deluded in thinking ourselves to be conscious—will surely continue to elude human efforts to fathom how the "wise blood" of Nature may have participated in writing the Book of Life, from whose latter page of civilization, where we perch, can be ascertained but snatches of the rest, and of that mostly the what and not the how or why.

The actual nature of "understanding," however, depends upon what is being addressed. If the subject is black holes, then there are excellent reasons to believe that these entities "leak" radiation—mathematical analysis seems to show that if every photon is a pair, one of which is a "virtual" photon, then one half of this pair, presumably the virtual half, may be able to escape from the black hole's event horizon within which all radiation is imprisoned, after the photon and its virtual counterpart have been captured within the horizon.[1] Thus black holes, having gulped huge amounts of energy and mass from ambient stardust and radiation may eventually lose all their substance in the form of escaping energy and finally disappear. Mathematical models show how this kind of process can happen, despite observational evidence as yet being unable to reveal if it does occur. And of course, beyond that "event horizon" of uncertain knowledge there dwell less tractable mysteries such as what greater role black holes themselves may or might enact in their astronomical domain. Even so, the nature of the subject does not completely discourage speculation, which indeed can veer wildly between poles of the bleak and the bountiful—a Cosmos either of final futility or endless regeneration.

But regarding the most puzzling biological phenomena, such as the complex life cycle of certain wasps that fits the category of which Darwin himself said, "we cannot see how an instinct could have originated" [2] science has not even tried to fathom them, nor does the baffling nature of the subject seem to permit, much less encourage speculation. A striking example is that of the ritual enacted by Pepsis marginata, a Caribbean species of "tarantula hawk" which preys upon a tarantula called Cyrtopholis portoricae. That spider's body, after being paralyzed by a calibrated dose of venom, becomes an extended meal for the wasp's developing larva. But after first locating its victim, the wasp investigates it carefully with its antennae while the tarantula passively awaits a doom that instead it could at least try to resist. The wasp then digs a hole to entomb what will shortly become a living corpse, and having done so crawls on its back underneath the spider, which offers little or no resistance to its impending, surgically delivered fate. The curiously acquiescent victim is typically stung exactly in the abdominal nerve center with a sub-lethal dose that will not ruin the exercise by producing a dead corpse which would rot before the larva had fed sufficiently. Then the insect drags its victim to the hole and shoves it in, covering it with dirt after laying an egg on the body and tucking in the limbs to prevent any chance of escape should the tarantula regain its powers of movement. Soon the larva will hatch and start consuming the flesh, saving the vital organs for last so as to keep alive whatever tissues remain until the grisly meal and the larva's growth have been completed.[3] Clearly, this awful sequence is precisely orchestrated to always produce the same result, else the wasp's genes would not survive in its progeny and the species become extinct. But how each step in this complex behavior, including that of the larva's careful partaking of the feast and, perhaps, the tarantula's odd acceptance of a role as the passive partner in a symbiosis that does it no obvious good, came about would seemingly defy all rational explanation in Darwinian or any more imaginative terms. Of course, constant genetic factors must be involved because the same procedure has been repeated over millions of wasp generations, while natural selection will also expurgate the genes of any tarantula hawks (of which a variety of species occur, wherever tarantulas are found) who fail to do their gruesome job precisely and effectively.

Nevertheless, the psychology of human striving towards greater knowledge has ever demanded explanations that can obviate any chance of some ragged twilight zone abutting the manicured borders of science, like a slum crowding against an elegant shopping district. And, as often in cases of vastly complicated issues where a semblance of knowledge is provided by what modest ideas may strive to represent the stupendous reality, such biological bafflements as the life cycle of parasitic wasps can be stuffed into the same generic packaging as first offered by Darwin. For the basic principles presented in "The Origin of Species" and later updated by genetic discoveries do in fact encompass those living phenomena which they cannot fully explain, just as the universal forces of gravity and sunlight drive unpredictable storms. Hence what is called the theory of evolution, that in essence simply points toward an immense four-dimensional organism whose body is that of all terrestrial species past and present and is rooted in abyssal time, has pretended to have tracked that creature to its shadowy lair and then dragged it forth into the glare of reason. Yet the latter faculty is one which that same creature has bestowed upon its human progeny, who shall hopefully now begin to use it more wisely and thereby avoid perishing from the Earth. However, as with many scientific questions emerging from basic discoveries like gravity, whose theoretical framework (as exemplified by the yet to be observed "gravitons" thought to carry gravitational force) is shiftier than once imagined, what has been captured and put on display is not the live animal but a desiccated facsimile from which some meta-rational essence has been drained to leave a barren husk, like the chitinous remains of a dragonfly. And having been rendered from a host of data of which the more awkward (whose numbers are legion) have been put aside, this pallid replica of a living truth which holds our own fathomless beginnings is then proudly displayed on the shelves of academia. Yet it might be foolish to suppose that slender human understanding, or what semblance of knowledge our minds may entertain, is unworthy when compared to the overweening abundance of Creation. For those same minds are also imbedded in a matrix whose proportions transcend the measure of time and space.

In other words, what evolutionary theory says simply conforms to natural limitations on what the mind is able to grasp, an ability that falters when confronted by the boundless ingenuity of Nature herself. Thus, for example, there is no conceivable explanation for the coordinated character of genetic changes which determined that one of the first creatures to emerge on land some 350 million years ago, Acanthostega, should have gills as well as lungs, or that its fully aquatic ancestors had already started to develop the limbs later used for walking on land.[4] Both adaptations—the appearance of primitive lungs and of crude limbs and feet which allowed for terrestrial forays—quite fortunately happened at about the same time, as if the creature's genome somehow foreknew what its descendants could become (although it may have been some other species whose subsequent lineage included dinosaurs along with mostly smaller and presumably reptilian creatures ancestral to modern reptiles and mammals). Of course, the originating cause of these mutations may have been a purely fortuitous rearrangement of DNA which just happened to encode a superior degree of order or physiological adaptation as compared to the less versatile creatures ancestral to Acanthostega and whatever brave amphibians may have joined it in emerging from the ancient seas

But the concept of "randomness," which could seem compelling in a Universe devoid of mystical proportions nor imbued with any metaphysical support for subjective experience, is shredded by the observation that mutations can hardly attain the higher degree of order that allows for new species to excel above their ancestral lineage without the additional information required for that superior order to obtain. Hence there must be a place from where that information comes and a reason and means of its doing so—a "virtual" order becoming real whenever the dynamic reality of evolving Life may invoke its manifestation. That Nature's call invited fish to become amphibious and venture onto lands where no animal, or at least no vertebrate had yet appeared, while that summons resonated in the DNA of those already restless creatures in a way that brought about the required genetic adaptations, would be a poetic way to interpret events that transpired over millions of years. Science of course interprets them more objectively, by indicating for example that some of these adaptations had already existed in a crude form, such as fins that were used for walking on the ocean floor and therefore primed for the enhancement of ambulatory ability via natural selection. But if all living things do not possess a subjective nature, a spiritual essence whose inherent power imparts to species the quality of evolutionary aspiration as it does to individuals an appetite for new frontiers—one version of the "élan vital" that is a bogeyman for orthodox biology—then neither do human beings possess such qualities, and all feeling, all human aspiration and subjective sense of self are simply gratuitous pretence of a heap of dust seeking to permanently enfranchise its illusory existence. Which of course can lead to questions such as the "real" difference between "illusion" and "reality," versus the semantic difference which itself becomes significant only within the virtual reality of a web of words wherein the mind can be ensnared as a victim of the spider of a "real" reality whose larger endeavors and whose love and strife, mere words indeed may help to implement. Hence, from the above, the philosophical ramifications of biology and organic evolution can more plainly appear. For not only the voice of God or of reason but "the voice of the blood," inform and empower our quest for understanding.

12. Information and Enigma

Even if, however, information theory tells us that biological machines that are self-reproducing and maintaining—as are even single cells that can repair their own DNA—belong to some incalculably more sophisticated domain of order than humanly-designed mechanisms (as could be said also to belong the non-self-reproducing yet impeccable order of the atomic and molecular constituents of those machines) it cannot suggest where non-random information might come from. Hence to posit the latter's necessity as in the phrase "intelligent design" is hardly scientific, however rational to claim that same requirement exists. And in fact the scientific theory of evolution neither insists that mutations must be random, nor can it rightly maintain they are not—let alone define what "randomness" actually means. Hence like all other science the theory is "God-neutral," however one construes the immense and exquisitely detailed proportions of Life as extended through the space-time continuum. Nor by its own rules should science ever compromise with facile ways of thinking or be content with comfortable ideas concerning what fragmentary glimpses of natural mysteries our species has obtained. Hence the philosophical comfort of either rejecting evolution, or else accepting some easy explanation that is substantially insecure (as opposed to the basic principles of selection and variation which are quite awkward to deny) offers a kind of temptation contradictory to the progress of human understanding whether scientific or religious. For, from a religious or spiritual point of view, from God has proceeded a complicated world of endless change at every order of magnitude, including the grandeur of evolution, whose subtleties would require an infinite time to explore. And from a scientific point of view, those subtleties that may at least in part submit to reason, such as nuclear energy or how Shakespeares evolved from hominid Calibans, border on a realm of others that do not—such as of what finer stuff are quarks and electrons made, how some parasites can program the behavior of their hosts, or why some persons fall from grace while others rise from adversity. And whether one may favor exhaustive study of an infinitely divisible and complex Creation, or simple faith in the all embracing Infinity of its Divine source, these two views are not mutually exclusive but instead complementary.

And indeed, that argument continues on whether evolution has occurred at all, whereas other tenets of modern science like the place of Earth in a Universe that may harbor countless other planets with intelligent life, or the atomic nature of matter, not to mention the mathematically fearsome arcana of quantum physics and relativity are not met by religious opposition, seems to indicate not only the rational insecurity but also the psychological corruption of views that seek to enlist evolution as the main challenge to faith and most potent weapon in the arsenal of atheist belief. For these same views appear to have drafted the basics of Darwin's theory in support of a simplistic cosmology and meaner concept of human nature than other science can pretend to be able to wrest from its highly impersonal discoveries For investigation of the elemental laws and building blocks of Nature has revealed a stark wonderland whose inhuman austerity can hardly be claimed as "meaningless," since it supports human life whose own meaning is enhanced thereby, just as the lives of penguins are rendered especially miraculous by contrast with the bleak Antarctic waste they inhabit. Yet the genetic keys of life, having been revealed as behind what Darwin knew only as variation and inheritance, have not been rightfully construed in their own context of wonder, whose magic cannot be shown to derive from the accepted canon of natural law. Nothing in physics or chemistry is able to indicate how Life began, let alone became what it is today—a pile of squirming puzzles that bewilder its crowning production, the human brain. Hence the enigmas of biology have been implicitly acknowledged through expressions like "irreducible complexity" or "intelligent design," which simply mean that hopes for any real understanding of how cells and their genetic mechanism can behave as purposefully as human governments face even tougher obstacles than efforts like that of combining gravity with quantum physics. For the latter could conceivably be shown to conform with some hypothesis like string theory, whose mathematical rigor matches the impeccable precision of Nature. But no scientific speculation has even attempted to guess how, for example, a cancer cell is able to invent molecular defenses against the human immune system, an ability not dependent on natural selection since it manifests in full development with the first appearance of cancer cells in the body. The more information that science may acquire, the less that data seems to fit a rationally coherent structure than to form a translucent screen increasingly transmitting the puzzling light of an enigma whose nature will never be fully revealed.

13. Channeling the Flow

Thus it is disingenuous to present such examples as the nearly self-evident role of natural selection in shaping adaptations like the variegated beaks of finches in the Galapagos Islands as proving that principle to be the quintessential guiding force or "mechanism" of evolution. For clearly natural selection was required for evolution to have gotten past square one, while even the weirdest bio-phenomena have been "selected" by the same unforgiving hand which only allowed the Brontosaurus to survive until its adaptive powers—already expended, as it were, in having attained its gargantuan form—were overwhelmed by changes more drastic than Life had confronted for countless aeons. But just as Life could not advance without natural selection, the Sun could not shine without gravitational pressure raising its core density to the point where nuclear fusion can occur, and yet that pressure alone does not suffice to explain stellar nuclear combustion. Hence, just like gravity, natural selection simply constitutes a "formal cause" which supplies a context wherein the "effective" causes of change involving the origin of new species can operate. But genetic mutation also falls short of fully representing that effective cause, because mutations are themselves the change of which the true effective causes remain concealed. New species and their altered genes arise as a unit, while the initial factors provoking the suite of mutations required, for instance, to have afforded the polar bear its resistance to cold, remain obscure To be sure a variety of profoundly subtle reasons for why many of these mutations occur have been identified—for example, the doubling of genes during cell division or their transfer by agents like viruses from one species to another can provide fresh genetic material that can be usefully re-assorted. But that still leaves the unanswered question of where the logic of usefulness has come from. For since the assortment of genes found in a lemur for example, constitutes a pattern that intracellular chemistry is able to maintain through many generations, why should some new arrangement encoding for example the phenotype of something closer to a monkey not have been forged as deliberately as the former genetic pattern had been preserved by Nature's wisdom, until that particular species of lemur decided to head in a new mutational direction that may have ultimately led to homo sapiens? Thus the wellspring of progressive genetic change can just as easily be conceived as the instinctual mind of Nature as dismissed under the rubric of randomness. And in that case, our human minds are scarcely hindered from conceiving that mind of Nature to also be inherent in every quantum of matter-energy, thereby reflecting a Divine Will whence all of Creation with its potential for dynamic change over countless ages sprang into objectivity, as suggested in Vedic scriptures—"having made this Universe from a fragment of myself, I remain." [1]

Clearly a variety of factors may bring about mutations, but the organizing principle that renders them meaningful is an open question in such cases as the "ant-organs" of caterpillars that use these specialized anatomical features, that can serve no other purpose, to play a kind of music as a call to summon ants, who in return for the privilege of drinking a nutritive syrup that the caterpillars exude, will protect them from predators.[2]. There just isn't any logical way to explain this fairy tale marvel of Nature, whose interacting anatomical and behavioral features including the ants' inherent tendency to respond, must involve many coordinated genetic factors—other than to apply the blanket mantra that they were "selected." But of course non-linear or metaphysical explanations which are not verifiably scientific are equally futile because whatever magical reasons they might invoke, such as nature spirits at the behest of "intelligent design" tweaking caterpillar genes to produce the ant-organs, are as deeply buried as the subconscious and cerebral sources for dreams and hallucinations. Thus there remains the paradox that intensive study of evolution, which has forged from unicellular beginnings the physiological basis for consciousness and the sort of mind that is drawn to such pursuit, may confront the need to admit that many biological phenomena are eventually revealed to be, like the fairy brides of mortals in mythology, at least partial denizens of a metaphysical twilight zone which should then have to be recognized as also woven into the fabric of consciousness itself—as an ineradicable contaminant of reason. Otherwise, any fuller comprehension of organic life must await refinements of the strictly materialistic scenario, which in turn is compelled to deny any power of consciousness per se to invest any human spiritual identity beyond the stream of temporal causality. And if that scenario is correct, the specter of unvarnished oblivion looming before each individual might seem of greater concern to him or her than acquiring whatever fleeting semblance of knowledge could help to lend the swiftly dwindling span of years an illusory sheen of the quasi-immortal. Hence a "formal cause" for seeking that semblance and what temporary gloss it might put on corporeal selfhood could be seen as the specter of Death itself, an event that will either erase all personal knowledge or replace it with something unspeakably different, perhaps as per St. Paul "raised a spiritual body" into some larger dimension that is closer to the source of all that is. In any case, the role of natural selection can be conceived as a "formal cause" that channels the flow of both evolution and human history

14. A Thing in Itself

Paradoxically, however, if consciousness is a "res ipsa" or thing in itself, it is also not a "thing," if the latter is an entity that has to be defined by known quantities or ideas—as consciousness may become when regarded as an "emergent property" whose manifestation depends entirely on neuronal structures and processes within the brain. Clearly, these mechanisms are required for thinking and self-awareness, or for that matter even the unconscious behavior of a sleepwalker. And in lesser neuronal complexity of the brain of a dog or a crow, that are only capable of solving problems far less difficult than calculating the mass of the Moon or composing a suitable Andante to follow the opening movement of a work like Beethoven's Fifth or Mozart's Jupiter symphony, a similar framework supports the narrower awareness of those creatures. But to claim that identifying and mapping out cerebral architecture and its functions tends to prove that consciousness and its dreams of immortality is simply a tour de force of a physical brain whose demise shall obliterate all of its late owner's religious fantasies, is a logical fallacy. The fact of a system like the brain being internally consistent in its workings, or that the latter include self-referential "feedback loops," hardly demonstrates that the same system or in fact the whole body of natural laws and phenomena discovered by science, is completely autonomous and independent of any factors which in terms of those laws cannot be described nor identified.

For the unsolved riddles of biology are strong indicators that such "x" or meta-factors do in fact lurk behind the canvas of purported modern wisdom—as a dimension that the latter is unable to portray—and may therefore apply to"consciousness," however problematic to define that term, as well. Otherwise, if science could even hypothetically be able to unscramble the writhing Rubik's cubes of consciousness and evolution, then the "x-factors" are nothing more than part of a deceptively comforting mirage that also includes the entire host of metaphysical entities and "prospective properties" such as the human soul, the benevolent and wrathful deities of Buddhism, and the Supreme Being of Judaeo-Christian theology and scripture, all of them soothing lullabies constantly whispered in the ear of the dying patient that we instantly become on being born. On the other hand, no scientific system of knowledge has the power to demonstrate that any pixie-dust or ghosts in the machine, however airily labeled as "intelligent design" or with names like "universal mind," the Dharma, or Godhead, either do or do not exist. The system of scientific law cannot be proven to represent all things in Heaven and Earth, or to be immune to influences working from outside that system, for much the same reason as in Godel's famous theorem, which says that no finite mathematical system can include irrefutable proofs of its own internal consistency. If the world or Cosmos in its largest sense is the "set of all sets" from whose overall and major truth all minor entities—whether gazelles, galaxies, or Space itself derive—then it is a thing in itself as well, encompassing every aspect of such indefinable yet real existential facts as consciousness. Or, it could be said that metaphysical "things" like consciousness that elude reductive definition are also interpenetrating aspects of each others' nature.

15. Mind Fields and X-Factors

Whereas the question of what the "x-factors" are may have no scientific meaning, however, the philosophical meaning which could be called spiritual as well, can hardly be very different in biology than in physics, where in quantum mechanics the "x-factor" of consciousness of the observer appears to play a role and where such riddles as the galaxies seeming to rotate more rapidly than Newton's laws are supposed to allow, suggest a connection with deeper or more ultimate determining factors than what are currently identified. To be sure, these hidden parameters may lend themselves to rational explanations that are based on new interpretation of known science, as in evolution evidence of impact by a comet gave an excellent possible reason for extinction of the dinosaurs, although these creatures extreme vulnerability to stress that mammals, birds and reptiles were able to endure has not and may never be explained. Both an invisible cloud of hypothetical "dark matter," for example, and a revision of Newtonian physics[1] may explain why the galaxies can rotate faster than seems possible without flying apart like an exploding flywheel. But the factor of consciousness, being the basis of reason itself, can hardly be reduced to the status of a rational outcome of a theory which also explains evolution. For insofar as consciousness is both major ingredient and agent of human experience, our connection with Nature suggests that in some unrecognizable form or manner non-human life may be permeated by a so-called "field of mind" that is only expressed more perfectly or fully through human self-awareness. Thus, that field retains a potential which is realized through the informational content of DNA and its transformations towards ever more autonomously behaving and gracile life forms, that have culminated in a species who is now embarking on what could be called "post-Darwinian" evolution. But for the latter to add any larger meaning to anyone's personal existence, demands that the living truth be greater than what intemperately reductive thinking and the psychology of its advocates may be willing to allow. For narrow definitions of mind that also pre-suppose a human capacity for godlike wisdom in being able to decide what kind of world-view is correct and should therefore prevail in society, can lead to narrower hearts as well that are prepared to impose or obey the rules of a Kafkaesque government where the State is God and its citizens mere pawns, whether economic or military.

And of course that living truth remains oblivious of human inclinations to shrink from its dreadful immensity, which might not even be comfortably scaled down by the actual absence of a Deity or "divine milieu." For the sketchiness of physics combined with the self-evidently more egregious complexity of living phenomena suggests the utter remoteness of evolution from human understanding with or without enlisting metaphysics. But the deeply psychological denial of the true extent of those wonders wherein we are imbedded like bedbugs in the fur of certain African bats on which some species of those insects feed (while displaying bizarre sexual behaviors and adaptations)[2] does not only typify many anti-religious defenders of ultra-reductionist evolutionary dogmas. For "intelligent design" is a form of reductionism as well, first by simplifying the elusive "x-factors" working in evolution to the unspecified actions of a personal God shanghied from a quite larger context. For that context transcends any readiness to meet the need for faith-based explanations which reduce the role of a Deity to that of a designer or "prime mover"—to posit which should obviate any further quest for more specific knowledge. But such attempts to cut the Gordian knot of natural enigmas are disingenuous, not only because Darwin's original theory and later versions of it do not themselves venture to speculate upon the possible existence of any "x-factors" including consciousness let alone a Divine parent of all of them—"I deeply feel the whole subject" (of religion) "is profoundly beyond the human intellect"[3]—but also because, in conflating faith and science, advocates of "intelligent design" and similar pseudo-scientific excuses for irreducible human ignorance of the Magnum Mysterium, would have us believe them to be exceptionally acquainted with the mind of God. Yet it is not irreligious to believe that God's plan may allow some mortal understanding of the Creation and its history insofar as that is possible, a possibility clearly defined by the limited capacities of human intellect. And in such case, both religious and scientific surmising shrinks to insignificance beside the glaring relevance of living Nature and its "immense journey" towards whatever, at least in the space-time continuum, that we are or may become. As to the "many mansions" beyond that dimension, whose existence grows more certain as efforts at reductive or mechanistic explanations of consciousness continue to splatter against the wall of higher truth confronting them, there are no better than what slender clues appear in Scriptures such as St. Paul's report of hearing angelic voices in a "third heaven," or Koranic accounts of Paradise and perdition. And these were written, in language whose rhetorical virtue may bear on their validity, less to captivate sophisticated philosophers than present to a broader audience the elements of a sacred cosmology—albeit dismissed as mythology, though perhaps of redeeming social value, by many scholars today ensconced in their towers of reason whose cubicles are lit by the glare of synthetic enlightenment.

16. A Dynamic Duo: Psychology and Philosophy

Whereas we cannot test the ultimate truth of such perspectives, however, but only the facts on which they may or not be actually grounded, we can certainly examine their psychological meaning and what the latter signifies from a philosophical standpoint, which can also reflect upon the further prospects for personal and human destiny implied by these outlooks themselves. At their two extremes, said views maintain that (A) the fact of evolution should compel recognition that religion is a fantasy whose proper place was in the childhood of the human race (and perhaps as entertainment for the "inner child" of believers) or that (B) there is a God, whose hand directly fashioned all of Nature without any intermediary mechanisms (except for those that allow for minor changes as shown in the breeding of animals) and therefore, evolution itself is mainly a fantasy, "the great cosmogenic myth of the 20th century"[1] whose deception arises from unwarranted faith in human intellect and knowledge. But in between these opposite poles of certainty there is a land where (C) evolution is a fact of Nature that says nothing, one way or the other, regarding any spiritual realm beyond Nature or where (D) there is a Divine agent who does have some connection to Nature in a manner that cannot be ascertained yet cannot therefore be scientifically rejected. All of these perspectives, however, are related to human psychology of the observer who, for reasons often not completely rational, may happen to prefer one or the other. That subjective preference and the objective truth or falsehood of what is preferred, amount to two separate issues. But the larger implications should be quite obvious.

First, if A. is correct, the observer himself or herself is merely an evolutionary byproduct whose very existence—and herein falls the crux of yet another argument of some scientific import—either is or is not a matter of happenstance.. It may be, for example, that natural law as the only factor responsible for the Ascent of Wo/Man, could not have had any different result, because by their own inherent tendency that is blind yet sure as gravity, those laws were bound to foster life, and the latter to evolve towards human awareness and civilization. Or instead, sheer serendipity may have steered those laws in a direction that could easily have ended differently with a dead heap of scorching stones, a desert of lizards, spiders, and thorns, or a timeless Dream-time of primitive hominids whose destiny was to keep hunting and foraging, and perhaps drumming and dancing and telling stories, till solar changes or celestial impacts ended all terrestrial life. In either case, the idea that science is worthwhile and superior to a faith whose object is purely imaginary is not only after the fact that science came a long way before starting to provoke any doubt on religious issues, but also depends on neglecting the plain observation that if there is no God nor any better prospects than temporal dissolution, then value assessments of human endeavor become quite arbitrary. Those endeavors, for example, may have secured a more comfortable existence for us and our descendants at the expense of repealing a selective process that could work more effectively in an environment less buffered by technology. For in having to face a more primal challenge, as a species homo sapiens might be safer than we are today under the shadow of nuclear and other threats that have flown out of the Pandora's box opened by modern technology, even while distracted by the toys that same technology has provided. Hence the ideal of knowledge in and of itself as a worthy goal for a mature humanity with no further need of metaphysical crutches or opiates remains no less dependent than religion on the self-same psychology of faith. And because spiritual belief may have deeper roots in the psyche than reason whose conclusions, as many scientists could argue, must remain equivocal regarding religious issues, a resurgent faith in more sophisticated form that can fully embrace evolution and all other wonders of Creation that science may reveal, is apt to be part of the path that humanity is hopefully destined to pursue.

On the other hand, if instead B. is true and evolutionary theory therefore a grand illusion, we are left with a portrait of humanity nearly as diminished as in the case where (to paraphrase) "science has driven the spirits from the trees into the hills and from thence to the stars, where their final extinction is now possible." But not advisable, admonishes the author of these words, because "we cannot do without them."[2] Perhaps, in other words, these "virtual" spirits in the stars can serve as a sort of escapement for excessive pressures of faith in the power of unaided human understanding, whose continued success might also depend upon a ballast of humility even in the absence of any actual Deity. But (B) is diminishing not only because both God and the Universe are reduced, and in consequence we ourselves, by the notion that Creation was a swift and simple Divine gesture and not an extended process leaving plenty of room for free will and the autonomy of Life, but also because the idea that human beings can know Divine intention and operation well enough to say how S/He actually did create is inherently blasphemous. Meanwhile, the idea that the mind of God can be fully revealed in scripture as a source of absolute knowledge concerning mysteries like the origin of life, suggests a kind of limitation that is markedly similar to the narrowness of faith in science and reason as able to interpret the deepest issues of human nature well enough to vacuum away any pixie-dust precipitated into our brains by an imaginary God whose only real power is that of tricking us into thinking that He and/or She actually exists. And of course whatever philosophy on such issues anyone may choose to adopt, is a question covered by the psychological observation that people believe what they want to believe, irregardless of whether they have free will—a term whose meaning could be pursued endlessly through a semantic house of mirrors—in making their choice.

17. Simplification

However, the issues surrounding topics as vast and complicated as evolution, itself the most complex and difficult in all of science, often have simple solutions for the patent reason that no other kind of answers are possible. This is the case both with Darwin's explanation and its modern refinement that incorporates genetics. Things change, because they cannot stay the same, is the one half of the theory which is identified more specifically as genetic variance and mutation. The other half is, that things tend to change progressively because they cannot on the whole go backwards, which on the face of it would be absurd—for if that kind of backsliding were as likely as forward progress, how could overall positive change have ever become established in the first place? Of course, there may be planets like Mars where life has become extinct, but extinctions happen all at once or relatively swiftly. They are not a gradual retrogression of the original process towards primordial slime. This other half of the theory is called natural selection, but how the two halves conspire gets complicated when one tries to peer inside the machinery to try and understand how and why specific changes occurred—such as mutations giving rise to the exquisite bio-technology of a polar bear's coat whose hollow hairs provide superior insulation, or to the shape-shifting octopus that can mimic the appearance of flounders and other creatures[1]—or why certain species were selected while others like the trilobites, once ubiquitous throughout the oceans, were deselected instead for reasons that remain obscure (unlike the threatened extinction of polar bears which if it does occur will have done so for the visible cause of their icy habitat being melted away by climate change).

Hence an equally simple solution can address the main issues concerning the connection between evolution, assuming it happened, and a Supreme Being who in the context of this discussion shall for the sake of argument be assumed to exist. If the question is whether evolution tends to demonstrate that there is no God, or to the contrary that the God who is witnessed by Scriptures like the Bible and Koran—works whose rhetorical virtues are in large part responsible not only for their literary survival but also for the historical endurance of religious concepts and faith—is not compatible with evolution, then a fairly uncomplicated resolution can be as follows: If there is a God, then the material Universe amounts to a miracle. And in that case, inherent in matter itself there is likely to reside the miraculous power for Life to negentropically arise from inorganic molecules. And when it has done so in a Universe where the presence of a Deity would strongly imply a far greater likelihood of "x-factors" being inherent in both organic and inorganic substance, there is a greater probability for Life to possess the capacity of developing towards eventual production of organisms of sufficient complexity for supporting higher animal and finally human consciousness.

Therefore the presence of a Divine dimension in Creation should make evolution more likely to occur, not less. On the other hand, without a God the Universe remains a miracle or is even more so, but in such a world the evolutionary journey of matter to mind, absent any "x-factor" assistance in overcoming entropy or in somehow spurring improbable mutations as are responsible for parasites—typified by the "lancet fluke" that hijacks the nervous system of an ant in order to steer the hapless insect to the tip of a blade of grass to be eaten by a grazing sheep in whose body the fluke will then continue its life cycle by producing larva that the sheep will excrete in its feces which will then be eaten by another ant[2]—being able to control the behavior of their hosts, is clearly less likely to even get started. In other words, the greater simplicity of a Cosmos lacking any spiritual parameters or metaphysical dimensions, and where reason and rational atheists might thus have greater authority, should scarcely be able to demonstrate that "less is more" by providing superior conditions for Life to emerge than might be found in a world where those dimensions and parameters are prepared to lend their assistance. The exact opposite is more apt to be the case, and accordingly there is no real conflict between God and evolution either in theory or in those wondrous enclaves of Life from archaic ecosystems of the deep to the human cerebral cortex, that actually do obtain. In fact, rather than create Life all at once, as He did in the fatally simplistic abstractions of patriarchal fundamentalist dogma, one well might suppose that a God of the Universe Who could witness the Creation at every stage of its development upon a boundless diversity of worlds, might enjoy observing the gradual unfoldment of Life in Permian or Jurassic times just as much as human scientists enjoy scavenging, in some of our planet's harsher environments, for the remnants of curious creatures that flourished in those distant times. And as to just how curious, there may be much to learn. If dinosaurs are ancestral to birds, for example (rather than some animals that looked like small dinosaurs but were nonetheless altogether different) then it is entirely possible and indeed even likely that the respiratory system of dinosaurs was akin to the avian "through-put" lung, rather than the bellows-type lung of mammals and reptiles which in turn would have to mean that the dinosaur lineage, from its very first emergence on land, was separate from that of reptiles.*

Given the kinds of difficulty encountered in either of the two extreme hypotheses A and B, namely A) Divine creation without evolution as opposed to B) evolution without God or any of the metaphysical factors both dependent on and suggestive of a Supreme Being—factors that also more vitally frame the quest for knowledge itself—the logic of Life, insofar as that can be uncovered, may reside with other alternatives. The neo-Darwinian theory, however, as bears repeating again and again, does not belong to any of these categories because the two principles of mutation and selection that it invokes are facts which can and have been observed. On the other hand, the theory does not say that these two principles are all there is to evolution even though both are indispensable. For, while the science of psychology indicates that the mind may fasten strongly on whatever it is able to comprehend and fiercely defend the intellectual turf where that pet idea or mode of thinking has then become established, no theory or concept can leap outside of its own rational skin in order to claim the total autonomy of absolute explanatory power. Therefore the simplest explanations can be best, because they are less likely to be corrupted by errors and logical fallacies—such as claiming that modern knowledge tends to discount any chance that psycho-spiritual parameters might embrace the whole of what that knowledge is about.

*In fact, this possibility has recently received support from research described in an article in Nature magazine (486, 2005, pp. 253-6) Or see Internet, "Avian Lung."

18. Microbes to Mozart

Ironically, however, Life appears to have done the equivalent—to have surpassed the bounds of any logic human minds can ascertain—when by some ineffable process, its properties first were manifest in what had formerly been or appeared to be mere lifeless molecules, outstripping all humanly conceivable complexities. For the higher order of complexity that biology represents, started by transcending the seeming bonds of material inertia to achieve autonomy of the first unicellular organisms, and must have done so by ways and means which may forever elude all attempts to discover them, even if the most likely conditions for the initial emergence of organic life such as clays or hot springs, can be readily supposed. It can be said, of course, that the chemical complexity of pre-living molecules prepared them to be "quickened" by some external influence to provide new powers of self-assembly and replication, but obviously that influence cannot be further specified. To call it God or an agent thereof is more of a metaphor than explanation, whereas the alternative is to suppose the power of making the jump from chemistry to biochemistry is somehow inherent in matter itself, although that has to be true in either case. But if the quickening influence or "x-factor" is described as internal, an inherent attribute remaining dormant until triggered at some tipping point of molecular ramification, that same property or "virtue" as it were, could be conceived as able to assume the directive role embodied in genetic substance that choreographs the whole of intracellular activity. And if some innate Divinity accordingly resides in every atom and every cell, the poetry of life may have been written not by a mind external or prior to Creation nor by the magic of blindly burgeoning molecular complexity, but instead by Nature herself in a saga whose latest terrestrial chapter of human history is still dramatically unfolding in the greater context of a Creation that could then be seen as an emergent property of God. And of course, because the vagaries of hearts and minds—of human psychology—have become major factors on the cutting, post-biological edge of evolution whose effects are displayed as History, we have yet to learn if the bad mutations of mind that lead to social injustice, genocide and horror can be expunged by the moral immune system of an increasingly vibrant and compassionate humanity, or instead may spell a sorry ending to the story of our self-endangered species.

In any case, the fact of Life's origin from matter-energy—from "the dust of the ground" in Biblical terms—would seem to bear a logical relationship to the character of evolutionary change that followed. The same inherent ability of matter to don the raiment of Life, in other words, carried forward into the process of genetic mutation. If the origin of life was a so-called "random" event—be it noted that "randomness" and "God" bear the same informational content, namely one lacking any scientific meaning—then mutations in all probability are also "random," mechanistic accidents arising from a variety of causes none of which express any purposeful intent even in the short term, where genes could somehow sense and respond to changing needs of the species. And if so, the philosophical consequences are vast—human beings do not have a soul, and the real importance of religion, if any, therefore becomes social more than pertaining to non-existent spirit, despite the latter could still retain no less importance than the null quantity of zero has in mathematics, or serve as a conceptual place to park the mind, so to speak, every once in a while. And in fact that analogy illustrates how hard it can be to distinguish the ideal from the real, or to claim objectivity for views that are generated within the subjective worlds of thinkers and observers, microcosmic bubbles in a stream whose power and extent can scarcely be surmised. But if a Deity, an Entity who almost by definition transcends the scope of information, swooped down to nudge the chemicals of primitive oceans, ponds or clays to marshal them into the elegant arrangements and processes required for Life—or more likely, sent an angelic emissary to do the job—then the same would doubtless apply to further critical steps of evolution.

This could mean that the change effected through Divine intercession or involvement was of a "quantum" character—that is, the succession of angelic interventions or "quickenings" could be nearly continuous or in fact a seamless interface between physical life and some metaphysical context where dwells potential that in matter is destined to eventuate. This type of scenario clearly leaves a variety of options concerning the spiritual distance between God and evolution and the consequent degree of autonomy expressed by Nature. Parasites and other monstrosities could suggest that distance to be wide—thus leaving plenty of room for theological disputes that arguably are but one variety of the strife to be expected in a world that is a "school for souls" of whom the brightest are light years away from understanding biology in any better than the kinds of crude, linear terms that may, in fact, represent the limits of language beyond whose squishy barrier the truth shall ever roam unfettered by any explanatory manacles. Yet of course the metaphor of Divine intercession can be easily transposed into one of Divine activity ever working in a world from which it has never been absent, and where the presence of Spirit or consciousness would naturally tend to promote the dynamic change expressed in Life's progression from protozoa to politics, microbes to Mozart, bacteria to Bach—from germs to worms to wondering why.

Hence in the latter view it can be readily supposed that the spark of life is already bound within matter-energy that itself has derived from some unspecified spiritual origin or pre-existing condition. For if the nature of that origin cannot be rendered or suggested in any conceptual formula, then perhaps the inherent spark is likewise endowed with potential to behave in a manner that no workable theory could hope to account for. And if so, one might expect that same potential to further manifest through genetic mutation on a rising arc not only buttressed by natural selection, but lifted by Life's innate capability to invent ever more sophisticated organisms for whose support, in turn, the more humble and enduring (such as pollinating bees and waste-consuming worms) continue to serve. In such case, the oft-derided "teleonomy" or goal-seeking attribute of evolution is not only directed towards the organic abundance clearly pursued through reproduction of creatures like fish that produce thousands of eggs so that a few might survive, but towards the fuller elaboration and refinement that has become, at last, the vehicle for human consciousness—a faculty that may mistake its calling in trying to rationalize such inexplicable aspects of reality as, for example, consciousness itself.

In both of the above evolutionary schemes, however, what can actually be observed is no different than if in fact there are no "x-factors" or mystic dimensions whatsoever involved in Life's origin and development. Yet even then the mysteries of biology are bound to remain immensely more profound and elusively subtle than in any other field of science. But with regard to the difference between these two scenarios that could be posited by faiths not hostile to Darwin, that distinction could be clarified by saying that in one it is God as person or "designer" whose Divine agency upholds—in part through laws like natural selection whose needed cruelty that Deity does not restrain—the life and evolution that such a Being would surely prefer not only to the barren splendor of celestial bodies and lights without living things but also to a perfect and changeless world of angelic robots or of blissful bourgeoisie which He/She could conceivably have instantly created instead (and may, for all we know, be found on planets where intelligent life has attained an untroubled plateau and remains for countless ages in the Eden of a timeless "dreamtime") Yet in the other view what could be called the substance of Divinity, or an all-pervading consciousness ranging through a vast variety of stages and qualities, either lends to physical substance its innate tendency towards living manifestation, just as sunlight lends energy to the metabolism of plants, or else simply corresponds in its humblest degree to matter-energy, which then becomes in effect the most palpable aspect of a universal mind or Dharma, projected by or proceeding from a Being whose embodiment is none other than the Cosmos itself.

19. Vital Information

To say that Life is inherent in the Cosmos and in matter, however, is a view which has been criticized as "vitalism" or as invoking despised "vital forces" that are the bogeyman of orthodox biology. Thus in proposing a more scientific approach to examining the flaws of reductionism, which basically reside in the extreme improbability of chance combinations of inert chemicals being able to form living cells, or for intra-cellular genetic changes to randomly hit upon the complex formula involving more than a single gene that corresponds to a stepping-stone of evolutionary advance or vital adaptation—such as the hollow hairs of a polar bear's coat that provide superior insulation, or the hollow bones of a bird that became stronger and lighter in the course of the avian ancestral lineage gradually evolving all of the other precisely structured anatomy also required for flight—it has been suggested that the "x-factor" seemingly demanded to supplement Darwinian principles could be identified as information. Information is a more scientific term than "vital forces" because, according to information theory in mathematics, the self-replicating and self-maintaining machinery of living cells cannot subsist or have arisen without an input of information in vastly larger quantity than required to produce a non-self replicating machine like a hair dryer or a can opener. On the other hand, the non-scientific concept of "vital forces" has been described as equivalent to "morphogenetic fields" providing the templates for living forms. If life is so radically different from matter, in other words, then just as electromagnetic and gravitational fields constitute a framework for molecular and astronomical phenomena, an additional type of field, operating according to or expressing natural laws too elusively magical to be measured or modeled, must be called upon as a hidden cause—perhaps a formal cause like the gravitational potential energy of a boulder on a mountainside rather than the immediate and effective cause that could trigger its descent—that the very existence of Life and its evolutionary consequence could seem to proclaim.

But in that kind of case, the prospect of fields, forces, or influences at work in living Nature that unlike radiation or molecular motion are inaccessible to scientific instruments, suggests the true picture of the Cosmos as being an hyper-dimensional iceberg of which only the uppermost layers of space-time and matter-energy have been or can be observed. Hence there can be sources of order, and perhaps of information whence biophysical phenomena derive those deeper patterns whose logic appears to transcend the laws behind repetitive motion of non-living matter. Hence it could be stressed, for example, that the self-replicating and self-maintaining quasi-intelligence of the living cell can hardly be detached from the biochemistry or mechanics of mutation. In other words, the latter can hardly fail to cleave to the same inherent tendency to self-ordering expressed by the intracellular activity of protein molecules—like the "chaperon" molecules that snip and then re-attach the strands of DNA to prevent their entanglement during cell division—that unswervingly perform their functions that in turn can be steered by the needs of some plant or animal within whose greater context those molecules and their cells may belong, as when cells of the adrenal gland secrete more hormones in response to stress. Thus in some unknowable fashion mutations—whose purposeful correction when they are accidental, erroneous and harmful by the intracellular machinery would seem to indicate untold dimensions of greater complexity than found in the "particle zoo" of nuclear physics—may also obey requirements not only of the organism but its descendants' evolutionary path, as was trod for example by those walking fish or fish-like amphibians that when first emergent on land simultaneously possessed lungs and gills, thus giving them a grip on both the future and the past.

Of course, there is no way to prove that mutations, and thus the crux of evolutionary change which has led to each new ecological phase up to that which now includes human civilization, are governed by anything other than known scientific principles, any more than it is possible to tell why a bird or a flock of them will suddenly decide, in the absence of any obvious threat or other survival need, to fly from their perch in a tree to a very similar place in the same vicinity. Thus the question becomes whether it is rational, or instead violence against reason and accordingly against knowledge itself, to concede any virtues or properties to Nature that cannot be identified and conformed to some reasonable hypothesis. And in the same context must also be included human nature, of whose own qualities some either may or may not be allied with metaphysical aspects of the Cosmos that shall ever abide beyond all rational understanding. (Although one such aspect could be that if the genetic template for a bear or bumblebee corresponds to an idea, and if ideas exist outside of Time, then the informational equivalent of species and their evolution is just as metaphysical as the concept of a cube or parabola). In other words, is it Life itself—for that is what evolution amounts to—that can or in theory could be grasped entire by the intellect, or only certain derivative features of the evolutionary pattern whose method of working can be recognized? One answer could correspond to an observation about the human brain, the crowning production of Nature—"if the brain were so simple we could understand it, we would be so simple we couldn't."[1]

20. Getting the Gestalt

That last quote may suggest an "holistic" view often associated with "vitalist" pseudo-scientific explanations that may be condemned as a threat to science itself and thus to civilization, whose continued progress is the highest conceivable goal and purpose for collective human existence on this planet, either with or without a Deity, especially when entrenched conditions of misery deny many members of that so-called civilization much chance to be more than suffering survivors. And a Deity's Earthly purposes, at least according to Judaeo-Christian theology, will best be realized through a civilization whose moral, economic, and ecological integrity are enhanced rather than diminished by science and technology, whose gifts then could work to repeal "social Darwinism," rather than further its harsh dominion by supplying the tools of modern warfare. But in absence of that Deity and His/Her attendant spiritual milieu, that is rendered less likely in a purely reductionist scenario (or rather, scientific materialist, since reductionism ultimately leads to the strangeness of a quantum reality which has lots of room for either ghosts or God) there is equally lesser cause for current generations to assume, even as their soulless forms prepare to pass away, responsibility for shaping a better society for their descendants to enjoy. Nor does the anti-spiritual philosophy leave any reason to suppose that the pursuit of knowledge, in and of itself, can carry the existential burden of justifying the lives of men and women who are otherwise, from a purely ecological standpoint, not always helpful to the rest of Nature or for that matter the human nature of a self-endangered species. Nonetheless, the twin imperative, both moral and Darwinian, to cherish and protect Creation has become so compelling that advocates of either religious or strictly secular perspectives can understand that the natural world must be integrated harmoniously with civilization in a way that favors grace and beauty over short-term expediency of commercial interests. Otherwise, a civilization that fails to ennoble human nature, will eventually find that the latter can become Nature's agent of destructive Darwinian imperatives, should all moral imperatives have been ignored.

But if spiritual dimensions of the Sacred or whatever label is used are sufficiently real to help us bear that burden, then its further implications also have to be accepted. For a Gestalt whose metaphysical substance is more than the dumb and invisible clay—perhaps described as the "quantum foam" of spacetime or in other highly sophisticated terms, and that was transformed into stars and the stardust whence our bodies were formed according to the strange logic of laws imbued by some ineffable magic—is then the fathomless framework for consciousness, life and evolution. And the choice whether to accept that view and its expansive suggestions or instead to meanly misconstrue the purpose of knowledge and reason by rejecting all but the most dryly rational picture of a Universe which then well may "appear to be more meaningless the more it is investigated,"[1] is matched by a more vitally practical decision now faced by society. The latter is whether to acknowledge and act upon the pressing needs of global interdependence that binds human destiny and the welfare of nations together with the non-human biosphere, or instead keep submitting to the Darwinian dominance of social and economic forces whose moral deficits are plainly manifest in poverty, conflict, and increasingly dangerous fouling of our environmental nest.

For the global interaction of those dire effects compounds their menace to where humanity shall now have to "seize fate by the throat" simply in order to survive, let alone make further progress on the path of post-Darwinian evolution whose promise is the only beacon of a brighter future. And only if and when that challenge is met will philosophical and religious issues related to the topic of evolution and of what science may learn concerning our Cosmic situation—such as concerning life on other worlds or if and when "the Heavens shall wear out like a garment"[2]—have any chance to be sorted out. In fact, they would then largely sort themselves out. For somewhat ironically a collective decision to detoxify and soften the winds of change that should else rise in unstoppable fury, would also demonstrate a firmer grasp of humanity's rightful place in the Cosmos, than could any bookish "measure of man" or of his/her surroundings. And that is because in a world of social justice, environmental sanity and consequent freedom from fear that lack of reverence for Creation might finally provoke what powers may be to pull the plug on homo sapiens, each person might more readily perceive that his or her connection to a living Universe and to Divine reality is no less actual than the link between mind and body, thereby gaining a kind of organic assurance of greater value and immunity to disputation, than any rational assurance based on scientific knowledge or whatever kind of wisdom is proclaimed in churches or the temples of academia. Faith in its least corrupted form, in other words, says that this present world is ephemeral yet meaningful, because it derives from that same eternal source that by any name is never beyond the reach of anyone longing for communion with a Truth beyond all human understanding.

In a Universe where the Supreme Being remains "outside," as it were—in Her own interior dimension wherein the purely outward measure of the Universe does not participate—the laws of evolution must proceed autonomously, and thus possess some inherent directing principle of their own. For a universe conceived as lacking any metaphysical parameters, this directive tendency has been identified as natural selection but as can easily be demonstrated, the same principle is indispensable, no matter the place or the reality of Spirit. For just like quantum mechanics and relativity, evolution has to work in much the same way and follow a similar path in each of two hypothetical worlds, one with a Divine or non-objective origin and support and the other without. For clearly, without natural selection of the more viable members of a species and of useful adaptations that are stepping-stones towards entirely new species as in the case of small dinosaurs or dinosaur-like creatures that gradually, (although just how gradually an insoluble mystery) conquered the skies with ultimately greater skill, swiftness and endurance than presumably clumsier and less resilient pterosaurs that were fated to perish, the whole evolutionary process could just as easily regress to primordial slime or further, to the square one of complex chemicals. But that very need for the dynamic order upheld by natural selection, a feature that life can no more do without than matter could subsist without the precise uniformity of sub-atomic and atomic structure, does not obviate the existence of a living intelligence whose interior dimension dwells within Nature herself. For that same intelligence, whose essence is no harder nor easier to identify than that of human intelligence which still struggles to fathom the neurological microcosm wherein it is grounded, is what manifestly guides protein molecules to perform their tasks within the living cell, a fertilized cell to multiply along the ascending track from embryo to organism, and the cells of organs and tissues and those organs themselves, as units, to maintain the whole organism's vital functions. Therefore it is hardly irrational to suppose the same sort of instinctive intelligence that manages our myriad bodily functions, and that is clearly a deeper faculty of Nature than what science can apprehend, could also have played a part in promoting whatever genetic changes accompanied every step of Life's ascent from germs to worms to wondering why..

Hence those bodies to which our spirits are linked—unless those spirits, to our enormous disadvantage in many respects, do not exist—are endowed with a complexity fully worthy of the wondrous process which has brought them forth "from the dust of the ground" over billions of years. And that of course is no less true, even if no mysterious instinct has from Life's beginnings shaped a genetic path ever prepared to match all future needs and possibilities, than also true that some virtual wisdom of the body clearly does perceive and respond not only to such immediate needs as for vomiting tainted food or pumping more blood, but can also perform miraculous cures as in the rare expurgation of deadly tumors. Nevertheless, anyone willing to grant an innate intelligence or "wise blood" to all of life while also wishing to attribute its likely source, could find mention of the latter in Vedic scripture— *"I watch and in its work of creation nature brings forth all that moves and moves not: and thus the revolutions of the world go round."*[3] It doesn't say how that work is accomplished—only that the task was delegated to Nature, whose own capacities and qualities being of Divine provenance no less than ourselves, should while challenging our understanding also "bewitch us body and soul."

21. Too Much Reality: The Ubiquitous Other

Thus Voltaire remarked concerning the science of his day—the day of the "clockwork universe" of Isaac Newton (who nonetheless also immersed himself in alchemy and the Bible)—that to study Nature, not "divine her," was the proper approach to natural phenomena. And indeed that same approach is virtually forced upon those who in attempting to divine the non-living kingdoms of particle physics and astronomy have found that every new discovery demands that further study is required, whereas trying to "divine" what these discoveries mean leads to theories so removed from the everyday kind of thinking that science still seeks to apply to seemingly friendlier facts of biology as to become almost terrifying. Animals, plants, and even single-celled organisms are accessible to the senses and carry on in a manner that makes perfect sense—beginning with the obvious need for survival that in human beings is often transferred into the psychological sphere, where the symbolic victory of "winning" or of "saving face" can become more precious than life itself. As indeed it should, for lacking the will for moral and spiritual survival expressed in such phrases as "give me liberty or give me death," all virtue, character and meaning would be drained from human existence.

But the weird otherness of theories invoked to try and resolve such riddles as presented by the daunting conceptual gulf that separates quantum mechanics from relativity affords no purchase for the kind of straightforward analysis that was applied to tangible geologic and fossil evidence in order to conclude that Life has incrementally ascended from abyssal Time, but instead can only be approached by a rare mathematical imagination that very few possess. Yet Life itself is no stranger to an otherness of its own, as fully beyond ordinary conception as the infinitesimal "strings" of energy vibrating in many dimensions that modern physics has proposed as the ultimate pixels of physical existence. For countless examples can show that no hard explanation for how many of the stranger facts of biology—more so even than the marvels of the eye that Darwin himself regarded in fear and trembling for the possible insufficiency of his theory which that organ's complexity suggested—could have evolved, is even remotely possible. And in that sense, the deepest riddles of biology appear more baffling than those of physics, where explanations, however arcane, for the mind-bending perplexities encountered in examining matter-energy and space-time, can at least be attempted.

A prominent paradoxical observation that helped give rise to quantum theory was of course the "double slit" experiment that shows how particles of light are also waves, and not simply small pieces of energy, as could hardly be otherwise. For if photons were merely spatially bounded units of substance then what would be in between them, other than nothingness which by definition cannot be described or explained, and what would the boundary of those units consist of? If the boundary were a two-dimensional surface it would then be effectively abstract as the "nothingness" that boundary divided from the actual particle itself. Clearly to have any real meaning, those kinds of abstractions at the very least must depend on the reality of space itself, but the latter's existence then calls for further explanation that our minds have not by any Darwinian principle evolved in order to obtain as they evolved to track game, to find edible plants, or to make tools and fire. Thus the non-local property of a wave must be invoked to account for the particle's energetic properties—its own inherent capacity for action and for operation in the time-space milieu with which it is continuous rather than separate from. And that continuum is the same in which there must occur the phenomena of genetic mutation, and if that continuum is temporal as well as spatial, may not the possible future affect those changes within the living cell that lead to transformation such as once forged shrew-like mammals into bats and whales, or the forelimbs of small dinosaurs, or animals resembling dinosaurs, into the wings of crows and owls? And if so then certainly humanity's possible future, whose dim outlines are at least more evident to human imagination than its possible descendants to the mind of whatever kind of lungfish first began the terrestrial chain of begats that finally became ourselves, may affect our hopefully choosing to build a society that values more abundant life above the grim survival needs of prideful nations and clueless ideologies. For that kind of choice, however problematic to conflicted minds, can come naturally to human hearts whose proper functions should include mediating a deeper interpersonal, ecological and spiritual communion, the latter being what could be called the marriage of Earth and Heaven. Else what lesser and meaner criteria should propose what the course of human life is ultimately guided by or aspires toward—while Life itself disposes and our words keep fading away into the wind.

Yet, if Life's belonging to a time-space continuum and not simply one of space alone, is what finally compels acceptance of Darwinian principles—no outline more finely drawn being possible for how the works of Nature have unrolled—then every challenge to those principles must be addressed. An easy example that like many others proclaims the "otherness" of the many biological kingdoms everywhere around and within us, is provided by what is called the "through-put" or flow-through lung of birds[1] These lungs incorporate tiny tubes, sometimes called parabronchi[2] through whose walls respiratory gases are exchanged in similar fashion to how they are filtered through the walls of tiny air-sacs or alveoli in the lungs of mammals and reptiles. It is quite difficult and probably impossible, since no scientist has made the attempt, to imagine some intermediate form of lung in between that of a lizard or reptilian dinosaur and a bird. The lung must be exclusively constituted of either parabronchial tubes that air flows clean through or else of alveoli where the breath dead-ends before subsequent exhalation, in order for the creature to be able to breathe. A mixture of the two would not function, unless they were separate in parallel sets of lungs. But even the latter would seem impossible, because all associated respiratory structures must be adapted exclusively to either one or the other scheme. In birds, the breath is pumped in a unidirectional flow by a system whose details are not spelled out in most textbooks if at all, but which provides for the greater respiratory efficiency needed for avian flight (whose powers of speed and endurance surpass those of bats with their mammalian lungs). The insoluble riddle as to how the avian respiratory system could have evolved from that of a lizard-like animal whose lung was analogous to our own has been posed as a major obstacle to the Darwinian concept of evolution and thus to evolution per se, since no theory can even be imagined which does not include variation and selection. But in fact that obstacle is an illusion. The avian lung is not more nor less of a natural wonder than our own, and could just as easily have evolved from creatures of a lineage separate from that of the reptiles and mammals from the very beginning of animal life on land, pioneered by stubby-legged walking fish that in some cases possessed both lungs and gills.

Thus the respiratory system of whatever air-breathing creatures were ancestral to birds would have employed parabronchial tubes instead of alveolar air sacs. Meanwhile these creatures themselves could and most likely did resemble small dinosaurs, unless of course actual dinosaurs were the true ancestors of birds, in which case they would have to have had the avian type of lung—as recent studies in fact reveal could well have been the case.

If the latter is not so, then that lung and its associated structures could only have sprung into being by virtue of a single massive mutation, occurring in many individuals simultaneously, and switching in a single generation from the tiny air sacs of the parental generation to the parabronchial tubes found in modern birds, along with all of the associated anatomical changes that would also be required. The notion of any type of lung combining both alveoli and parabronchi in a series of transitional forms that over the ages gradually swung towards a purely avian type with its supporting physiology (like the large air sacs in the hollow bones of birds) is plainly preposterous. However, the clear and simple way around the evolutionary paradox claimed for the avian lung by detractors of Darwinian theory has never been proposed, for reasons that themselves are extremely obscure, thus leaving evolutionary biologists to carry on an argument as to whether birds did evolve from dinosaurs. One noted biologist indicated this was unlikely, because the wing bones of birds do not appear to match up with bones in the forelimbs of dinosaurs from which the wing bones would have developed as the forelimbs were slowly transformed into wings over millions of years,[3] But that additional twist to the puzzle of avian origins does not obviate the clear and simple solution to the question of the flow-through lung, which could also have been present in dinosaurs even if birds did not arise from whatever those creatures were, but instead from something else that merely resembled them. Consequently, the riddle of the avian lung simply becomes an exception serving to highlight the rule that Nature—an alien "other" on whose hide we reside—abounds with many far more baffling bio-enigmas that defy even tentative and hypothetical solutions.

A number of these puzzles involve not only physiology but behavior, whose being wired into the genes over many generations of selecting whatever mutations had to occur would seem hard to choreograph through chance alone. In this regard it bears repeating the grim tale of how certain kinds of wasps are genetically programmed to attack and paralyze with a sub-lethal dose of venom a large insect or spider of species depending on that of the wasp, whose body shall feed the wasp's developing larva. Success of this behavior demands that the attacker sting its victim in the abdominal nerve center, and in the case of a tarantula hawk wasp it must crawl under the spider's belly on its back in order to deliver the poison. Therefore in whatever wasps first managed this gruesome task successfully, there must have been encoded in genes that were relayed to future generations, the instinct towards such behavior and innate awareness of how to do the job correctly. Wasps able to inject a calibrated dose of venom precisely into the spider's nerve center would be selected above those who failed to subdue their prey or else killed it outright, leaving these incompetents no other adequate means to provide for their offspring. Anything smaller than a tarantula, in the case of tarantula hawks could be harder to paralyze without killing it and would not suffice to nourish the larva's full development. Nor does the choreography of instinct end with the victim being rendered helpless, for the wasp must also entomb the living corpse, after depositing the egg on its surface, in a hole which may be prepared in advance. And finally the growing larva must enact its own horrid role correctly by saving its victim's vital organs for the last, so that the arachnid will not perish and start to decay before its own miserable mission of nourishing the larva's growth has been fulfilled (the story varies somewhat among several different species of tarantula hawks that belong to the genus Pepsis, and different genera of similar wasps prey upon other kinds of victims)[4] This entire routine clearly fits the category of behavioral adaptations that Darwin viewed, and dismissed, as a possible challenge to his theory but more seriously to notions that a merciful God could also have created or allowed the peculiarly awful horrors of invertebrate existence. In any case, the wasps' life cycle must be genetically ingrained so as to recur in each generation whose instinctive knowledge guides their precise reenactment of the same pattern, including the larva's care in eating to avoid killing its host.. But to imagine how the entire drama was either pieced together over time from pre-existing adaptations, like a poisonous stinger, that by themselves already served a useful purpose, or else was manifested all at once in a superior new generation of wasps, could tax intellect well beyond those limits already marked by the arcana of modern physics, even if specific genes involved could somehow be identified. Clearly, then, if "man cannot stand too much reality"[5] biology is an especially likely place to encounter that unwelcome abundance.

In fact the question of behavior and of how the insect knows what it is doing can be analyzed just as intensively and with as little hope of arriving at any conclusion as problems of a very different nature but comparable difficulty arising in quantum theory, where the meaning of what certain experiments appear to indicate has been debated for nearly a century.[6] How and when for example did a wasp first conceive of laying its egg on the body of a tarantula, along with the whole choreographed sequence of actions necessary for the scheme to work? What suite or sequence of mutations fostered a behavioral pattern subsequently encoded in the wasp's genes for countless millennia, so that, for example, each new generation instinctively knows how to sting its victim in the proper place with a calibrated sub-lethal dose of venom? No part of the entire behavioral sequence, for instance preparation of a hole for the victim, could have arisen by chance due to a random mutation somehow favoring occurrence of such action. Nor could anything less than the whole sequence of actions prove useful, and therefore the wasp's predatory pattern had to initially emerge in its final form in order to be preserved by natural selection. This problem has no bedrock where definitive answers like Newton's laws of motion could be obtained. Hence a more general and rhetorical solution, which of course is not scientific, appears to offer the only attainable means of understanding. That kind of solution—and there may be others of no greater validity than science fiction—could indicate that the insect in some respect knows what it is doing well enough that in the distant past, an ancestral wasp discovered a mode of survival that subsequently in accordance with natural law, became wired into the genetic code of the entire genus of tarantula hawks. Yet precisely how these genetic factors might interact with the wasp's tiny brain to guarantee the generational re-enactment of its gruesome tradition, is just one of those questions that allows for no better than such holistic or even mythological explanations (holistically, the wasp and its victim are bound together within an ecological web where their traditional roles emerged as naturally as mythic rituals like human sacrifice first began in ancient societies) in those metaphysical mists that swirl chaotically wherever no chart or chain of rational connections can either be drawn or identified.

22. The Size of Bio-Complexity

Indeed, if taken within the framework of a mutual interdependence of Life and inorganic matter-energy as part and parcel of a cosmic Gestalt that cannot be more precisely defined, many physical theories become nearly as open-ended and approximate as the broad principles that constitute the theory of evolution. The Big Bang theory, for example, says basically that the Universe came from a tiny seed, but precisely how this happened is not entirely clear. And, while the micro-worlds of atomic theory and of chemistry possess many features that are clearly identified, especially those mathematical laws which have to be true in order for matter-energy to provide a reliable platform for physical existence, it is far from obvious what atoms and their sub-atomic pieces really "are", as epitomized by the now defunct designation of atomic pieces like quarks and electrons as "point particles." Nor do such questions as to the ultimate nature of substance even make any sense, given that the limitations of language and thinking would seem to render them utterly futile. Points are zero dimensional, of which nothing can be said other than their relative position in space. But if the least constituent parts of matter-energy are not actually nothing, they still remain engulfed in the paradox of being more physically basic than anything else and yet completely indescribable—black holes for knowledge as it were, although these irreducibly tiny "things" fleck the blank wall of No-thing-ness that is the "white hole" from whence all existence including the human inventors of language and of words and ideas like "existence" has originated.

But in the case of Life such contradictions are simply magnified, insofar as biological complexity transcends in both degree and kind that of non-living phenomena. Hence the distinction between existence and non-existence—the "thingness" of the familiar material world and the "no-thing-ness" whence it sprang (and wherein it still consists, insofar as the quantum constituents of "things" are not classical objects and the volume of those objects themselves consists mainly of intermolecular spaces that are, like interstellar and all of space filled with energy)—is easier to identify or to frame in philosophical terms than distinctions between the living and the non-living. Yet if the latter is identified as the difference between the self-replicating and self-creating autonomy of biological organisms as opposed to non-self replicating and other-created character of machines, then a similar distinction could be posited as dividing the evolution of living from that of non-living Nature. And so doing would appear to demand non-mechanistic reasons why and how progressive genetic mutation can forge new species, while conceding that to understand such reasons or modality of change is probably impossible. For that kind of transcendence, that separates the laws of biology from those of physics, could be crudely modeled by the mathematical analogy of a transcendent number such as pi that the endless string of digits 3.1417...only approximates, inhabiting a region surpassing that of ordinary numbers by dint of more than mere quantitative proportions. Numbers like pi elude arithmetical definition and by similar token, the exquisite pattern of the least living thing is of a meta-complexity transcending any sum of all of its discrete elements, factors and connections. For while the total number of parts may for example be larger in a computer than a bicycle, or in a car than a can-opener, that quantitative difference can more easily be defined than what elevates the workings of Life above any system fully described by the laws of chemistry and physics. Thus, hypotheses concerning the origins of the physical

Cosmos are more precisely formulated and better supported by observations like the background microwave radiation or the red shift of light from retreating galaxies, than are any conceptions of how the first living cells could have emerged in the dawn of terrestrial life. For while the mysteries of matter-energy assuredly gave rise to or were translated into those of Life, just as ordinary arithmetical numbers are transformed into transcendental ones, exactly how that translation occurred is a question that keeps reverberating within the cosmically localized sphere of our human understanding.

Yet complicated questions can be simple ones, amenable to simple and straightforward answers, when all that can be known are basic outlines of an issue such as how complex chemicals combined to form the first living cells, or why dinosaurs both great and small could not survive ecological consequences of the impact of an enormous comet 65 million years ago, whereas equally primitive reptiles including crocodiles far larger than those of today were able to overcome whatever those disastrous consequences must have been. The simple answer is that the chemicals did combine into the substances of Life, and that the dinosaurs, even small ones, clearly lacked some vital resilience that was possessed by their more adaptable reptilian cousins, along with primitive mammals and birds. For if the alternative would be that Divine intervention must have accomplished every step in evolution that intervention becomes an x-factor which is logically equivalent to all that we cannot understand concerning evolution, and that factor or sum of them being by definition unknowable as any presumptive mind or purposes of God, there is no logical way to assert those factors must have been Divine as under the rubric of "intelligent design." All we can say is that evolution must have been at every stage at least imbued with the virtual intelligence or vital instinct clearly at work in the living cell and its indefatigable protein constituents that know how to do their maintenance, metabolic and reproductive jobs as surely as does the human body on a grander scale of operation, that marshals every cellular element towards service of the whole. Therefore insofar as "wisdom of the body" is not a theologically burdened phrase, neither should be "the wisdom of evolution," words that suggest a Supreme Being only because the existence of natural wonders which defy explanation may indicate still greater wonders, that could be called supernatural in that they appear to transcend all human conceptions of natural law. Yet, if the concept of Deity is not totally absurd, it becomes reasonable to suppose that Creation is the body of that Deity and therefore sacred. And in that case, evolution becomes a function of that body which is just as natural and yet easily as remote from understanding as concerning how the myriad interlocking functions of the human body are collectively coordinated. In either case, whether evolution or human physiology, the real dimensions of organic life splash over and beyond the edges of any picture of the natural world that human intellect may entertain or shall ever be able to attain.

And that of course is no reason to not keep expanding and improving upon the picture, for in so doing science may help instruct us how to more deeply "consider the leviathan" as Job was divinely advised in the Bible, and thereby acquire a fuller appreciation of humanity's place in a Universe whose greater Life pervades and embraces our own. And a part of that appreciation could be to realize that as compared to physics, even to quantum physics whose own peculiar logic is beyond all common ways of knowledge, the incalculable proportions of bio-complexity are virtually transcendental.

23. Gazing Inward

Yet simply to imagine that super or supra-natural dimension, perhaps of untellably greater quality and magnitude than any mind is able to suppose, may constitute a kind of evidence of its reality having helped us to recognize a deep connection linking brain and body with mind and spirit. And a reason for such evidence being so constituted is, that in a world whose interior dimensions recede into deep subjectivity, whatever we take to be real may blend the inner and imaginal realms of existence with those we call external or sensory, in ways that logic is unable to discern, any better than reason is able to tell how all the human factors on which it rests may alter its path and affect its conclusions, which themselves of course are always transient, and are fancies whose degree of being bred more in heart or head is virtually impossible to tell. And of course the very nature of what may be called states of mind or spirit, unavoidably corresponds in terms of irreducible ambiguity to that of any language applied to them. Hence evolution, if conceived as a para-physical process that has generated the human vehicle of consciousness, must partake no less than we ourselves in some inherent property of awareness at work throughout the Universe, and concerning which such tautological words as "mind" and "consciousness" are nearly all that can be said unless one wishes to ascribe awareness to the sheer wizardry of neurons ever weaving our grand illusion, that necessarily includes all such theories and any reasons for entertaining them as well. And indeed, whatever supernatural or instead, blindly causal factors may substand all fretful tissue of seemings in the mind, those cerebral mechanisms that either weave our consciousness or else simply constitute the physical garment of its incarnation from a place outside of Time, could hardly be much different from what they are and still be able to perform their function.

But if consciousness itself is equivalent to the "x-factor" ultimately sustaining Life and driving its sequential progress through a pageant of forms whose leading edge, whether amphibian or anthropoid, has ever displayed a growing awareness—then the latter's physiological underpinnings (such as "mirror neurons" that model important patterns in the external world, patterns closely followed and copied by infants in developing their power of speech in a manner that provides a clue to the biological roots of culture[1])—says nothing either way as to whether the source of consciousness may be not simply biological complexity, but a metaphysical Entity that our lesser selves reflect and thereby serve to mediate or interpret more than to fathom or understand. Yet if we ascribe to that Entity the ultimate support or ground of all natural processes, that need not imply those processes have been stamped from the template of Destiny nor programmed by "intelligent design" of a Divine engineer who envisioned and then projected from His/Her mind the entire Cosmos both past and future, so that our personal lives only seem to be unfolding from a future that in fact has already happened. For instead, the evolutionary journey and our personal part thereof can as well be conceived as being led from moment to moment by the same kind of immediate intelligence that plots the path of a sonata or the strokes of an artist's brush—and that shall never disclose either its ultimate origins or exactly how Nature works. For to do so, would mean translating the lightning subtleties of living transformation into far cruder and more static terms of intellectual thought, whereby the pulsating secret would disperse and only its brittle bones remain.

Thus the creative impulse driving cultural phenomena like music and art, whose internal dynamic reflects the minds of their human creators may well be akin to the mainspring of Life's development by sheer aspiration to express its own inherent nature, whose manner of derivation from a deeper Source is likely to remain as great a mystery as that very Source itself. And just as music ever retains those simpler yet vital elements whose emotional authenticity is evident in the best of popular and indigenous works whether of past eras or today, so has evolution carried forward and kept from extinction such relatively simple animals as beetles and nematodes, whose ecological roles have remained irreducibly important ever since their first appearance in the biosphere. Yet sadly and perhaps fatally, the native intelligence of Gaia and the web of Life is now being compromised by the clever perversity of a self-endangered species, whose own ecological duty should take precedence over trying to justify ideological views that were better set aside until that crucial obligation has been met, which in fact is the only way our species can hope to justify its continued membership in the terrestrial ecosystem. And following that way more earnestly will also help alleviate anxieties and fears that impede pursuit of the spiritual paths that are found by gazing inward.

24. Immanent Causality

Nevertheless, both our picture of evolution and its philosophical significance alter in some regards, though in others hardly at all, depending on whether one posits any Supreme Being or metaphysical ground. For the latter imparts to mortals some portion or degree of immortality and the Eternal that cradles Time, absent whose real existence any concerns for ideal truth, whether scientific, philosophical or religious, become either quixotic, dubious or quaint. Yet if such concerns are meaningful, then whoever may speak of them should take care to not "confuse language with reality," as they seek for certainty in the labyrinth of tongues. The reality of language that can easily shift from sticky to slippery—from a glue that clogs the mind to a lubricant that sends it spinning gaily through rhetorical bazaars and alleyways—is quite other than those deeper realities it purports to address as for example in the use of words like "consciousness." For if God is consciousness or else the basis of its many forms, from emotional awareness of a domestic animal to the dreams of a hermit writing poetry in a rural cabin, and well beyond such limits towards lesser or greater degrees of freedom that might be found in ants or angels, then that same consciousness surely enfolds the realms of both Nature and civilization. Hence the reality of evolution dwells within a living tapestry of influences that are not simply blind or random but partake of an inherent awareness that permeates a Cosmos which itself is altogether "more like a great thought than a great machine."[1] And as biological organisms have a greater degree of freedom than so-called non-living matter—whose own intrinsic life is manifested by the fact of inorganic molecules having long ago combined to form the chemical infrastructure of living cells—so does evolution, it can be readily surmised, consist within a field of universal consciousness no less than molecules and atoms swim in those fields of force which, as "frozen energy," they also embody.

Thus, putatively, could evolution draw from that universal field the power of meaningful change which can bring about, for example, the uncanny adaptation of a sea-slug, Elysia chlorotica, that extracts chloroplasts from the algae it consumes and thus acquires a plant-like ability to extract energy from the sun.[2] And while speculating on the role of consciousness or omnipresent universal mind in natural processes may not be scientific, the strictly rational mantra of new species being plucked from a brew of random but useful genetic changes by the hand of natural selection can hardly explain how Elysia's rare ability to extract the chloroplasts and implant them in its own skin could have been genetically encoded in the first place, even though it may be undeniable that those mutations were indeed selected because an improved sea-slug possessing Elysia's talent displaced a more primitive ancestor which had a harder time feeding itself. Hence the evolutionary panorama appears to show how Nature's instinctively creative path is ever being expressed and revised through positive genetic change, as opposed to simply driven forward by impersonal blows from all sides of a Darwinian gauntlet.

For assuredly, it is not by chance that cells of the immune system find their way to the site of an infection or proteins within the cell infallibly escort others to where they are needed, or copy and transmit important information encoded in DNA. Hence by the same token, the accelerating progress of Life, whose ages ever shortened until the culminating "ascent of man" (which took only a few million years as opposed to hundreds of millions for the Jurassic and Cretaceous eras of dinosaurs) has been impelled by more than a sheer concatenation of causes springing from the context of a physical and chemical complexity periodically jolted by enormous catastrophes yet lacking in the purposeful character of moment-to moment activities within individual cells or bodies themselves. And in this picture the conundrum of "irreducible complexity" as represented, for example, by the rotary flagella of bacteria that would seem incapable of having any more primitive antecedents[3] (unlike the wings of a bird which apparently evolved from cruder modifications of the forelimbs which had rendered them useful for gliding from tree to tree or instead perhaps, leaping high in the air to catch insects) could come about because the requisite genetic changes were deliberately initiated through the organism's dimly conscious or instinctive recognition of immediate adaptive steps upon the path its descendants were to follow. Thus for example, insofar as temporal cause and effect is bypassed or abrogated at the quantum level, perhaps at the genetic level the shadow of things to come might help to shape the process of mutation. Changes in the genes of a fish, in other words, could be influenced by waves of information flowing backwards in Time from the genome of an amphibian species that descendants of that fish were destined to become. Or to put it another way, an ever-evolving concept of Life in the Cosmic mind or some aspect thereof, could gradually precipitate into physical matter. Here it should be noted, that some have suggested that the flagellum was originally a separate organism that formed a symbiotic association with the larger bacteria but if so, the picture of whatever sequential steps would have to have been involved in this miniature metamorphosis and its subsequent perpetuation is one of stupendous intricacy, as indeed are all cellular processes choreographed into the dance of Life.

This concept of mutation suggests a cellular or even molecular consciousness that can apprehend some fragment of a larger evolutionary scheme, in the same sense as how the needs of the body are sensed by individual cells that behave accordingly, for example, by increasing or reducing the flow of hormones, a suggestion highly incompatible with conventional views whether religious or scientific. Nevertheless, those views prevail for psychological rather than rational reasons because, quite simply, not only is the thinking that would be required to completely grasp the issue far too difficult but the information on which that kind of reasoning could operate is not obtainable. There is no way to observe or understand the process, for example, that transformed the fur of the bears from which polar bears evolved into the hollow-shafted insulating fur that along with associated physiological alterations allowed a specialized ursine species to survive in the high Arctic regions rather than migrate southward from advancing ice and cold. Thus if many puzzling facts of astronomy and physics appear to indicate the limits of understanding or to hover at the edge of hypothetically attainable knowledge, the same then surely applies still more convincingly to Life and its evolutionary dimension. And such being the case could just as well concern the nature and meaning of existence and of human life on this planet, with more hopeful connotations than could be extracted from a leaner and meaner context less perturbed by the sort of enigmas and paradox that arise near the borders of Infinity.

That simpler context, however, cannot exist except in the imagination, wherein was formerly conceived a "clockwork universe" affording the possibility that science would someday succeed in penetrating to what were then presumed to be the rational roots of all natural law, thereby nearly obviating all further reason for scientific progress, except towards fuller understanding of tricky phenomena like weather whose basic causes are known. Indeed, even in the modern era such hopes have continued in the shape of prospective "theories of everything," that could only succeed by relegating biology to a place subsidiary to physics, whose own laws might then be enlisted to account for origins of the first living cells. Yet the non-mechanistic but unfailing rule which says that Nature's surprises are not confined within any rational boundary keeps overturning such expectations, which in the context of the "dead" universe they presume to be the case can hardly seem hopeful. For the prospect of every primal secret someday falling within the finite grasp of a human mind which in Darwinian terms did not evolve to do that anyway, is a dismal one indeed, on which existentialist advocates of angst could feast like jackals on a dead giraffe.

Nonetheless, while physics has boldly vaulted forwards into a twilight zone as yet but dimly sketched through quantum mechanics and relativity, whose mutual incompatibility still awaits resolution by a hopeful expansion of the "zone" into hyperspaces able to accommodate infinitesimal vibratory "strings" and/or a "quantum gravity" which would mesh gravity seamlessly with all other forces of Nature, evolution remains mired in arguments that can stoop low enough to question whether it even occurred at all. Yet while that last view may seem preposterous in its dismissal of the fossil and other evidence that only unbending ideologues dare try to explain away, the somewhat more rational disputes over issues framed in slippery terms like "intelligent design" still provoke a polarization of opinion that in being more politicized than scientific fails to squarely address the problem (which includes the question of whether it can be meaningfully addressed at all) of what constitutes the mainspring of evolution and accordingly of Life itself, within whose throbbing tapestry we are embodied and imbedded.[4] And if the answer turns out to be a tautology—namely that the mainspring of evolution and of Life is "life, and life only," just as the core of matter is "quantum stuff," then the bulk of the subject resides in a region where human symbolic language retains what only an "emperor's new mind" might pretend to be more than a hollow semblance of meaning.

For example, the "design" debate really depends on just two basic questions, one of which could be posed to proponents of "intelligent design" and the other to defenders of stringently non-metaphysically burdened accounts of how evolution works. The first question asks that if the "intelligent designer" is a God or supernatural agents carrying out a scheme preconceived in the Divine mind who foresaw that human science would discover many curiosities of His/Her scheme (such as a wasp that while laying her eggs in the body of a caterpillar also injects a virus that disables the caterpillar's immune system to keep it from attacking the eggs, whose security thus guaranteed will hatch into larvae and devour their hapless host)[5] then did Divine intervention promote every stage by manipulating or even creating fresh DNA to spur each incremental advance so that, in effect, the stream of Life gradually oozed forth into time and space from its conceptual beginnings in the eternal Divine awareness? How exactly does "intelligent design" operate, and does it replace or simply mesh with the evolutionary process? Without clearly rational and thorough answers to that kind of question, there is really no valid debate—whereas any purported answer could only, in lieu of quite improbably knowing the mind of God, be sheer speculative indulgence. Nonetheless, that same indulgence might be the best to be hoped for in confronting the living truth of biology and evolution that is even more difficult than quantum reality. Thus it has been said that by the same token that phenomena governed by the "quantum logic" of "the dancing Wu Li Masters" or subatomic particles are more subtle than classical Newtonian mechanics, organic phenomena such as mutation are equally inscrutable, because they follow what has been called "immanent causality" whereby intracellular activity appears to have a mind of its own. And since that activity includes genetic mutation, the genetic heart of evolutionary change is no less purposeful or more accidental than the self-regulating biochemistry of every living cell.

25. Upon What Stage

On the other hand, to dismiss any Divine association with Creation on scientific grounds is to reject all spiritual hope for humanity as well. For in actual absence of a Supreme Being, already dismissed for the sake of protecting intellectual aspirations towards better understanding of the Cosmos, there can scarcely remain any niche for a personal spiritual essence except as a comforting fiction of meaning and purpose not simply engendered by a self-referential neuronal network, whose accidental grace grants capacity for making believe that mortal dreams and longings may reflect a higher and more lasting state that some individuals claim to have realized as salvation or enlightenment. In other words, it is quite awkward to try and defend what is seen as the rightful territory of reason from licentious incursion of the supernatural, by denying all possible linkage between God and evolution, hence excluding that God from a Universe which can hardly be other than Divine at least in provenance if not in essence should any Deity, Godhead, or Buddha-mind exist at all. Yet should a similar rationale of protecting science from the sloppy kind of thinking that could try and cram it into a cage of ironclad theology flatly reject that Existence—which in truth is a meta-existence if to be is a humanly-designated attribute of things, or of "bound variables,"[1] distinguished by differences amongst themselves—it becomes less awkward than capriciously arbitrary. For that same rejection clearly denies all immortal hopes for any whose concerns for truth, that led them to scoff at faith, are likewise destined to perish along with them or their descendants. And in such case those same concerns that rational science be protected from any spiritual contamination, become as frivolous and vain as any mystical concerns they had decried should also prove, were it that we dwell in a Universe whose surest promise is oblivion. Yet the truer dichotomy of the human condition is not one that divides such conceptual possibilities as that there is or is not any mystical Reality. It is the apparent dichotomy between the actualities of subjectivity and objectivity that in truth are inseparably combined—so that the very idea of objective truth is compelling in subjective terms. And the objective world could become as beautiful or divine as any persons might subjectively perceive, were that perception shared among all humanity.

Hence we arrive at a major talking-point involving evolution—namely, its relation to the Universe and thus to ourselves and human self-knowledge, insofar as that universe cannot be severed from its metaphysical connotations. For, to rephrase one conclusion of the last paragraph, if there is no God or some equivalent such as "universal mind" or "cosmic consciousness" to serve as the para-physical framework of human experience, then there is also nothing more than the ephemeral appearance of a self—whose "strutting and fretting upon the stage" obtains no higher importance in debating weighty topics like evolution or religion, than by watching a film or discussing politics. And in that case the significance of evolution along with that of knowledge in general becomes virtually moot, although of course its functional character remains the same, namely that of representing the temporal dimension of dynamic change without which there could be no existence whatsoever.

But the importance of so-called Darwinian arguments in supporting an atheistic philosophy is close to zero, should that philosophy be correct. For in the lesser and de-Godded universe that indefatigable explanatarians may prefer, the human animal can well dispense with all but practical knowledge, in favor of more earnest epicurean enjoyment of its fragile moment in the sun. Yet if arguments against religion based on evolutionary science—the only kind of science that could work in such regard—are false, their significance paradoxically then becomes much greater, because within the context of a spiritual universe whose Divine drama heavily involves the pageant of human history and of post-Darwinian social and cultural evolution, the role of belief is all-important. Moreover, when religions uphold the idea of a static universe where evolution did not take place—and where instead, such noxious creatures as lice and tapeworms presumably were injected into the ecosystem instantly when Eve and Adam fell, by a God whose mood had thereupon darkened considerably—they have to be corrected simply because faith, whether in a Deity or in the scientific progress that Being might hopefully wish for us both to enjoy and to employ for the sake of improving Her/His kingdom, is crippled when its rational foundations are insecure. And those foundations clearly include an understanding of the web of Life and its deep evolutionary past, from whence all mortal vessels of the human spirit are derived and in which they are imbedded.

One connotation then of removing God from Nature for the sake of enabling science by vacuuming away the pixie dust that the actual presence of any spiritual factors would tend to deposit everywhere, is clearly that, religious fantasies aside, there cannot subsequently remain any room for spiritual reality since even Eternity and Time, in other words Heaven and the evolutionary time-dimension, cannot be totally separated. Thus Darwinism could be credited for helping to reveal the theoretical possibility of God's non-existence as more credible than once appeared in former and more "demon-haunted" ages of human history.

And of course there are many religious or faith-based alternatives opposing that starkest interpretation of evidence that the ascent of human consciousness required a long and painful journey, but these alternatives typically misconstrue or dismiss the same evidence for a reality larger than the mind, whether slanted towards faith or reason, can more than begin to nibble. Thus if evolution is governed only by hypothetically knowable scientific laws that could in theory fully explain, for instance, how human self-awareness arose from the blind instinct of bacteria, our existence cannot include any transcendent properties but instead, both rational and religious dreams and longings are fated to be ground down by relentless entropy. And that fate can only be opposed rhetorically, in words such as "Love's not Time's fool, though rosy lips and cheeks within his curving sickle's compass come."[2] But a sunnier view of evolution is equally possible, namely that its improbable defiance of entropy, as notably displayed in myriad biological examples such as the bower-birds of Australia which stylishly and lavishly decorate their nests in a virtually purposeful manner[3] derives from an actual power of consciousness as intrinsic to a Creation that constitutes the embodied nature of Divinity. And if that mode of Being somehow substands what we experience as mind or awareness, there is no great distance towards supposing that powers invisible to science or even beyond surmise may support all natural processes in the visible world, including those molecular phenomena that constitute genetic transformation.

Furthermore, any living or hidden powers of Nature as may exist, can only manifest in bodies whose quantum essence has been shaped into atomic and molecular structure by the fundamental forces already scientifically identified, namely gravity, electromagnetic radiation, and the so-called strong and weak nuclear forces. But so-called vital forces, morphic fields, or whatever labels might be applied to hidden aspects of Life that could be varied as the known properties of matter, are unlikely to function in any manner that could be formulated under known scientific laws or rendered even as accessible as the mysteries of quantum mechanics—despite that many influences or patterns in biology like the progressive tug of natural selection or cyclical swings in the population of species such as lemmings have been identified. Therefore a living Universe whose Divine aspect is embodied in physical Creation is bound to present a picture quite similar to that of a Cosmos lacking any metaphysical embarrassments (quite possibly as inconvenient for religion as for science) whatsoever. For the consequences of existence per se deriving from the rather obvious requirement of there being something instead of absolutely nothing, not to mention the almost equal certainty that material existence should spring from the "no-thing-ness" when "darkness was on the face of the deep," can hardly be less rational than those overriding reasons for Being. Accordingly it would be quite illogical for Life, society, and the psycho-spiritual nature of human beings to simply cease evolving. And in that case the vital Cosmic tapestry of being and becoming has to be sufficiently purposeful, whether literally or figuratively, to have shaped not only a stellar architecture that proclaims "the awful power of non-human things,"[4] but by an even stranger magic than what ignited a myriad nuclear fires far and wide across the heavens, has tweaked the blind regiments of inorganic substance into curious living observers who from their vantage of dubious security beneath a thin shield of air and of protective radiation belts are attempting to render rhyme and reason from a spectacle that while majestically enfolding them also constitutes the stage for the human drama.

26. Depths Untold: The Magnum Mysterium

Unfortunately while the latter goal, as many of its pursuers would admit, is apt to remain as far beyond their grasp and "the frontiers of our ignorance"[1] as the proverbial grapes that kept eluding Tantalus in the Greek fable, it may also be a delusional goal if the seekers of knowledge possess no self to receive it, beside what is cobbled together "from non-self elements,"[2] themselves perhaps devoid of any metaphysical conscious essence. For in that case, knowledge itself is but one of those elements, that helps to augment an illusory wisdom which is all that shall reward those who surmise that "knowledge is our destiny." Of course, it is true that while civilization continues, the sum of information will multiply geometrically, whereas knowledge as to what that information says may also grow accordingly. But in absence of a "knower" who can only exist in a universe whose spiritual dimension also supports the wisdom to measure and apply that knowledge, the latter cannot pretend to more than practical meaning without becoming as much of a vanity as whatever quasi-religious hopes might be placed in science and reason by those who have already argued that their own sense of conscious selfhood is completely conditional and fleeting. But if their being willy-nilly does incorporate or is centered upon a self that is "made in the image of God" or spiritually wired along with every form of consciousness that manifests in Nature including whatever instinctive wisdom is able to coordinate bodily functions and intracellular activity, then personal knowledge can never be more than a fragmentary reflection of what more properly resides in the Divine or non-temporal ground of being and intelligence.

And in that case, the Universe should, ideally, make sense in a manner that is virtually self-evident to anyone who does contain a Divine spark as the core of their "real" reality, thus nearly obviating any need to demonstrate or to argue as much through either theology or science. Hence further investigation of the Cosmos, should in fact it correspond to that mystical model, can only tend to confirm its owning no less of meaning and purpose than routinely ascribed to both our personal lives and the plans and objectives of human societies. And of course, both persons and societies may have good Darwinian reasons to act first and ask questions later—whereas positive answers to the inquiry into meaning and purpose can also be attributed to a similar cause, since hope is more germane to survival than the existential despair provoked by perceptions of formerly purported "meaning" as having been bled away by the ministrations of modern science. (A despair whose psychic tenor may differ from that of an angst intensified by confinement within the synthetic environments that scientific technology has fostered, that in turn may not be the same as Sartrean "nausea" that feels oppressed by the flagrantly writhing corpulence of Nature herself) But that does not have to mean that the stark logic of survival, however compelling in the realms of both biology and of human affairs, can exclude the more elegant rationale of an interior dimension, whose discovery and exploration may require a harder journey yet afford even bolder adventure than what has led so far to the quantum edge of where that same journey may now be poised to get underway collectively, for the whole human race, as it has ever done throughout the ages for any individual whose inward voyage has attained the gates of Eternity.

Nonetheless, modern physics has attempted in an imaginative leap as yet unconfirmed by experimental evidence, to suggest various ways whereby not only matter-energy but life itself can be fitted into an explanatory framework which totally obviates the need to invoke any supernatural foundations or spiritual support as prerequisite for physical existence. And in so doing, presumably the exposure of religious delusions as nothing more than purely psychological artifacts will compel us to face the true situation, although for a soulless animal that kind of truth may afford little solace nor serve any vital purpose. Hence, for example, "string theory" can imply the possibility of countless universes[3], each governed by some variant of physical law, of which our own particular version could be one of the very few to favor the appearance of life—although among an infinity of mostly dead worlds, that relatively few of the living could itself be infinite as well, just as are the primes as part of all natural numbers. And in this kind of scheme, the specific fabric of matter-energy in our world and perhaps a relative handful of others in a "meta-verse" most of whose members might be lacking the impeccable tolerances of a cosmic machinery engineered to produce squids and centipedes—for example, a planet at the proper distance from its sun and protected from asteroid or comet impacts by the gravitational shield of giants like Jupiter, and saturated with organic chemicals whose elements like carbon had been forged, against all odds, within the stars—could be bound to occur via probability alone, without any need for a supernatural Creator or Designer. In fact, most bioactive planets in our own universe may support only primitive forms of life, whereas many of those universes conceivably representing the different versions of string theory—said to number[4] in the neighborhood of 10^{500} although that stupendous figure does not alter the infinite totality of all worlds in the "meta-verse"—could contain no celestial bodies at all, or else but a bleak magnificence of scorched, frozen, and giant gaseous planets lacking any poets or astronomers to sing their praises.

But this concept presupposes that any spiritual agency that might exist would have to intervene in order to fashion life, by manipulating or guiding at every stage of cosmic evolution—including the alchemy that forged vital elements like carbon in stellar nuclear furnaces through a reaction that could not have happened were the values of physical constants like the force of gravity even slightly different[5]—a dead material clay that only a Divine Potter could assist in surmounting the hurdle that it clearly, in our portion of the "meta-verse," has overcome in beating entropy through transformation into the living framework of animal and human awareness. But if God, Divine Mind, or whatever spiritual principle is not outside of but involved in the Creation, then that principle becomes intrinsic to Nature and ineluctably alloyed with natural law, that accordingly can only work towards positive change that evolution, from its very birth in the dawn of time and space assuredly represents. Hence the physical world could be seen as having "phase-shifted" into its current condition from a higher spiritual state which could even be synonymous with those hyper-spatial dimensions already posited by quantum theory to account for the behavior of sub-atomic particles that observations have revealed as completely alien to all ordinary ideas concerning palpably objective things. And if that is the case, then the same might well apply for every other universe in the "meta-verse" as well. For despite the raw probability that could assign to many of them sub-optimal variants of physical law under which no form of life could hope to arise, it is hard to imagine that any of these alternate realities would lack the same metaphysical proportions of the Magnum Mysterium wherein we and our indefatigably explanatory minds are hopelessly imbedded like ticks on the back of a cow. Except that, unlike the ticks, we cannot let go and drop off from the hide of a Reality to which we are bonded more firmly than any reciprocal attempts of intellect can engage with That-which-is. Thus the human and Cosmic mind are like the two sides of a Mobius strip that are actually only one.

27. What Little We Know

None of the above, however, means to say that incredibly complex workings of the brain, however feebly understood, cannot help explain consciousness, or that Darwinian principles are not crucial to the fact of evolution having occurred. For clearly, whatever processes, laws or mechanisms science may identify cannot be any simpler or of less explanatory value than they are, either with or without the existence of a God who clearly and by definition must transcend the immediate sphere of whatever factors and influences that science can identifiy—a "beyond" whose very manner of remove can only defy all human conception. And at the same time whatever theories, philosophies. and equations that the mind may please itself to entertain cannot become much more arcane or complicated without exceeding all hope of understanding. Thus for example the reputed ability of certain pets not only to detect, perhaps by smell, the presence of a cancer in their human owner but to recognize and consequently warn that person of the danger is just one of a myriad natural phenomena that would seem to belong on an uncomfortably larger canvas than any standard rational picture of reality. Hence any apparent deficiency of neo-Darwinian evolutionary theory regarding such phenomena, for instance, is merely due to the story of Life being ridden with far deeper subtleties and more twisted turns than even the living processes of a single organism, which already rises to a higher order of difficulty than found in physics. Indeed, concerning those abiding mysteries of the latter, such as what may be the ultimate fate of the Universe, Einstein himself said that "The Lord is subtle but He is not malicious"—He could not have made physics and biology any easier to understand and therefore simpler than they are while still allowing them to provide us with functional body-minds in a suitable environment. Therefore evolution submits to nothing better than a relatively sketchy accounting which inevitably fails to do justice to its true proportions, to the same extent as intellect must needs fall short of whatever existential truth can be said to constitute Reality. Meanwhile, research will continue picking out additional evolutionary themes like the transfer of genes from one species to another by means of viruses[1], which must then be folded into an ever expanding data base subsumed by the convoluted history of Life dating back to its shrouded beginnings in the chasm of geologic Time.

Thus the true position of knowledge with regard to evolution, namely that of an outpost on the fringe of a wilderness, may be ignored by seekers of a rational framework for human experience that includes its biological roots in the soil of pre-human ages. But the fact of those roots proclaiming us members in the fellowship of DNA provides no reason to dismiss the greater mysteries of Life and of existence itself, which our species long ago began to face through philosophical questions that loom today no less compellingly than in pre-Socratic times. The very nature, for example, of Time itself whereof the evolutionary process clearly partakes, is hardly more obvious today than for the ancients, even if many time-related properties such as thermodynamic entropy have yielded more analytic approaches to the subject than formerly possible. For all of these pathways simply lead to further questions, where the new picture of the Cosmos that they roughly depict has become far more strange than once believed in mediaeval times, or even when a few adventurous minds began to peer into the temporal abyss where they discovered wondrous fossilized creatures nearly as ancient as the rocks themselves. And as those paltry bones compare to the "buzzing, blooming confusion" of the former ecospheres they attest, so does evolution theory compare to the immensity it tries to confine within the narrow horizons of mortal understanding that are only more constrained should that attribute lack any spiritual dimension.. Yet that same dimension is indicated even in sub-human organisms and their behaviors. For example, animals of the same species can have distinctly different personalities, more so in dogs than in spiders or insects but not entirely absent from the latter[2]. Thus in the subhuman kingdoms, psychology begins to appear as preliminary evidence of the mind and psyche that in humans could be regarded as the bridge between body and spirit—a place where science cannot venture and yet not entirely sequestered from the strictly objective reality that any rational attempts to conquer are themselves of subjective derivation, whereby all presumptive knowledge cannot avoid being tainted with the character of a dream. .

For in a world where faith is not merely a delusion, and consequently where any portions of that world accessible to scientific study are limned and/or permeated by unknowable dimensions of what could be called supernatural, the limits to human understanding are starkly evident in the case of all-embracing subjects such as evolution, which is nearly synonymous with the nature of Life itself. And the question of what is Life—as compared to the hypothetically more probable state of a universe not finely tuned enough to produce any living things who could appreciate its and their own existence—cannot be divorced from the issue of what is meant by consciousness, which in that perspective then becomes quite hard to explain without explaining it away. For if "unweaving the rainbow" of our dreamy lives should leave no more than a heap of untangled causal threads of what had seemed a fathomless complexity, then who might claim the knowledge of such barren truth without inviting a further query dating back to almost prehistoric times—"how can the knower be known?[3]

And if within the labyrinth of physical complexity alone, and with no further need for spirit, soul, or Deity, could be found the key to our grand illusion and against all odds that ultimate secret be unveiled, what profit to any knower of same, who then could only confess to an essential non-existence, amounting to nothing more than fleeting enjoyment of a fantasy that Death would shortly scatter to the winds? Yet, ironically, in a world enveloped and imbued by spiritual influences, cosmic consciousness, or a Supreme Being and therefore broader and more radiant than the kind of reality seemingly preferred by those who wield a rational sword against any looming metaphysical specter, our dreams are just as ephemeral and the formulas of science, however imperfect or incomplete, are equally true because that truth can only so be designated by the human mind and then appointed residence within the latter's limitations.

And yet those same limitations are, in being contiguous with the infinite boundaries of imagination and of reason when stripped to the bone as in mathematics that has expounded on the very concept of infinity itself, as vast as they are also often constrained by tendencies to seek the comfort of belief—even in believing that nothing awaits beyond the gates of Death except conclusion of all joy and sorrows finally and forever—or to remain safely within the territory staked out by custom and tradition. But the pressure of adventurous thinking ever wears away at the walls of orthodox opinion, just as life's improbable defiance of entropy can split and crumble granite into fertile soil. Therefore one is free to imagine, for example, what is meant by concepts such as entropy and order with reference to evolution and the character of human experience and destiny. For if low entropy and the high degree of order and freedom that Life represents, as compared to greater entropy and lesser freedom found on a barren celestial body like the Moon or Venus, is simply a statistical aberration that occurs on but a relative handful of the countless planets in our universe or among the larger host that may comprise the members of a "meta-verse," then human consciousness (or that of aliens who may or may not be recognizably humanoid) is merely the predictable yet rare exception to a Cosmic rule that seldom favors flowers, birds or children. And in that sorry case, no spiritual parameters of awareness would need to and accordingly might not exist at all, although in an infinite Cosmos the number of bioactive worlds could hardly be finite however sparse their distribution.

28. Across the Universe

Then again, it may also be that according to the rules of some domain of natural law as yet unknown to science, there are better than statistical reasons of happenstance why life must nearly always arise in any universe and by those same hidden rules subsequently develop sentience, that serves not merely to find medicinal plants or employ simple tools for catching termites as in the case of chimpanzees, but to venture on the wings of symbols, sounds and pictures into imaginary kingdoms that appear to be an eternal homeland for those minds inventing them, despite that what their fancy breeds shall vanish when the neuronal machinery that engendered it has likewise perished. For in this view which still excludes the soul and all immortal aspirations, a Gestalt embracing both life and matter manifests its rippling oceans of phenomena by a quintessential subtlety that no human or other minds should ever grasp, however long they vainly strove through long ages of the stable civilization that would favor such enduring effort, to learn the secret of their origin.

Yet it is equally possible to say—no less than also impossible to claim any knowledge of what the true probabilities of life's or human existence may be except they are clearly better than zero, and perhaps 100% if even very rare events are bound to someday happen—that in a third perspective matter-energy is not only the antechamber to biology, that in turn opens into human consciousness and psychology, but the latter also connect to the portal of a "far country" of spiritual existence where awaits the transforming of our mortal into an immortal journey. And in this view, Divine reality, human life and consciousness, and Life itself in its full diversity throughout both time and space constitute a trinity whose divisions are not separate and apart from one another. Instead, the enormous complexity and range of organic life and evolution do justice to the greater Life of God, and to the fullness of human potential both in this present world and in those mansions that shall unfold before whatever our former selves may become in Eternity. And seeds of the Eternal ideally may also unfold in the Here and Now to yield both personal and social transformation—"on Earth as it is in Heaven"—whose potential is prefigured in the greatest works of music, art and poetry, and of Scriptures whose expressive power is partly responsible for the lasting predominance of faiths that they help to proclaim..

For in fact, potential for that same unfolding is already apparent in our mental ability to consider such issues in conditions of more perfect freedom than the physical universe itself enjoys, insofar as the latter is regarded as the material or temporal substrate of all existence including what, according to "scima" (scientific-materialist) philosophies, are romantic but purely fictive notions of a so-called "spiritual" existence. Those philosophies, of course, maintain that the same illusion of a non-material world unfettered by relentless decay and grinding entropy is really nothing more than a mirage spun by Nature's magic in a brain which in animals lacks the neural complexity to generate and entertain such tales as presented in Dante's grand trilogy describing Heaven, Hell, and Purgatory as conceived in mediaeval times, despite those animals having personality and emotion as recent studies, not to mention common experience with domestic animals, appear to indicate.

And in a hypothetical Cosmos of abounding possibilities which free minds as opposed to those ruled by ideology can easily consider, such unforgivingly restrictive views might in theory be correct, at least for those who lack experiential evidence for an "imaginal" or psycho-spiritual realm contingent on everyday awareness. And even if incorrect, they can contain important aspects of a Truth whose larger or metaphysical proportions as may obtain are also far more difficult to formulate in any clear conceptual way, and thereby misconstrued, indirectly promote more egregious error—as for example so sadly displayed in episodes like the Inquisition—than might be committed by those who flatly dismiss all supernatural concepts and beliefs as relics of humanity's childhood. Then again, however, it could be argued that the underlying constant is not ideology or religion but human nature, meaning that children who are innately cruel may just as easily find, in an atheistic society, quasi-rational instead of religious excuses to display that tendency. And in that case, evolution itself becomes the integral of all derivative hopes for social reform, environmental sanity, and personal transformation, because that integral can only mean that the world as a whole—in whose currently post-Darwinian phase the role of human nature and consciousness becomes increasingly significant—is advancing in a positive direction.

29. Now and Then

In any case, the dichotomy of conflicting views on whether human nature is fundamentally spiritual—an issue reflecting, as it were from the top down upon questions involving evolution and in what degree of freedom what kinds of causality worked in the shaping of Life from its molecular beginnings—may seem to afford little hope for the cause of freedom, whose increase provides the course that evolution has taken and shall continue taking in what is going to become the post-Darwinian future of our species insofar as it has any future. Nonetheless, that same future will someday become a present that is also now—an Eternal Now whose recognition has been and ever will be a source of meaning and means of escape from the tyranny of a past outworn and of uncertain days to come wherein are likely to emerge whatever difficulties, including new versions of ancient troubles, that time and change are certain to impose. Thus the mind can borrow from the eternal realm of spirit—while putting aside the issue as to whether that realm is in cold actuality merely a gossamer production of the human bio-computer or is instead, the latter's metaphysically substantial context and mystically ultimate progenitor—in order to effect, however briefly, that desirable escape and thereby strike a blow for the larger freedom whose achievement ever remains a major goal of human striving whether in physical, social, or psychic space.

For instance, one can escape from the tyrannies of information, theory and ideology by contemplating a "talking point" that has bearing both on evolution and on the nature of thinking and consciousness, namely what is meant by "freedom?" The universe is said to have begun in a state of what is described as low entropy, or high order according to the laws of physics[1], despite the minimal complexity of an indescribable speck of Ur-stuff that at first was no bigger than the smallest measurable distance or "Planck length" of 10^{-33} cm.[2] that soon differentiated into subatomic particles and radiation that in turn coalesced into clouds of hydrogen and other light elements and thence by the influence of gravity, into stars and galaxies. Thus in terms of physical law, the current state of highly ordered complexity and of freedom, as compared to insentient substance of the incipient Cosmos and as manifested through life and civilization on our planet and perhaps many others, has derived from a formerly lesser degree of entropy and of disordered randomness. But at the same time the virtual self-creation and consequent ascent of Life has displayed an ever-growing liberty, as embodied in species of superior mobility and intelligence to their ancestral forms, or in the case of plants like sequoias and roses, more beauty and elegance than plainer types of vegetation like ferns that predominated in the early stages of life's emergence from the seas. And today that living degree of freedom has attained in the human species the conscious ability to entertain such concepts as that of freedom itself, in consequence of having discovered the ideal realm or "mindscape" wherein also reside the keys to a new and post-Darwinian phase of evolution.

Many of these keys, of course, have already been found—as for example in mathematical concepts like the square root of minus 1, a so-called imaginary number employed in the formulas of electrical engineering, or even the number zero without which much or all of modern mathematics and science and their contributions to the highest hopes and worst fears of society—the abolishing of poverty, disease and ignorance versus nuclear annihilation—would not exist. And while mathematical abstractions like the calculus which became enablers of practical science may not be philosophical keys to human nature, they do indicate a deeper and more cogent connection between the real and ideal than debates about the nature and quality of that connection might seem to indicate. Thus Truth in its abstract incarnation may outstrip our thinking in the ideal realm—where for example can be found the many kinds of mathematical Infinity—no less than Nature in the realm of physical reality, where an incalculably intricate network of lightning-fast neuronal interactions underlies our every thought and weaves the tapestry of consciousness. And whether that tapestry completely constitutes or merely supports our seeming sentience may be in strictly scientific terms an insoluble riddle, but in philosophical terms it reiterates a question whose putative answer depends on how much freedom we imagine ourselves to possess. And the degree or quality of that freedom, in turn, could be said to derive from what lesser degrees have arisen in the course of evolution and are manifest today in animals whose physiology and behavior may be simpler than our own, yet remain exceedingly problematic. For the greater freedom a system—in this instance the progressive ecosystem represented by all past and present life on planet Earth—contains, the less amenable it becomes to theoretical fossilization. And thus insofar as that same system includes ourselves, whatever kinds or levels of freedom it may happen to display, as in ability of the genes of apelike creatures to reconfigure those species into modern homo sapiens, are also inseparable from any consideration of whatever existential issues we regard as meaningful.

The expressiveness of Life for example can be described as strictly channeled by the Darwinian demands of struggle and survival, but is more evident in playful bears or dolphins than in more sober sharks or iguanas. And for the human condition, existential consequences of those same demands have been explained as proceeding from the fact of human life in its prehistoric state of nature as having been "nasty, brutish and short," a state of affairs only partially alleviated by a social contract that provides leverage in dealing with necessities while shifting much of the burden of the most brutish aspect of survival, namely defense, from individuals to governments. Nonetheless, that contract also exhibits an equally Darwinian property of cooperation which occurs in Nature no less than competition and conflict—as for example in the case of beneficial guest bacteria that inhabit the intestinal tract of people and cows, or fish that clean the teeth of crocodiles. Thus the social contract is not only natural, but is basic to the intellectual and emotional liberty attained in the course of social and cultural evolving towards a psychological state of lesser constraint than obtained in past ages, when humanity not only cringed before the ever-looming specters of famine and disease but was often in thrall to weird beliefs and murky superstitions, some of which according to extreme views of how the mind can alter reality, may have helped to generate materialization of horrors, the sheer dread of which accordingly lent actual substance to monsters that could then stalk the night.

30. Performance Artistry

Yet non-human Nature also exhibits an uncanny versatility that science has scarcely dared to recognize, because of what today is the psychological equivalent of superstition, namely an apparent belief that the conventions of current knowledge mark the boundaries of a reality that for reasons not easy to explain, has been conceived more narrowly for biology than physics—perhaps in part because the latter is more closely allied with mathematics and its realm of boundless possibilities. But in fact the opposite is true, which is why the stunning immensity of evolution is more simplistically addressed by current neo-Darwinian theories—to which assuredly there are no viable alternatives—than are the deepest riddles of physics and astronomy by a host of alternative concepts whose empirical resolution, if any, lies far in the future. Thus the utmost nature of matter itself has received a tentative explanation in the form of "string theory"—an hypothetical turtle on whose back the more definitively established turtle of quantum mechanics may be standing—but the nature of Life and how it evolved, is a question for which, aside from the long since evident factors of mutation and natural selection, not even a ghost of any hopeful answers has been sighted. For how Nature is able to function with a degree of freedom well beyond mere blind response to constant pressures of necessity can be shown through examples like the following.

A bird called the African Crowned Crane, or Balearica Pavonina, has a crown of feathers whose only conceivable purpose is simply to express or to represent the essence of this creature, to proclaim its uniqueness as a species and freedom of an existence perhaps more joyous than that of many humans who are oppressed and tormented by their fellow men. The crown feature can scarcely have arisen by chance combination of genetic factors accidentally improving the bird's appearance and consequently favored by natural selection, because the various features involved derive from separate genetic factors and yet are closely coordinated to produce the total effect. These features include, for example, the twisting of every crown feather to provide stiffness, the appropriately varied lengths of the feathers, and the black, red and white colors of the head, neck, and crown. The latter are derived, respectively, from melanines—the same chemicals that darken the skins of humans—hemoglobin, and the structure, rather than pigmentation, of the crown feathers which causes them to appear white by reflecting the full spectrum of light.[1] Hence what appears in the crane as in many or indeed all other animals and plants, is Nature's display of ingenuity and power, attributes at work incessantly not only in the process of evolution but in the neurological machinery of the brain, wherefrom derives the capacity to form those opinions and ideas which may wander far from reality in attempting to account objectively for what are the simultaneously objective and subjective phenomena of human thought and consciousness.

Thus, attempts to characterize Nature herself as intelligent and therefore the "designer" responsible for what cannot be otherwise explained might be equally misguided, insofar as what is meant by those words cannot be called science but instead, simply a muddy ground for endlessly futile debate. However, in such a perspective, or "talking point," the dancer and the dance or designer and design are one and the same, and evolution happens through reason of an internal and constant guidance over countless generations, akin to the equally autonomous and inwardly directed process that governs the growth of an actress or a penguin from an embryo. But if that is not the case, and instead the "wise blood" of Nature a mere figure of speech bearing no true analogy or connection to human intelligence, then the latter only exists as part of an illusion of "mind" so total and complete that the whole point of any philosophical disputes on that very issue or others including evolution and the difference between life and matter becomes either moot or else tantamount to wishfully redecorating the illusion. On the other hand, if evolution springs from a power inherent to Life in a manner which cannot be humanly explained, that statement is not far from saying that power has flowed from a Deity who is less the immediate "designer" of living things than a necessary condition for their coming into being, in similar sense to a "divine spark" in human nature being regarded as the essence of finding beauty in another person or in artistic expression. And in such case, the role of a Deity could be defined as follows: "I watch and in its work of creation nature brings forth all that moves and moves not: and thus the revolutions of the world go round."[2] In other words, if Life is no less an aspect of Divinity than consciousness, then exactly how Nature brings forth "all that moves and moves not" is especially likely to remain an enigma, for "if we learn anything from the pursuit of science, it is that even things as "elementary" as atoms are quite hard to understand."[3] And if the natural world shares in or has derived from the same spiritual source as we could hardly wish ourselves not connected to, it cannot be surprising for living Nature's performance art to retain a degree of freedom that eludes all attempts at theoretical restraint or explanatory incarceration.

31. Degrees of Freedom

According to physics, however, that freedom—which we possess more fully than does a cell of our immune system or a protein within that cell—is not the same as order, because the history of the Universe actually entails an increase in entropy, and thus a decrease in the order which the primordial orb of undifferentiated substance/energy contained in preeminent degree.[1] The original cloud of hydrogen, which evolved very quickly from the sea of subatomic particles and radiation that in turn was rendered from an initial undifferentiated state where speculative journeys end—"an absolute limit to any credible backward extrapolation is set by quantum theory"[2]—was broken down by gravity into separate regions of greater density, which then became galactic whorls of stars that started to shine (and still in the immensity of space are being formed) when their internal pressure grew strong enough to initiate nuclear fusion. Hence the evolution of life from matter, though clearly defiant of entropy involves a different concept of what order represents. And it lies in us to choose how hopefully that concept and its kin may be regarded.

For in fact as social order and its regime of cultural and intellectual complexity has reached a pinnacle scarcely dreamed in any former times (although the poet Tennyson foresaw modern civilization—"for I dipped into the future far as human eye can see"[3]), the current order and its unpredictable future are threatened by an equally modern form of entropy as never before. Wars, weapons, and ecological destruction hold over us a sword of Damocles that should it fall, could largely undo the gains both of Nature and History while returning humanity to a primitive state far worse than once prevailed in prehistoric ages of innocence and biological abundance—ages whose needful departing from was assailed by dangers perhaps quite similar to those that may have confronted and sometimes overcome civilized societies on other worlds. And the sum of human suffering, that was once inflicted by the likes of Imperial Rome or the hordes of Genghis Khan, in addition to all the plagues and diseases of former times, may in sheer quantity amount to less than now endured by all the "wretched of the Earth" today, from the child slaves and prostitutes of Asia and the oppressed of Africa to the disenfranchised Mexican peasants who have perished in the desert in their search for a living wage in the United States. Not to mention those nominally privileged millions eking out their sickly lives on a medical treadmill whose mercies cannot remedy the blight inflicted by an over-industrialized civilization. These are the grimly ponderous facts against which concepts like order and entropy must be measured—prospective entropy of a global wasteland as terrible recompense for greed and neglect, versus aesthetic and moral order that a humanized technology in harmony with Nature could help to bring about. And the key to surmounting the entropy of desolation rows ruled by barren logic of survival—a desolation encompassing not only crime-ridden ghettoes and grimy sweatshops but the vacuous opulence that gleams in the temples of commerce—exists only where human minds and hearts envision higher than flatly utilitarian hopes for future generations. For that key depends on an understanding of human nature as ultimately grounded beyond the sway of entropic temporal powers that mock mere pretensions to freedom.

Yet far in advance of fully realizing those socio-economic reforms whose longstanding moral imperative keeps growing more relevant towards the stark issue of sheer civilized survival, the same kind of freedom needed both to dream and to implement such practical ideals can also serve towards examining various concepts and modes of thinking that currently prevail in a modern world where many opinionated, biased and otherwise psychologically tainted layers of the proverbial Socratic onion still beg to be stripped away in any quest for more essential truth. To be sure, that quest may never reach its goal, especially because in every conceivable field that same truth is just as fluidly dynamic as in physics, where the untellable nature of "quantum reality" constitutes an ultimate rebuke to the vanity of fixed ideas and entrenched ideologies. Yet reason, which at best is a gift of our spiritual nature rather than rightful source of support for any lesser "mismeasure of Man" as a fancy bag of chemicals or self-deluded biocomputer, can at least keep making progress towards purging the most egregious fallacies and errors from our "demon-haunted world." And imaginative use of that gift may even manage to identify a few rational landmarks and trace potential pathways through a "mindscape" that in many respects shall ever remain a wilderness.

For example, religiously based thinking may especially invite hard scrutiny, which of course is apt to be dismissed given that such opinions typically spring from the kind of psychology whose objections to being challenged may achieve the level of deadly force, as happened for example in early Christian conflicts over the "filioque"—"and the Son." The Holy Ghost, insisted one faction, proceeds not just from the Father as their opponents claimed, but from the Father "and the Son." And in bloody violence of the ensuing struggle the sense of what the Son had taught, not to mention human decency itself, was entirely forgotten.[4] But a voyage in the "mindscape" far beyond harbors of conventional thinking where shelter preconceptions both of faith and of science, might try to address such issues as the concept of order, which from a scientific view is the opposite of entropy, or disorder that according to physicists has increased since the start of the material universe. Overall, that universe, once a ball of pure uncorrupted fire is running down, a concept found in the Bible—" the heavens...shall perish...and wax old as doth a garment."[5] But this very concept itself exists in an ideal space which is, in effect, eternal. And in that realm the meaning of "order" can take on many forms. For instance, in mathematics the system or pattern of the natural numbers begins from the pure abstraction of nothingness, to which can be assigned the number zero. Placing zero in brackets identifies it as a digit* that marks the beginning of a procession that advances incrementally in the series of 1,2,3 and onward to infinity. From these numbers can then be derived the whole of arithmetic, algebra and geometry which in turn are all related to one another as, for instance, the familiar case of the Pythagorean theorem which says that the square of the hypotenuse of a right triangle equals the sum of the squares of the other two sides—as when one squared plus one squared equals the square root of two times itself. But the square root of two cannot be expressed in any finite decimal or fraction, thus it becomes a so-called irrational number. Already, a whole new order of expanded complexity, that of the irrational numbers such as the cube root of two or the square root of seven, has arisen as if by magic. And this magic is part of an endless variety which is greater than can be reckoned by the natural numbers themselves. For even if the series of these is continued forever, it will never reach what is only one of the infinite kinds of Infinity, whose true proportions are shown, for example by proofs that the number of points on a line segment of any length is infinitely greater than the non-finite sum of all natural numbers.

32. Seeking the Source

And our realization of this fact, or meta-fact since it is not physical, is enabled by some aspect of human nature partaking of a state which is immortal. For all such theorems would be just as true in the minds of any creatures who might happen to discover them in any universe. Thus one is free to consider--in a higher degree of freedom than typically constrains most everyday decisions--this present Universe as having sprung from some ideal state or principle wherein may also be located the secret of our spiritual nature if the latter is also a valid principle and source of our ability to know and reason, insofar as these gifts are properties of consciousness. And to grant the reality of that source also links it to the physical universe and thus to the evolution of life, despite the latter's also clearly depending on those rational principles first plucked by Darwin from the ideal domain where they reside. And in such case, any aspects of life those principles per se cannot fully explain though remaining a vital prerequisite, invoke a deeper than rational source not only for them but for any extra-temporal dimensions of human nature that could be attributed to a soul or spirit whose homeland abides outside of Time. Indeed, one could further suppose that the formal structures of living things including their respective genetic codes exist extra-temporally as well in the form of information, insofar as the latter might in theory represent all organic factors and relationships that comprise living things, for example the biochemistry of vision or metabolism of a fiddler crab or kangaroo and the place of those creatures in a wider ecological scheme and branching network whose common descent proceeded from the very dawn of Life itself. And of course it is important to remember that information in the abstract or ideal state whence it can be found and retrieved by intelligent beings on any planet in any universe—as versus the concrete form of data stored in texts or encrypted in computer memories—may also submit to the integrative concept of wisdom whereby the entire plan of Life and evolution might reside in a seed, within whose Protean potential akin to but surpassing that of DNA, an extra-temporal Mind could be assured that stars and flowers and children were poised to unfold.

One of the more obvious of those features of the biosphere that could be expressed as information is clearly the overall body plan of animals whose appearance is based on significant attributes like size, the number and types of limbs and appendages and the kind of covering whether of chitin, shell, or skin and fur, and these outward elements are what people may picture when they suppose these creatures to have been "designed" in the mind of God, although of course the total sum of information required to specify every detail of the internal and external anatomy of a worm or a wombat is incalculable. But God could just as well have designed only the core features of each species or phylum in the form of its malleable genetic code, foreknowing that the outward forms would spring from this initial stamp of literally vital information with some degree of freedom as to what they might become. In either case, anyone subscribing to this kind of theory cannot ignore the problem of how the actual creature or genetic imprint was translated from its conceptual form in the mind of God into physical embodiment. However, if we conceive of God as beyond existence, since the Deity by definition is not a "thing" but the creator of all things both living and non-living, not to mention meta-things like time and space, we can say that God created Nature, or perhaps that Nature was projected or proceeded from God as the original condition of, and source of order for the physical universe with its four fundamental forces and entire array of subatomic particles which congealed into the lightest atoms that in turn were forged in nuclear fires of the stars into every element of the periodic table. And the physical order that resulted is subject to entropy, but the laws whose existence that order proclaims are not of Time, nor affected by its relentlessly degenerative process. Hence a flip side of order that unlike its physical counterpart is immune to entropy could be imagined as providing an influx of information and ideas from an extra-temporal domain that is the ultimate source not only of Life but for human inspiration and aspiration.

However, in the case of Life there obtains another type of order that works oppositely to entropy, by turning carbon and other elements into feathers, for example. And this ordered complexity could be seen as the manifestation of Being, or becomingness of its potential, not just at the cosmological outset of a temporal process governed by laws whose expression in formulas such as F=ma (force equals mass times acceleration) is not temporally corruptible but enduringly ideal—but throughout the evolution both of living and non-living things. Hence Life, while less deterministic or repetitive than matter-energy and thus not only possessing a higher degree of freedom but presenting a less definitive picture than the steadfast firmament or hills, may better reflect than insentient atoms or quarks the primal fullness of Nature that also masks or embodies the Divine—S/He who is greater than Creation, and is proclaimed equally, though differently, by humble grasses and distant galaxies.

Of course, because living organisms are self-replicating and self-repairing machines they also incorporate information of not only greater amount and density but of so fundamentally other kind than non-living systems as perhaps to evade attempts at being thus defined as information per se. Hence there are equations to describe the process of solar nuclear fusion, but not to codify the internal activities of a living cell. The biochemistry of the cell may be expressible in formulas, but not how that chemistry together with the physical activity of protein molecules—such as those which help to disentangle strands of DNA during cell division—is choreographed into the intracellular dance of life. And when the network of communications to be sorted out is an intercellular flux of messages that for example may signal the endocrine system to secrete more or less of a certain hormone like adrenalin or the flow of blood to increase in muscles under stress, then the level of difficulty is even further beyond what can be described in terms of a system or mechanism whose workings strictly conform to known laws of physics. Hence the order that Life represents is more subtle than what has shaped the stars and planets (although living processes have clearly altered the face of planet Earth). Living order is less strictly ruled by Time than is so-called non-living matter and thus at every moment more strongly connected to that source of freedom which may dwell within or beyond the primal state whence Time began, yet timelessly enfold the space-time dimension and the human condition it contains.

But the evolution of life has led to consciousness and to human psychology, wherein resides an even higher kind of order with more degrees of freedom, a good reason why freedom itself is one of the deepest principles underlying that psychology and its personal, cultural and social expressions. For while free will may be a debatable proposition, the liberty to consider such questions has but lately and uniquely emerged in the mind of homo sapiens, thus further distinguishing the phenomenon of consciousness.

Yet if there are different aspects or qualities of order—the order of a factory versus that of a ballet, or minimum entropy of the primordial fireball versus the maximal and purposeful complexity of a brain or an ecosystem, there are also different kinds or gradations of existence that arise from or depend upon them. For example, one can describe biological existence as a dynamic condition equivalent to survival—a constant avoidance of the death that will collapse that condition—whereas the simple persistence of non-living things is virtually automatic, the repetitive drone that underlies more subtle harmonies of the biosphere. A mountain range forged by inorganic processes such as folding of the Earth's crust will change over time according to geophysical laws, but surrender of its relative permanence to gradual erosion will not involve any phase shift from living to non-living. But to maintain an animal's existence requires intentional effort which may be called instinctive yet nonetheless displays a form of consciousness or mind. The mind of a dragonfly, for example, may not involve actual thinking (although a jumping spider named Portia Labiata apparently does have the ability to plan a course of action that it can retain in memory until carried out)[1] but does retain pictures of its environment and can make decisions based on how that view may vary, although its own degree of freedom falls well short of being able to reinvent itself. And in the instance of plants, immobility of the entire organism does not prevent the process of survival from involving adaptive response whose complex variability, and chemical wizardry is far from fully understood, for example in producing toxins to ward off harmful insects. Causes and methods of the plant's behavior like much else in Nature occupy a sphere that is only thrust even further beyond that of human understanding by claims to an understanding, or even its mere possibility, that does not exist.

What does exist is evidence that the virtual intelligence of Nature in plants and animals derives from the same source of mindfulness that is present in human beings, meaning that metaphysically, mind is just as common to all of Life as is physically the genetic code. And for what is meant by "metaphysical," one only need consider the motivation or mind-set of whomsoever might accept, contest or simply consider the rhyme and reason of that last statement, according to in what degree of freedom they are capable of voyaging towards new frontiers whose promise inspires longing to escape confinement of stale ideas and creeds outworn, or to flee a theater of "memes" whose tired shticks may present a sticky wicket for new and progressive thinking.

Yet for living things in general their willfully active survival reflects a different kind of order than what governs classical objects like baseballs, whose own mode of being is non-derivable from that of quantum particles which are not actual objects in any familiar sense and thus continue to elude rational comprehension (although their raison d'etre can be comprehended insofar as what is basic to familiar reality cannot be more of the same since if it were, the subsurface foundation of more ordinary things would still remain undiscovered). And finally, in the peculiar domain of human psychology, survival can assume such forms as "saving face" or achieving social status, reflecting laws of a social and psychological order which is nearly as vital for the meaningful existence that includes sentient beings as the ironclad rule of physics, insofar as any knowledge concerning the latter depends on support of human awareness that is nurtured by the social order. Hence, one kind of order and the form of survival it enables does not take precedence or pride of place in some explanatory hierarchy above any other, because all are mutually and seamlessly interdependent. And in light of that interdependence, one can envision how the laws or behavioral patterns of physics might become transformed into those of life, even if any actual understanding of how that transformation occurred, when complex chemicals first acquired the spark of autonomy that spurred their cooperative assembly into living cells, shall continue to dwell beyond any remotely imaginable horizon.

33. Essence and Entropy

Yet again, within those horizons we can at least attempt to understand what order is and how it shows itself—that is, beyond the obvious fact that it constitutes an idea that is realized when people talk about what it means in the abstract or apply it in reference to society or science. First of all, if order is an existential property inherent to Being and manifestation, then it should be present most directly in primal or absolute existence before so-called randomness or chaos has begun to arise along with, or between the gaps of, burgeoning complexity in the course of cosmic evolution. And in that perspective order becomes either, simply, the incipient state of the universe that also according to physical theory represented perfect absence of entropy[1]—since entropy can only grow with time—or is else most purely obtained in the eternal existence or meta-existence of a Deity or higher mind whence that primordial state was projected by the fiat, "let there be light." In the latter case, one could say that the existence of that putative Supreme Being is a condition of effortless and permanent survival, equivalent to perfect freedom and absolute security combined—with neither of those virtues having to give way in favor of the other as occurs in the case of society where setting a fair balance between the two can become crucial. But in the case of the Cosmos' initial appearance, the coalescence and subsequent differentiation and dispersal of matter-energy involved a sacrifice of perfect freedom for the partial security of what has culminated in the relative freedom of human life whose security is challenged by entropy, as when governments, in succumbing to the entropic influence of fear and/or temptations toward cruel abuse of power degrade the happiness of their subjects, or when Nature's caprice may deal a telling blow as did a volcanic eruption circa 1600 B.C. in wrecking Minoan civilization. The primary laws of Creation that initially produced the quantum world of subatomic particles and radiation and later built the stellar nuclear furnaces wherein the elemental blocks, like carbon and iron, of planets and organic life were forged were strictly deterministic and thus weighted heavily towards abiding permanence of the Heavens. But the latter having been established, subtler laws of change then began to favor greater liberty that allowed for organic evolution that in turn led to human self-awareness and capacity not only for affecting Destiny in the temporal sphere where determinism still exerts a powerful influence (as when former conflicts only lead to future strife or complex psychology confounds cold-blooded cost/benefit analyses) but for withdrawal from that sphere into extra-temporal realms that could be called the homeland of mind and intellect, insofar as the ideal essence of thought is incorruptible, and that also in even larger perspective are where the soul when its Earthly days are done shall return to continue an endless journey.

But the ramification of an order whose rippling complexities were channeled in a surge that finally crested to uplift the freedom of consciousness can also be analyzed in mathematical terms of an understanding fashioned in the "mindscape" where ideas are not subject to entropy. Hence the construct we envision can deal with what the concept of order means in a context not subject to temporal decay. Subsequently, that concept can be applied to the real world in a manner analogous to how by similar token the ideal can be seen as precipitating into the so-called real world whose very "reality" is a function of our subjective apprehension of an environment that in truth is continuous with consciousness. And so doing also confers upon a world including both the real and ideal a bridge between them, whereby what can or could be can become what is, so that what is eternal because it cannot be affected by entropy may enter into and affect a temporal process such as evolution, just as the laws of physics figuratively speaking enter into time and space, whose very properties are shaped by principles like relativity, in order to determine or become embodied as the actual and specific nature of physical reality. Thus for example the dream of an opera can be said to correspond in its ideal form either to information or to a non-specific concept that easily generates the formal data corresponding to physical realization. And consequently through means of written score, stage design and lyrics that are both real and abstract, the work can assume a fleeting physical appearance through the human agency of various workers and performers. That appearance is subject to entropic decay, but the ideal essence—however regarded—behind its or any material manifestation is immune to circumstantial or temporal change and as Shakespeare said of love, "alters not when it alteration finds." Yet the opposite is of course true for the dynamic stream of biological evolution, that changes course not only to conform with a changing environment but to alter that environment as well, as in generating oxygen and enriching soil. Hence an important task for civilization is to ensure that any environmental change our species may cause stops short of the slippery decline of irreversible entropy whose bottom would be bleak indeed. And advancing that cause could be helped by accessing a reservoir of values such as reverence for life—not to mention the strictly rational value of self-preservation—inherent in the essence of our human spiritual nature that ideally, both graces and is graced by the natural world.

34. Vital Order

Thus, the concept of order and its basic connection with Life as rational essence of a living process that is ever escaping the jaws of entropy, can be analyzed as deriving out of some indefinable condition lacking any shape, boundaries or number, nor any other identifiable properties such as temperature or spatial dimensions, any one of which would imply the presence of other, affiliated features as well But in that case such an hypothetical state cannot really exist insofar as certain characteristics must be assumed for anything whose existence can be claimed or discussed, or rather it can only be described as having the character of origin, or unity—"In the beginning was the Word, and the Word was God, and the Word was with God" which in physics corresponds to minimal entropy—a state that theologians could maintain still exists as the "divine spark" in sub-atomic particles, in symphonies, and in sunsets as well as in the embodied minds that perceive them and the souls therein incarnate, all of which explicit entities were once implicit in the primal Word that indeed continues to resonate and sustain all Creation.

In any event, one property or characteristic required for obtaining the distinction of order from virtual nothingness, or "no-thing-ness" could be that of separation or the drawing of boundaries to create a number of specific entities as for example in the carving up of geometric space into various ideal objects like spheres and pyramids—although in such instance it must be noted that space itself already possesses the innate geometrical order which allows those boundaries, or limits, to be drawn and thus to render such entities from the void, whose virtual non-existence is thereby the ground of being for all mathematical conceptions. Of course, however, since even space itself is such a concept, the so-called void must be imagined as more purely nothing than an empty space that can be defined mathematically. And in fact, if the "void" is really nothing (which clearly makes it non-real) then it could be described not as emptiness, but as a point of zero dimensions. But then it has at least been identified and accordingly does exist after all as the cornerstone, so to speak, of a geometry that can easily be generated simply by establishing additional points, an exercise whose accomplishment could lead us to identify the most absolute void imaginable not as a point, but rather Infinity—and in that sense perhaps analogous to an actual pre-existent state from whence precipitated the space-time universe. Hence nothingness, whether mathematical or physical, instantly implies being-ness as well, and a primary component of being-ness is the principle of order as defined by unity, an existential value that retains within itself all consequent existence whether in terms of numbers, equations, or living things.

Thus it is easy to see how the beginning of mathematical order and of consequent complexity models the birth of the universe whose initial unified state rapidly differentiated into a sea of quantum entities and forces. And that primary order, whether ideal or physical, can be ramified or acquire fresh layers of complexity as new qualities and relationships are incorporated into the various kinds of entities and their combinatorial associations. Yet all of these semi-individual existences are bound to have something in common as members of the same set or bounded region of Reality which may be called a universe, because all are subject to the same set of laws or conditions whose warp and woof, by definition, cannot be other than universal across the whole breadth and depth of the cosmic tapestry that upon those principles has been established. And in a broader context, that universality applies not only to the laws of physics, but to less provisional truths such as the link between the ideal and the real—whence can be taken rational possibility of a deep and vivid metaphysical milieu that is reciprocal to and yet imbues a poignantly wispy world whose creatures have not long to savor their evanescent days of wine and roses.

However, even in a hypothetical model, order having once been established is not going to stay the same, if it has been formed by the same dynamic principles which brought forth material worlds from a transcendental state of pre-existence. For these principles then become incessant forces that drive the process of change that is irreducibly inherent to the real world and thus keeps generating new patterns of an ever-increasingly diversified order. (Whose character is, of course, quite unpredictably different for Nature whose multiplicity of things and relationships cannot be completely specified by any finite quantity of information, than in the case of mathematical objects in a space of known geometrical properties, or obeying the simple instructions of a computer program). Nor shall these patterns arbitrarily begin to shed complexity and sink to lower degrees of the freedom that every individual node of being has attained by virtue of the powers of change which are bound to prevail in any physical universe which has not, quite unreasonably, been denied them—as could be the case for a 'perfect world" with no slop in the system and where bad things never happened either to good people or to the bad ones who would not be around to do such things in that unlikely kind of world. That observation, however, need not obviate the hope of an Earthly paradise arrived at by the kinds of positive change, like towards wiser use of technology or eliminating hunger and ignorance, that today are flatly imperative toward saving our species and civilization. Nor does it obviate the religious vision of heavenly realms free of sorrow and suffering, in part presumably because their higher degree of freedom should transcend the all-pervading perils of change ever rife with decay that are inherent in a temporal universe.

For even when some fragile forms of order are compromised, as biodiversity has been by civilization, they are typically replaced by others as for example the psychological complexity of human life now occupies the space our species has, though often to its detriment, expropriated from the natural world. The ramification of evolving order, in other words, is not going to reverse itself at some arbitrary point and go back to square one for even a global extinction, as may have happened on Mars or on planets whose civilizations and even biospheres could have been destroyed through unwisely abused technology, is not the same as reversal. Thus evolution, constrained toward advancement by that open-ended rationale, is bound to express the ever-expanding ordered complexity and higher degrees of freedom that on favored planets can ultimately lead to conscious observers who even, beyond all strictures of Darwinian necessity, can contemplate questions such as free will or whether the Cosmos and human life holds any purpose or meaning rather than simply a semblance of these qualities in the fancy of self-deluded minds. And one form of answer to that query could be provided straight away—that in such context words like "purpose" and "meaning" are indeed delusional, insofar as reflecting a rational failure to grasp that Life itself is synonymous with the whole purpose and meaning of existence, to which an additional dimension being given by human life automatically endows the latter with that very meaning and purpose whose philosophical pursuit is accordingly in vain.

35. Igniting the Fire

From a bottom up perspective assigning pride of place to the shifting sediments and swirling currents of the quantum foundations of physical reality, life and consciousness can be viewed as a blind accident of random chance operating in the context of laws not intended or designed to produce anything so special as a singer or a centipede, even if, atop the pyramid of inorganic structures in at least one of countless galaxies or universes, organic life was bound to eventuate. But from the top down perspective assigning prime importance to consciousness as the most pervasive principle of all existence—one which, after all, can thus be identified only through the agency of mind—life dwells as a spark even within non-organic matter that is always ready to burst into flame. And that flame is alive in us as part of the fire of Life that has a mind of its own throughout the Universe. And in subverting ostensibly dumb molecules to the alchemy of its relentless purpose, that life assumes the myriad forms of creatures, who display the imagination of Nature but some steps removed from the mind of God, a Being whose own freedom is not diminished by some part of it having been vouchsafed to Creation. And in this perspective, human cerebral awareness is but one facet of the Cosmic mind wherein all physical reality resides as "a great thought rather than a great machine," yet is also a vehicle for spiritual consciousness that can enter into our world from those beyond through a portal whose widening faith may willfully facilitate, although already open to what extent derives from humanity's evolutionary attainment. Hence the reaching of civilization towards "values" whether conceived as ethical, spiritual or intellectual, that is ever in advance of the social Darwinism sadly manifest in politics and commerce.

Thus there are at least two conceivable kinds of order, as well, in addition to what is held to be the opponent of entropy and therefore doomed along with any "dreams of reason" that starkly interpret whatever appearance of rhyme or reason more spiritually hopeful dreamers may attribute to personal and cosmic existence. For example in quantum physics, there is clearly a kind of order manifest in "quantum fields" and their associated particles which is other than the classical order ever stalked by the relentless dying that not only wears down the human body but shall eventually cause the Sun, when its hydrogen fuel is exhausted, to become a bloated giant within whose sickly embrace our planet shall be baked to a cinder. For quantum particles like photons, electrons and quarks are not classical objects like pebbles and feathers—if they were, they would have a definite surface and form in three dimensions. And that surface could not be two-dimensional and thus perfectly smooth. Instead, it would have to be granular just as the surface of a macro-object like the Moon or an amoeba is composed from particles of dust or molecules of water, gas, or chemicals, or from proteins and other organic substances like oyster shell. And in that case, quantum physics would be part of the classical order instead of what it is, namely a category of existence whose nature we cannot fathom because it underlies and is accordingly more basic than the classical regime of elements and forces whose own laws sharply constrain our thinking and perceiving. Thus quantum particles, which are not pieces of stuff like a drop of water or a diamond but rather hyper-spatial nodes of vibratory energy insofar as any such classically slanted description of them is possible, are despite having been born at the beginning of Time, not busy dying nor subject to decay—at least not in any time-frame smaller than the current age of the

Universe—but instead belong to an order that is virtually no less eternal than the paradox it represents.

Then again, a more metaphysical departure from the realm of classical physics takes us into the theatre of mind where "order" in and of itself exists as an idea whose myriad forms—just one of which is the kind that is tremulously opposed to entropy—cannot be counted. In fact, some spiritual philosophies view the mind itself, whose "mindscape" includes both mathematics and artistic imagination, as subsidiary to a still vaster scheme of transcendental existence, beyond yet including what some philosophers may once have conceived as a realm of ideal forms like the several regular or equal-sided solids of geometry[1] whose immortal state was imperfectly reflected in the material world. Hence the spark of thoughtful awareness that has kept expanding throughout human history was, in those aforesaid views, first instilled in primitive hominid species from a source above and beyond the deathless mental domain of reason and imagination. And whereas it may be easy to say that the so-called mind and its ethereal landscape along with any wishful spiritual source are simply comforting fictions, that very opinion itself is generated in a mental world, that whether called real, ideal, or imaginary is just as immune to entropy as in the perspective where mind is a part of personal consciousness that occupies a larger field of cosmic awareness to which it is bonded inseparably as an electron with its associated electromagnetic field. And whatever passions fuel debate upon such issues, are merely flames of a fire that burns in the minds of those who have not ignited it, nor have any clue as to its origin or that of the larger Life that also in themselves is burning..

Yet another type of order, however, can be associated with evolution in a way that indicates the logical necessity for structures of life and its neural mechanisms of consciousness to arise from inorganic matter-energy. First of all, the pattern of order itself has already emerged in any collection of elements that bear distinguishing characteristics like the properties of atoms or sub-atomic particles and the forces they embody. That is true because existence cannot simply be a shapeless mass devoid of any character whatsoever (including mass itself) or of any definitive features that mark it as existing. Whatever constituted the original manifestation of the universe did have properties such as temperature, for example. But if that primal state becomes dissociated into separate entities, these must bear some relation to each other by the same universal law that brought them into being, and therefore share a common identity as photons and quarks, or whatever the primal elements may be. Thus the very beginning of physical existence implies a great deal of order—the universe, in other words, has to make some kind of sense to exist at all. And from that point if any change occurs as the dynamic nature of reality demands it must, that change is likely to follow the trend of increasing order at least in terms of the growing and coordinated complexity of whatever new entities such as atoms and stars may arise in the course of change. For if that process were as likely to go backwards, one would have to ask at what point it were reasonable for that reversal to happen and why it did not already take place long ago and bring the developmental journey to an ignominious end. Thus whatever actual causes provoked any of the major and often baffling transitions in the history of life—of which the greatest was the birth of unicellular organisms from complex chemicals—by the most sweepingly abstract understanding of the patterns that life and the universe represent these changes were bound to occur and in doing so to advance towards more complexity and degrees of freedom, whose pinnacle has been currently attained by homo sapiens. And even when change may seem regressive, that appearance can be deceptive as in the case of some mammals that after evolving from fish that crawled onto shore, returned to the sea to become dolphins and whales. For the latter creatures high intelligence and aquatic grace may well represent considerable improvement over their terrestrial ancestors.

In other words, insofar as Nature or the Cosmos is a unified entity as can hardly be otherwise if all its parts are in mutual agreement, then it must incorporate a single set of interacting laws by which the character of its individual parts and elements is also determined. Hence that character must exhibit common features shared by all those elements as indeed happens to be the case—all electrons are alike and also share with other quantum particles common properties such as charge, mass and spin. Thus the establishment of progressive order is guaranteed. And as that primal pattern ramifies into the grander aspects of Nature such as stars and planets, those larger composite entities are no longer exactly alike but continue to share recognizable similarities such as stellar nuclear combustion and adhering to the forms of solar systems and galaxies within the overriding context of time and space, the vast arms of the Cosmos that embrace all it contains. And finally, because order cannot stay the same but is dynamic insofar as the story of those changes that shaped the firmament could only be the prologue for further changes to come, the inorganic astrophysical and chemical order leapt in the only direction open for continued progress, across the gulf that formerly divided insensate molecules from a new phase of living complexity expressing ever more radical freedom, whose continued expansion is today the keynote of human social and cultural evolution. And it is also true, of course, that the background for this kind of change remains the growing entropy of the physical Cosmos, just as a body increasingly ravaged by syphilis was the physical framework for the genius of Franz Schubert in composing his last and greatest works. But the difference between the material kingdom that entropy will someday overthrow and the higher kind and quality of order whose roots are conceptual and therefore eternal is shown by the fact of evolution having culminated in the burning awareness of beings, by whom that very difference can be recognized.

36. Rational Pursuit

Just as there may be countless universes, many or even all of which express its own variation on the theme of Life, there are many ways to define what is meant by "order." Or to put it differently, many meanings can be ascribed to a word that is being employed to clarify understanding of a reality whose constant fluctuations also keep swaying the consciousness of those who seek a deeper acquaintance with what no words or equations can securely grasp. But insofar as science has identified the opposite of order, or entropy, as the ultimate outcome for change in the physical universe, it can still be pointed out that at least a bit of order is necessary for anything to exist at all. Thus the principle of order which is wedded to that of existence may be even more basic than the concept of a physical order that has continued to slide downwards from its peak of minimum entropy ever since the dawn of Creation, just as a baby starts to die from the moment of its birth. In fact, just as the person who grows from a baby gradually loses innocence and acquires knowledge, so has the evolving Universe lost its initial purity of an absolute quantum essence while gaining the sophistication of self-maintaining and autonomous living things. And in a universe consisting of only a mixture of subatomic particles and photons of radiation—as was briefly the case for what is now this present world—the laws of relativity, the wave-particle duality of light and all of the parameters of physical existence that are inherent in the very nature of time and space must still prevail and thereby yield the kind of order that may nearly always be sure to blossom into Life whose full fruition then is realized through genetic magic, combined with evolutionary sifting of the wheat from the chaff in each succeeding generation.

And even if we must accept that evolution of the Cosmos also represents a net gain of entropy, as species and civilizations arise and perish until in the long night of Time that no conscious minds remain to observe, the stars themselves burn out into chunks of ash adrift in virtual emptiness, the very character of that hypothetical void may offer further clues as to the nature of the physical Cosmos. For while such emptiness might be even more profound by dint of lacking any witnesses (unless future science could discover some means for continued human survival) it would also be more virtual than absolute by reason of containing not only photons but "virtual photons" as well, that are held to be the agents of transmitting magnetic or electrostatic force.[1] The attraction between a magnet and a nail or a heap of iron filings cannot, unlike heat or light, be measured as consisting of photons of a certain frequency. Therefore magnetic force is assigned to what amounts to another dimension, where perhaps may also dwell those mysterious principles that seem to manifest in biological phenomena that continue to defy conventional evolutionary dogma. And while the cosmic harmony revealed both in equations and in viewing the skies, mountains and oceans may inspire wonder, evolution rightfully should do so even more. For the story of Life remains less likely than the deepest riddles in physics and astronomy to give up its secrets, despite what explanatory fig leaves may try to conceal the naked meta-truth by which biology and evolution, above other science, continue to challenge excessive faith in the faculty of reason that they also keep luring into realms of ever-deepening fascination (that include the neuronal machinery of reason itself). And that is because the vast multiplicity of Nature is far more daunting in its living aspect to human understanding than even the unknowns of quantum mechanics and relativity still seeking resolution through some theoretical embrace that could connect the sweep of gravity with all the blurry quantum bits that constitute our nominally substantial being. Meanwhile no sign of any dawning theory has yet been glimpsed on any horizon, whereby the wonders that science has revealed could be gathered up in a manner that could vitiate their existential indication as to the true proportions of our nature being interpreted in those countless ways, whose restless pursuit is hardly at odds with the open-ended character of reason itself.

37. Threads of the Tapestry

In fact, the existence of hidden relationships in physics whose disclosure awaits discovery of a more deeply binding order than current knowledge has yet been able to resolve, cannot but further indicate a profoundly concealed current of higher causality in biology and evolution as well, to which science may never attain. Thus, for example, in pierid butterflies, there are many substances related to uric acid, which is a product of excretion. One of these substances is guanine which produces both "the white spots on a spider's black coat and the glittering white of many fishes."[1] Therefore it has been supposed that excretion through the skin of many animals has caused these substances to have accidentally begun to play a role in creating skin patterns which only later were preserved for their selective advantage. But in the pierid butterflies, part of the pattern consists of colors derived from melanin pigments which are not a product of excretion. Furthermore, "there are scales which produce a variety of scintillating effects and which, again, have nothing to do with excretion."[2] Thus the total appearance of the butterfly depends on a variety of factors whose coordinated emergence can hardly have been dependent on mere collaboration of chance and natural selection. The phenomenon requires considering that "the colors on the wings of butterflies, the colors of spiders, etc. do not get there as the chance result of excretion"[3] but instead are "specially diverted into the skin"[4] according to genetic guidelines of the organism which did not arise simply because of natural selection having preserved the initially random tendency for certain colors and patterns to appear. Similarly, biologists long since attempted to explain certain basic patterns like the stripes and spots of zebras and leopards "which occur not only in mammals but also in many birds, insects, fishes, and reptiles"[5] as "growth patterns" whereby "different phases in development of the skin can be associated with alternating tensions and variations in pigment distribution."[6] However, "all attempts to explain specific patterns in terms of specific phases of ontogenetic processes break down when it comes to the study of species that are closely related but differ in their patterns"[7] Nonetheless this type of explanation has been accepted because nothing else works and because any admission of ignorance and bewilderment would be unacceptable. For what remains, is that what does appear to be at work could only be called the mind of Nature, inventive as any human abstract artist (who as the painter Jackson Pollock said of himself is also part of Nature) and manifest in the outward appearance as well as structural physiology of an organism or species.

The evolutionary role attributed to the "mind of Nature" clearly does not, however, qualify as science in any sense deserving to be taught in schools or to be added onto the broad Darwinian outline which, aside from the fine tuning provided by new genetic and other findings, is scientifically speaking the best conceivably possible. Nor does that outline contradict any metaphysical approach to evolution as, for example, is taken in suggesting that the all-pervading presence of a mind of Nature or the Cosmos is a "formal cause" underlying or pervading all phenomena including natural selection itself, no less than electromagnetic fields are responsible for lightning. Nor does the fact of natural selection ensuring that each living species representing a thread of the ecological tapestry remains viable enough to pass on its genes to future generations say anything about the truth or falsehood of religious faith, since clearly God would wish His/Her creatures to be strong and healthy as possible in a necessarily imperfect world. For almost as clearly, the Deity might well prefer allowing natural selection to do the job of leveraging progress, rather than issue forth a world already perfect—assuming it could be determined what "perfection" means. For in a perfectly safe and happy world—at least in one like ours under the sway of natural laws like death and entropy—the only alteration would be for the worse, since change for the better would imply that before it occurred things were not actually perfect after all. Therefore science is able to elucidate that wherever its laws prevail there must be sorrow and suffering, for only in a dream world, or a mystical paradise whose reality can neither be confirmed nor disproved by mortal minds, could all change consist of neutral fluctuations within a state of unalloyed happiness. And perhaps the mythic "dreamtime" of the Australian aborigines was such a state whose innocence endured for thousands of years and perhaps involved forms of awareness of which modern humans know little or nothing, yet was fated to conclude through unforeseeable circumstance whose perils are inherent in the very nature of our space-time Universe.

38. Post-Darwinian Evolution

However, should humans evolve spiritually to the point of acquiring the power to die at will, then those laws would be partially abrogated and change indeed become mostly neutral, as in a film whose characters dwell in a world of imagination immune to entropy. To repeal entropic corruption altogether on the other hand would mean, in effect, the uplifting of matter into another dimension comparable to the mythical Shamballa or the Biblical Eden. And finally, if a quasi immortality could be conferred by medical means, those who chose to pursue such a path could hardly be considered the most noble of humans, since their choice would imply a lack of faith in any spiritual existence whereby Death itself can acquire redemptive power transcending the cycles of mortality.

But of course if the "mind of Nature" is sufficiently spiritual to fashion its human components towards containing aspiration that in turn reflects the longing of Spirit—whereby "God so loved the world"—to be more fully realized in the physical Cosmos and its intelligent life, then the accordingly inherent "goal" of evolution in its largest sense can hardly be a static perfection, but instead a self-transcendence of its own heretofore necessary laws. And that same transcendence which in fact is partly manifest through the phase-shift of consciousness ascending through the various stages of animal and human psychology, is also happening through the "post-Darwinian" progress of human understanding and society which has established at least a slender foothold in the world for eternal values and ideas such as "Beauty is Truth, and Truth is Beauty." For practical application of the latter towards ending the ugliness of destitution and protecting the beauties of environmental treasures would clearly help to realize the most worthy and enduring dreams of civilization, and in so doing close a deal with whatever agency of God or Fate might then less grudgingly allow our society and species to survive. Thus to realize the moral imperative, that our species and civilization become humanely human and enlightened, would also meet the Darwinian imperative, which is to adapt or perish.

Yet to view that moral imperative as inherent in some post-Darwinian phase of evolution hopefully to be more fully expressed by future humanity, rather than as a mere figure of speech or rhetorical fancy, may depend on understanding the evolutionary past in some deeper sense that borders on metaphysics. For that is what is needed to allow continuity between the pre-human past and a fully civilized world which a glorified animal lacking any spiritual source of inspiration might be hard put to attain. And that understanding is virtually compelled in contemplating that while genetic mutation as required by Darwinian theory for the blueprint of evolutionary change is logically indispensable, there just isn't any way to account for how and why the multiple and coordinated mutations behind any radical adaptation, like conversion of wings to the function of swimming together with acquisition of insulating blubber and down by the birds that evolved into penguins, are able to occur in the non-random manner that they must have done.

Thus to arbitrarily designate such mutations as "random" is the same as saying that their basis has not been identified even though genetic change in general may often derive from various known factors such as the impact of a cosmic ray or the reshuffling of genes during cell division. In this context, an expression like "the mind of Nature" is a rhetorical way to indicate how these simultaneous mutations are forced to make sense not just by natural selection, but in being vetted by the same intracellular sorting process that weeds out bad DNA[1] and maintains integrity of the genome. And the further step of describing this process as intelligent—and in a manner perhaps responding to larger patterns of ecological or climate change that offer fresh opportunities, as for example when loss of forest habitat may have forced tree-dwelling primates into the more dangerous environment of the African savannahs where survival called for new skills and thinking ability—is no different than to describe ourselves as intelligent. And certainly the conceivable evolution of our primate ancestors from dim-witted tree-dwelling, fruit eating climbers into smarter hunter-gatherers insecurely roaming the plains might be explained by selection alone, with lions and hyenas helping to breed what became modern humans by picking off the slow and unwary.

But there are far more problematic cases that basic evolution theory does not suffice to explain. Just one example of many is an Australian bird that constructs an incubator to maintain its eggs at a constant temperature for several months until ready to hatch. Moist vegetable debris lines the bottom of a hole so that decay will produce heat to maintain a temperature in winter months of about 90 degrees. The male bird monitors the warmth with its beak, and adds or removes insulation above the egg chamber to keep the relatively constant temperature value that the embryos' development demands.[2] Clearly, how this whole sequence of behavior could arise and be genetically encoded transcends the realm of chance mutation or any conceivable explanation, beyond observing that any bird parent doing a sloppy job of caring for the eggs is unlikely to pass on its genes to the next generation, and in that respect natural selection plays a part in preserving this avian species and its lifestyle. It is the question of how some set of genes can spell out complex nest-building behavior that also involves the bird's knowing what temperature must be kept in the egg chamber, or how the requisite mutations could occur haphazardly or without the aid of the "wise blood" of Nature whose ingenious powers greatly surpass human intellect, that rebukes any scientific hope of fathoming what kind of magic it takes to produce the special effects that Life displays everywhere in plain sight and even in the neural machinery of those for whom reason and knowledge are important deities..

As in human thought, however, the role of the genes can be regarded as subservient and the bird's behavior, repeated exactly from generation to generation, a function of its actual knowing or mentality just as in the case of human ritual traditions or modes of living. Although the bird's knowledge is presumably not learned from its parents but somehow programmed, it nonetheless appears to know what it is doing in caring for the eggs as consciously as any human performing a daily task like cooking or driving. An even more puzzling example where the role of genes would be harder to identify is that of cricket mothers that convey to their unborn young to beware of wolf spiders, something that only occurs when the female cricket has been familiarized with this danger during pregnancy. Thus hereditary instinct genetically ingrained by selection is ruled out, as shown through more careful spider avoidance behavior by the progeny of crickets exposed while pregnant to what for them must be as terrifying an enemy as were cave bears and saber-tooth tigers for prehistoric humans.[3] Yet scientific neglect to consider the meaning of such riddles is less reprehensible than psychologically indicative, because it calls into question the nature of knowledge itself and what psychological role is played by the standard modern picture of reality and the Cosmos. For facing that question squarely could find that picture to be a reflection in a warped house of mirrors, and current knowledge, paradoxically, though manifestly superior to ancient superstitions still infinitely far from attaining the boundless horizons of a Magnum Mysterium wherein unfailingly shall ever emerge new things and more radical perspectives undreamed before by any philosophy.

Yet description of humans as intelligent presumably confers upon our species not simply autonomous functional capabilities but desire for knowledge that is meaningful and purposeful in the sense those very words imply, namely one of moral superiority to some autonomic or robotic tendency on the part of some to collect and assort information just because they can, while others commit the yet more egregious foolishness of constructing airy castles of fantasies and theories to provide a sort of pseudo-immortality akin to that momentarily attained by doomed though mighty kingdoms through their conquests and colossal works But such a tendency is all that words like knowledge can refer to if we do not have souls and are thus, quite arguably, not really conscious in any deeper sense than when some neuroscientists and philosophers seek to identify personal consciousness as a pure illusion draped on a framework of factors that are, however apparently magical, strictly mechanistic rather than "spiritual" in any other sense than that of what coldly atheistic views might regard as a falsely glittering word. Then again, the spiritual paradigm does not necessarily uphold any greater hopes for knowledge and science to be less a "vanity of vanities" than when "the heavens vanishing away and Earth wearing out like a garment"[4] represents the barren sum of our fates and not simply what happens on the lowest floor of a house wherein are many mansions. And of course one could also argue that without taking sides in favor of either paradigm with its own peculiar illusions of certainty, the knowledge industry has both economic and cultural significance. The meaning of "meaning" as applied to evolution or any other subject blending scientific and philosophical import, is found within a here and now whose Author, whether person or principle or both, shall ever remain inscrutable. Yet beyond any limits of knowledge and reason, is ever the possibility of non-intellectual acquaintance with subjective spiritual worlds within ourselves. And to better recognize and be familiar with these inner dimensions of the human micro-cosmos is surely a goal of post-Darwinian evolution, if only because the richer Cosmos that would readily include them is surely a safer one, even in Darwinian terms, than the starkly simplified non-spiritual universe where no better than a harshly unforgiving fate is more apt to await our species and civilization.

39. Bridge to Erewhon

Yet in a metaphysically proportioned Cosmos there is also a less tenuous bridge between the naked facts of evolution and biology and the far deeper study of psychology and personality wherein reside such questions as the role and significance of "knowledge," a study that is also, for those willing so to accept, the portal to psychic and spiritual worlds inconceivably greater than any canon of what can or could be codified as information. Concerning these, the Erewhon of psyche is for many persons evident in dreams, especially those that afford a glimpse of coming events. If the dream can be shown to correspond closely enough to some subsequent event, one might presume that some channel of communication allows the dream state to extend into future time—and is therefore not temporally bounded but has transcended the flow of events in a manner which obviously cannot be described since understanding Time itself is already supremely difficult. However, the criteria for establishing whether a dream exhibits any precognitive features are fairly straightforward. What could be coincidence, for example, can explain many instances of dreams corresponding with subsequent occurrences. Thus it would not be unusual to dream of an airplane crashing into a building or a tidal wave sweeping over coastal regions since the possibility of either event is quite conceivable. But to dream of two airplanes crashing into two adjacent buildings at nearly the same time could seem distinctively psychic if that dream took place before the terrorist attacks on the New York World Trade Center on September 11, 2001. Yet if the criteria are strict, then ruling out coincidence in this hypothetical case might seem arbitrary. But if, instead, the terrorist attacks were cryptically foreshadowed by a dream scenario quite unlikely to ever happen in reality or even be imagined while awake, yet in hindsight clearly symbolizing the subsequent actual events, a compelling case can then be made that non-physical parameters should be included in any valid picture of the Cosmos.

Suppose for example that the dreamer finds himself in a room on one wall of which appears a mural of the New York City skyline. Standing before the mural are two men, one of whom is aiming at the picture a kind of gun with a wide aluminum-colored barrel. The other man raises his hand and then drops it, saying "fire." The first man pulls the trigger and part of the skyline image is erased. The same actions are then repeated once more. In retrospect the symbolism is clear but was totally obscure when this curious dream occurred, as it did in this writer's experience, over a year before the terrible events. Had any hint of its meaning been evident at the time, then it could have been recorded in a notarized document and thus acquired some semblance of credibility as evidence of a psychic dimension. But on the other hand, there may be slight reason for trying to drag that ill-defined region into the manicured temple of proven science, thereby straitjacketing the former like a harmless madman who were better left to wander singing and shouting over hill and dale, while encumbering the latter with a burden even more awkward than such bafflements of the strictly physical world as the wave-particle duality of light or various loose ends of particle physics and cosmology as are currently entangled in a debate between string theory and "loop quantum gravity" with their alternate explanations of how the ineffable micro-cosmos of quantum particles is connected with the forces of gravity that bind the macro-world of planets, stars and galaxies.

Even stranger facts than found in the quantum world, however, are rife in biology and still more so in its evolutionary time-dimension, whose further linkage with psychology is shown not only by the Darwinian ascent of Wo/Man, but because both subjects often involve phenomena lacking any definitive explanation—as opposed to the kind of rhetoric of a scientific mien that often feigns at resolving the kind of puzzles presented equally by human psychology and evolutionary biology. Dreams are of course a prime example, having been "explained away" as wish-fulfillment, brain processing of superfluous information, sorting of imagery left over from the day's events, and in various other ways that seek to impose a rational framework on the psyche, despite that the faculty of reason itself subsists within a larger psychological context whose underlying forces motivate human thought and how it is directed. And in biology, a survey of strangeness could begin with the quasi-scientific tale that birds evolved from dinosaurs—which certainly may be true if it can be shown that the creatures ancestral to birds actually were a species of dinosaur and not just of similar shape as are some fish when compared to dolphins or a hummingbird to the hummingbird moth. But if that popular view of the avian lineage happens to be the case, it might be necessary to attribute to dinosaurs the same internal anatomy as birds, including the unique avian respiratory system.[1] The "flow-through" lung of birds is not harder to explain than the bellows-type lung of mammals and reptiles, insofar as either can be, but accepting the logical necessity of its totally separate origin and lineage vastly expands the already monstrous size and complexity of the evolutionary panorama.

Yet that particular example is relatively simple as compared to countless others, for instance how intracellular mechanisms made the leap to what has been called the "irreducible complexity" of structures like the rotary flagella of bacteria whose movement is propelled by a molecular motor. The fact of that leap having occurred does not, of course, preclude the molecular features involved from having achieved the requisite feat of self-assembly on their own, since the biochemistry of human and other cells performs virtual miracles at every instant of their lives. But dispensing with "irreducible complexity" by reducing it to readily rational dimensions, if that is possible, still leaves many other less noted yet even more problematic examples, such as the variety of parasites that were able to evolve the capacity to program the behavior of their hosts. Nevertheless, psychology often dictates that inconvenient facts be set aside in shaping whatever mythology is best suited for the times and to illuminate human experience. Thus, the crucial understanding of evolution as having been the prologue to civilization instead of simply "the great cosmogenic myth of the twentieth century"[2] or a cosmological accident of which we are the lucky beneficiaries may deserve higher regard than the enduring enigma of how and why many major evolutionary shifts like that of frogs to lizards actually took place, or how many of Life's more curious passengers, such as mites that cling like slippers to the feet of ants[3], have found their way upon the broad but rugged highway of natural selection. Yet the meaning of human life is only diminished by dismissing evolution in favor of God or vice-versa when both of these mythologies being based in truth, lend more favor to that meaning when in mutual alliance. For to say the hand of God somehow working through the evolutionary process implies that same hand to actually be Nature herself, simply admits the untellable proportions of a Gestalt that is equally the natural and supernatural context of our lives. And supernaturally, that same context holds an Erewhon from whence may flow a re-enchantment of the world that could also enable its purely physical salvation.

40. Adaptive Thinking

Hence, the chain of Being linking biology with psychology also extends backwards in time through the non-living antecedents of life to the very beginnings of a Universe that itself may have sprung from some meta-condition equivalent to, derived from or allied with the worlds of psyche and spirit that transcend psychology—including the psychology of faith and its adherents—and whose true proportions, as perhaps dimly suggested by the hierarchy of mathematical infinities,[1] beggar the physical Cosmos. But while psychic phenomena may be for many, excepting those rationalist gurus who adulate the symbols of their linear beliefs, a matter of common experience, the true spiritual realm is apt to only manifest through a sense of contact with some quality or form of consciousness whose actual nature cannot be identified more precisely than as given in poetic or allusive words of scripture. For if that kind of consciousness is also an aspect of ourselves, it might be expected to manifest more and more or become more freely acknowledged insofar as its holistic properties also address the growing demands of globalizing civilization for a broader awareness of common survival interests.

On the other hand, it is also true that while the psychic realm can be but poorly defined, as one should expect for what lies at and beyond the paranormal fringe of human psychology, its nature is also occluded by superstitions whose grip upon the mind has persisted since prehistoric and mediaeval times, when "every bush was supposed a bear" just as natural phenomena are frequently mistaken today for UFOs. Of course the latter, if and when they represent actual extraterrestrial spacecraft whose occupants are deigning to visit us, are not truly paranormal but rather examples of magical technology—unless as sometimes claimed the aliens have briefly materialized from etheric or imaginal dimensions that also provide the source for other psychic phenomena. Yet at either end of the chain of being, whether in the past at the very dawn of Time and birth of the physical world or at some transpersonal limit whence human consciousness might clearly apprehend a timeless ground of being, there appears a virtual absolute, whether at the temporal origins of physics and cosmology or at the non-temporal boundary dividing physical from spiritual reality. For in each instance, the intellect must confront either an infinite wall of pre-existence at the far edge of quantum reality, or an equally daunting barrier that could be taken to separate the existential or contingent from the sacred and eternal (although that separation may be false if "all that lives is holy"). Yet conceptually, as versus the truer perspective that concepts can scarcely begin to address, both extremes also inhabit a common point on the tautological cliché of a circle that vain quests for certainty are fated to follow endlessly. For any superior assurance than given through concepts and rationales baked to ceramic hardness in the furnace of psychology, can only be won by jumping off the circle into an abandonment of no direction known.

In that same abandonment, however, can also be found more freedom that allows for new ideas and ways of thinking that can apply to a real world whose constraints upon the mind—like the thought police of consensus reality—may then have to relinquish their repressive influence. And clearly, evolution is a prime target for the sort of exploration that can open a territory of kaleidoscopic fascination that had long been buried under a crust of ideology—derived from what once were new and radical ideas in the context of their times—grown weary and outworn. For ideology, whether scientific or religious, dwells in a separate universe than true realities which cannot be altered by opinion. But of course the effect of those realities on that imaginary universe may also be limited, given that the quest for truth concerning a subject so vast as evolution is unlikely to ever reach any clear destination. For the subject of life in the Universe, which is key to human nature and of incalculable existential import, is one where any search for answers is fated either to keep wandering a tangled maze of paths or else to finally encounter our former selves coming from the opposite direction. For the nature of Life and thus of evolution cannot be divorced from that of consciousness, whose essence is either the illusory aura of a fathomless complexity or instead ineluctably a mystery beyond time and space and accordingly immune to any intellectual captivity or arrest by the wardens of reason.

It has been said, that when species maintain a stable form for long periods of time, they may still accumulate genetic variability through mutations that remain latent and are not expressed, so that when the environment presents an unexpected challenge that species can respond accordingly by plucking from its reservoir of stored genetic potential whatever adaptation is either needed for survival or can exploit the opportunity of environmental spaces that were not available before. Hence, the evidence suggests that extinction of the dinosaurs removed all barriers to an explosion of mammals (though fossils from the late Cretaceous of mammals larger than previously thought to then have lived have lately been discovered) drawing upon deep reserves of long accumulated potential, into freshly opened ecological niches for a staggering mammal diversity, replacing an equally abundant variety of dinosaurs and that today is crowned by a primate who may well be evolving in step with a world for whose increasingly rapid changes that same primate is largely responsible. And part of that evolving may include freshly adaptive ways of thinking and perceiving that shall flourish even while ancient ideologies and their associated passions remain doggedly entrenched in haunted and bitter ground.

And by similar token even while the public debates over evolution continue to repeat, over and over again, the same tired themes of a conflict whose roots are more psychological than scientific or religious, and whose expression more politicized than inventive or astute, creative and adept approaches to the vast enigma of Reality—the so-called "new paradigm"—are building just below the threshold of consciousness of a human species that simultaneously needs to marshal all its powers in response to the mounting challenges to civilization and even raw human species survival. Unmistakably, these challenges are spelled out by universal ABCs that are equivalent to five Es of Environmental sanity, Educational adequacy, Economic stability, Energy sustainability, and the Ending of starvation. And to realize these in practice requires only a sixth E—human post-Darwinian evolution towards being able to capture the elusive quarry of a seventh E in the form of a post-modern Enlightenment. For the latter will hopefully supplant or build upon initial enlightenment of the Renaissance and subsequent Age of Reason (one of whose chief exponents, Isaac Newton, also pursued strange byways of alchemy and dubious Bible decodings) which inaugurated modern scientific objectivity. And here it can be reiterated that rightly and objectively considered, organic evolution lacks for nothing in potential to inspire the subjective attribute of wonder which scientists themselves have often extolled, having learned by observation that Nature's kingdom is an endless tide of miracles.

Just one of these, for example, is the sequence of deliberate steps that must be followed by a metastasizing cancer cell when it leaves the site of a primary tumor and undertakes a risky journey to some other part of the body to establish a metastasis[2] that subsequently helps to carry out the purposes of Nature through balancing life with death. But to recognize the true import of such examples, whose numbers are legion, would necessitate adaptive thinking that can also acknowledge the true nature of Reality as not only more beyond than accessible to explanatory powers of intellect, but as the ultimate source of those wondrous phenomena, many of them noted in the annals of biology, that tend to show how ineffable that same Reality really is, despite its having room for human minds that often like to tell a story many wish to hear, namely that the world is not so terribly mysterious after all.

41. Life and Life Only

But if the "new paradigm" seeks to embrace biology and consciousness under the same post-Classical rubric that applies to quantum physics, it may have to be satisfied to remain no more explicitly meaningful than pre-Classical ancient Greek philosophy, thus demanding a fresh outlook as much or even more than new ideas—an outlook that is able to accept radically greater parameters for a Cosmos that has become less comprehensible than ever before. And that paradigm must also wait upon the dissolution of archaic nationalistic, religious and rational mind-sets just as bats and whales, lemurs and jaguars, had to remain mere potentials in the genes of their cruder ancestors until the once dominant dinosaurs had been reduced to heaps of bone. Yet by planting a flag in the barely charted regions of biology and evolution just as it has already done in the wonderlands of quantum paradox, that paradigm may be able to accumulate still greater potential for an eventual glorious emergence. However, the latter will only occur if and when environmental sanity and social concern can gain enough currency and conviction to drain the slough wherein humanity still is haunted by the fearsome bogeyman of Darwinian obsolescence. For that specter might take the solid form of an actual monster, should our species decline to assume a fully human responsibility for its destiny but instead charge like panicked cattle over the precipice.

Nonetheless, that paradigm can also be regarded as a "top-down" phenomenon rather than a flower which will finally bloom from the richer soil of full social justice, a phrase which can have at least two meanings. First of all, the growth of human consciousness corresponding to spiritual evolution will increasingly favor cultural, spiritual, and scientific changes that will in turn promote collective recognition and unopposed application of whatever it takes to maintain Spaceship Earth, for example protecting marine life by ending all fouling of the seas with the runoff of agricultural waste. But from a completely different perspective, one could view the phenomenon of consciousness as either having acted from the future, or from outside of Time to bring about the evolutionary process, which thus might be seen as feeding upon a non-temporal domain of information—or instead, in its physical manifestation as outwardly representing a principle ever inherent in Nature and germane to Life insofar as living cells and even complex chemicals may possess some level and character of sentience and thus embody a fragment of Cosmic mind. And on a planetary scale of the global organism called Gaia whose life embraces evolutionary time and space, every cell and its molecular constituents including DNA obey an instinctual awareness of their proper place in a four-dimensional ecology that includes not only their parent organism and its environmental niche, but that creature's evolutionary role as well, in similar sense to how every cell in the human brain and body is instinctively attuned to play its part in serving the varied needs of the entire organism. Hence new species constitute an instinctive rather than fortuitous response to shifting environmental pressures and opportunities, not only because those shifts may favor the expression of mutations hitherto dormant, that had lain in wait for the proper time to exchange scales for feathers or to switch from gills to lungs, but because the overall evolutionary dynamic penetrates every corner of the biosphere and shapes its destiny, analogous to how the biodynamic of a single organism guides its maturing from a seed or embryo.

And of course that kind of perspective has been criticized as "teleological" in attributing to evolution the non-provable metaphysical property of being oriented towards a goal that presumably resides in the mind of God, or in some supernatural or angelic repository of ideal conceptions that endow the visible Universe and shape its course. But that same criticism simply says that interpreting Life in any other way than by means of scientific explanations that have purportedly refuted any supernaturally slanted philosophies constitutes a sin against the intellect which, in the rationally proven absence of any God should be all we have, our only candle in the Cosmic dark.

Furthermore, the slippery concept of a goal of Life is not more abstract than the concept of Life itself, nor necessarily more distant than what the immediate future holds. And in fact, in the eternal Now which was present at the dawn of Time the "goal" of human consciousness can be said to have always existed in the form of information ever latent in the developmental potential of DNA, whose message can no more be separated from its chemical structure than the dancer from the dance. Hence, given current knowledge that human life was implicit in the first living cell, the obvious goal for evolution has been at every point exactly what its next stage could reasonably achieve, and thereby realize an expression of Life itself as worthy to exist as any human work of art, for example flowering plants or pollinating hummingbirds, while each incremental advance has expanded biodiversity and its roster of possibilities. And today, the latter affords a categorically different and more conscious hope of post-Darwinian evolution, whose achievement depends less on being lifted by impersonal tides of Nature than upon our lucidly dreaming it into reality—to "dream of things that never were and say, why not?" Otherwise, the human cerebral capacity for consciousness has been an evolutionary objective of no greater value in terms of improving higher mammal awareness than the advancement of mammals over their distant reptilian ancestors, or of the first living cells as compared to the clay or chemical broth from whence they sprang. But to say that Life does not have a goal or that evolution is not teleological is just as illogical or mistaken in its human judgment of matters where our ordinary ways of thinking do not apply, as to claim that creatures do not actually wish to survive but are programmed or driven to do so. And at the same time "It is life, and life only" that embodies the goals it appears to have realized, and from our partaking of that Life has derived our own inherent purpose, whose accordingly primal grounding should render it immune to being gainsaid, or gratuitous fancy of an accidental tourist in a meaningless Universe whose inherent deficit of meaning should render the very word "meaning," and therefore its opposite, as utterly nonsensical. And that may be the case if Life, including human life, simply is what it is to the extent of not even demanding the quality of meaningfulness often invoked to excuse the existence of lesser things and occupations..

Yet life is expressed as fully as could be desired in creatures like a hummingbird, a dragonfly, or a golden weasel, all of which may well rejoice in a physical being and animal consciousness that incorporates, beyond mere grim determination to survive, "a world of delight"[1] whose inward treasure our own senses cannot perceive. Accordingly, all living things on this planet have realized as great a purpose as could be imagined, short of some higher destiny for the human species that sprang from them and whom they support, in part by serving as reminders of the true intensity and beauty of living things unsuppressed and uncontaminated by intellect. But in humanity appears a categorical departure from its non-human ancestry, by virtue of newly emergent aspects of consciousness that are not well understood—and perhaps need not be, any more than a crow or falcon, joyful in mastery of the air, needs to know about its evolutionary history. For while Life has fully manifested through those kingdoms whose ultimate, human metamorphosis now reaches toward higher, trans-biological domains, so shall consciousness increasingly realize greater depths of understanding together with a broader psychological and cultural diversity across the spectrum of a human race that can manage to achieve the clearest immediate goal of our inherent purpose—namely to quell the menace of its self-engendered monstrosities that are equally dire whether construed as separation from the Good, or as savage relics from the Darwinian past

Yet the word "Life" is clearly a virtual axiom that makes sense without further explanation, because failure to grasp its basic meaning would amount to lacking all semblance of consciousness. Nonetheless, it is also nearly a given that the "talking point" concerning what actually differentiates Life from the inorganic structures and processes that support and substand its serendipitous existence, is a perennially crucial question in both philosophy and science. In the latter, the twilight zone of viruses may harbor a transitional region or evolutionary bridge between complex chemicals and living cells, whose incessant alchemy finally produced the cerebral theatre wherein that question is presented. But in the former, namely philosophy, the same issue can assume a very different shape, because what is at stake are no longer such facts as by what specific process matter was goaded up the trail of burgeoning complexity that was soon co-opted by the magical appearance of living things. Rather, the philosophical issue involves examining what principles may distinguish Life as an irreducible property of existence that accordingly is bound to externalize its active potential, whose all pervading essence of the Universe is thereby certain to obtain physical expression in a spider, a flower, or entire living cathedrals of wilderness.

42. The Nature of "Things"

Clearly, the dynamic potential of matter-energy, which includes its ability to be transformed into living substance, is no less inherent to existence than space-time which itself is not simply an abstraction—except perhaps in the mind where even abstract ideas must nonetheless be embodied as an electromagnetic impulse in the neural network of the brain. And because these dimensions are not purely ideal conceptions, they contain intrinsic potential that becomes physically realized as quantum fields and their associated particles. And at this point, the challenge to any hope or pretence of grasping what existence is—a Gordian knot wherein are bound all lesser issues of science, philosophy and faith—becomes extreme, because it is difficult or impossible to say what the smallest known particles actually are other than in terms relating to their properties of mass, charge and spin which, perhaps, could be said to represent the very first actual differences to separate out from the primary field of undifferentiated space-time or of some pre-existent hyper-space. Hence the nature of these particles cannot be clarified any further than by describing them as the building blocks of the larger blocks called atoms and molecules. Subatomic particles, in fact, have little in common with ordinary objects, as we normally understand the latter, insofar as they do not have a spatial boundary but are continuous with the fields they embody, vibratory entities that must themselves consist in some untold number of hyper-spatial dimensions—as indeed shown by experiments where a photon or electron is revealed as having the properties of both a particle and a wave. Of course so-called ordinary objects do not have a clear spatial boundary either, since their surface is made of atoms whose outer layer consists of electrons that themselves are nodes of electromagnetic force whose spatial location cannot be specified more precisely than as roughly forming a shell surrounding the atomic nucleus, whose own internal nature is equally problematic, since the quarks of which protons and neutrons are made do not have a clearly definable surface or external boundary. Hence the smallest bits of stuff are energy rather than substance, unless those two are considered one and the same, and if so are not exactly "things." And in that case perhaps there are no "things" except in the mind, which nonetheless enjoys sufficient freedom to label anything including itself as something rather than nothing

Yet in one sense ordinary objects do coincide more closely than photons, electrons and quarks with our ideas of them (and in another sense do not, because those particles correspond exactly to their mathematical descriptions) and thus, because living things also belong in the category of everyday experience it is sometimes assumed that human reason, though humbled by its glimpses of the alien quantum world, can comprehend the phenomena of life and evolution. However Life is equally an embodiment of the same existential dynamic—the power of Being itself—that is expressed in non-living substance, whose nuclear fires have forged those elements, like carbon, that constitute the physical framework of living systems. But the progressive realization of Being through becoming via the evolutionary path that has led to the very juncture we now occupy on the brink of a post-Darwinian journey, involves a transformational modality whose rhyme and reason transcend what is called "complexity," in the sense of that word being used to describe how the interactions of physical law have built upon themselves to ever more deeply elaborate upon the multifarious weavings of Creation. For despite the miracles that same complexity has wrought, the ways and means of biology and evolution express a "meta-complexity" whose level of difficulty surpasses that of physics to at least such degree as calculus is beyond arithmetic, or in more visual terms, to the extent that factors behind a dream or hallucination are incalculably harder to comprehend than the scientific causes for a mirage or a rainbow. And of course, the patterns and meta-patterns of material and biological complexity spring from the subtlety of space-time and its interwoven quantum fields, in which they and their human observers are immersed.

Another sense of what "meta-complexity" could mean might be as follows: "without a consistent theory of the mathematical infinite there is no theory of irrationals, without a theory of irrationals there is no mathematical analysis in any form remotely resembling what we now have…"[1] lacking which most of modern mathematics would not exist. And, "what has escaped philosophers and logicians is that from the moment a system of symbols becomes independent of the objects designated it is itself subject to displacements that are incalculable for the logician."[2] In other words, what is beyond comprehensible complexity in the physical world, for example some hidden basis for the myriad inexplicable phenomena that are especially rife in biology, plays a role in the real world analogous to that exercised the Infinite in mathematics. However in the latter case there are theories and explanations, as developed by Georg Cantor, while in the former there are not even guesses as to how, for instance, there can occur the suite of simultaneous mutations that would seem requisite for the forelimbs of a small dinosaur to become an effective agency of flight, combining extra power with lightness, grace, and an integument of feathers specialized far beyond whatever their former purpose might have been. And ironically, those who might propose some tentative outline for how some of these baffling transitions could have happened, are using a talent bestowed on them by Nature whose neuronal functions are as mysterious as whatever elusive facts such thinkers may purport to comprehend, and whose abstract and theoretical creations are, as Einstein remarked, inexact insofar as they conform to reality yet insofar as they are exact, correspond all the less to the actual world. And if that statement is equivalent to some permutation of the quantum uncertainty principle then perhaps in the vast and nebulous gaps of that uncertainty is where the dynamic of Creation roams with more than human freedom and transcendent power.

43. Wizard behind the Genes

Such irreducible meta-complexity is why, for example, the original explanation for the ornate pattern on the tail of a male peacock does not really work. That particular application of the Darwinian principle called sexual selection, was the basis for claiming that peacock hens are attracted by brighter displays and therefore more apt to mate with males so adorned, thereby selecting the genes instrumental in producing the gaudiest displays. Of course in many species a similar explanation can be justified because brighter plumage may indicate superior resistance to parasites and overall fitness. However, "the white peacock, which lacks the colorful effect of the peacock's 'eye,' is nevertheless preferred by many hens" and therefore the view of sexual or aesthetic selection as the reason for the peacock's display being so gorgeous "was criticized so violently that it was dropped even by the Darwinians themselves" because "there was no valid experimental proof that aesthetic selection did in fact occur" Furthermore, the whole subject of the peacock's display and the part it plays in mating is quite complicated, and not only in terms of how the feathers develop in the adult male to produce the total effect—"the ornamental feathers are governed by special laws of development—as they grow longer, they also grow looser. Thus all ornamental feathers have a strong shaft, but lack the downy part which normally provides thermal insulation This role is taken over by special down structures in the region—one further provision that shows how complex a phenomenon the peacock's display really is." But to get a fuller picture of what is happening it is necessary to take into account the behavioral factors involved—"the display goes hand in hand with a complex type of behavior" in which "the hen is not simply a disinterested spectator but an active participant in the display. In the presence of the courting cock, she begins to peck at her food with great intensity, and as she pecks at her food, the cock becomes visibly more excited—the two partners are actors in one and the same drama."

Clearly, genetic factors are involved in producing both the appearance of the male peacock, and the behavior of both sexes in the mating ritual, but "The fact that the peacock's ritual as a whole has both behavioral and structural components poses the problem of the particular role of the latter" as indicated by the preference of many hens for white peacocks seeming to indicate that the more typically colorful "fan" pattern of which "all the feathers which participate in it are so many variations on a single theme—the eye feather which shines forth in all its splendor on the central axis"[1] is irrelevant as far as aesthetic or sexual selection is concerned, even though natural selection has at least not weeded out this particular form of extravagance. Thus, however desperately is felt the need to find some way to account for phenomena like the peacock's display and many others of equal perplexity—parasites that program the behavior of their hosts being one outstanding instance in such regard—in which biology abounds, that deficit cannot be squarely addressed within limitations of proven science, that offers no conceivable way of even asking how the deepest wizardry of life and evolution actually does its magic. Nature's far horizons, in other words, remain at some unthinkably greater distance than the explanatory powers or conceptual boundaries of intellect can rightfully hope to attain. And that of course is because the mind, being but one of the myriad productions of Nature, can far less hope to resolve the Magnum Mysterium of which both its rational and neuronal processes are but a fragmentary part, than adventurers who braved stormy oceans in creaky wooden ships could guess what dire contingencies might imperil their lives or rich and strange discoveries reward their courage.

And that is why, having left the tidy garden of a theory that does provide at least "a good general approximation"[2] of how, or perhaps rather why evolution works[3] and entered a teeming jungle of phenomena for which any explanations have scarcely been attempted, we are no longer in the level territory that some might wish could extend not only across the seemingly known world but even beyond those horizons ever in perpetual flight from aspiring knowledge and the dreams of reason. Thus a dedicated rationalist unwittingly offered an amazing example of such phenomena—the "lancet fluke" that somehow evolved the weird ability to program the behavior of its host. The latter is an ant that thus victimized is accordingly compelled to keep climbing up and down a blade of grass till eaten by a grazing sheep in whose body the parasite can continue its life cycle. This bizarre tale from the more obscure annals of biology was oddly cited as a metaphor portraying the futility of repetitive religious rituals that the human race, this author feels, badly needs to overcome.[4] But while the ant may be as deprived of whatever choice or wits it once possessed as any fanatic member of a cult or dutiful adherent of crusty dogma, the parasite's uncanny talent cannot be disingenuously explained away by the pallid pronouncements of an atheistic orthodoxy that seems quite dreary beside the wealth of Nature's magic, that could be said to effectively mirror the depths of spiritual existence. Nor can the fluke's uncommon ability or a similar gift found in other parasites, let alone how that talent evolved be fairly accounted for even in the speculative terms that can be applied to issues, as in physics, for which mathematical models are able to be constructed. In other words, close examination of bio-phenomena, far from assisting any reduction of homo sapiens to the same status as any other subject for research, instead illuminates the wizardry that lurks in every living cell to be well in conformance with any non-reductive interpretation of human nature as reflecting or focusing a greater Life and consciousness that embraces and enfolds the Universe, in accord with the "perennial philosophy" whose timeless wisdom eclipses any squeaky pronouncements skimmed from the shallows of current knowledge.

44. True Magic

At this point, however, it grows needful to pre-empt any possible misunderstanding by defining such terms as "magic," whose usage skeptics may decry as teetering on the brink of a gloomy, dank ravine wherein the "magical thinking," superstition and taboos of our progenitors, and sadly even today, was and is, in a variety of forms, a philosophy of willful ignorance whose premises are scarcely examined. Of course when those premises are an irrational reflection of warped human psychology, or constitute a deliberate abuse of reason, there may be little point in examining them. And indeed, such thinking has often hindered or bloodily opposed the progressive vision toward whose gradual realization both science and the rule of law have in recent centuries tirelessly albeit erratically striven. Yet, while that effort may ultimately help to implement a global vision of social justice and a sound environment bequeathed to coming generations, absent which all hopes for them are shamefully aborted, science itself has come closer to the brink of perceiving a magical Gestalt whose greater Life lends power to our own, and whose clarity can penetrate even those murky swamps of the collective unconscious, or the reptilian backwaters of planetary human consciousness, where monsters of a myriad species breed and bellow their fury and anguish. For if that is not so, and research thus progressively deletes from growing knowledge all hopes of faith for human nature to contain a positive potential whose depths cannot be codified, the only vision that should remain is of an emptiness that vitiates the very sense and sensibility of its discovery. Hence evolution, albeit its rules be ironclad as may befit what is, to paraphrase, of Nature more than Grace[1] cannot be rightly excluded from the metaphysical portrait of a living Universe whose rhyme and reason reify our lives. And that rhyme and reason spontaneously choreograph a dance that if not designed, is yet no less and doubtless more intelligent than we ourselves, who cannot think outside the infinite box against whose measureless walls the mind can only beat its glittery wings in vain.

Therefore, any meaning for words like "magic" or "life" is less akin to arrant superstition than pertaining to irreducible axioms human understanding needs must rest upon. For in fact while modern technology might appear magical to savage tribes, or that of aliens to us, thereby inviting comparison of Nature's supposed magic to artifacts whose workings might in theory be explained, that analogy is deceptive and cannot suffice. For reason can at least imagine what outlandish kind of physics, for example, might allow a starship to venture through interstellar space in quest of other bioactive worlds and then return to our planet in one human lifetime—time warps, wormholes, and anti-gravity being among the ideas that a creative bending of physics can manage to extract from the puzzle palace that sweeping yet sketchy scientific knowledge currently constitutes. But for many of the baffling characteristics and behaviors of living things, such as the coordinated cooperation of a termite colony in building its nest, there are no definitive concepts nor have any been suggested .regarding how, for example, these insects can communicate amongst themselves to shape their collective destiny. Chemical communication is a likely medium, but how these messages consistently convey any specific instructions is something else again, thus lending credibility to phrases like "morphic resonance" or collective instinctual consciousness that whatever rational substance they lack, at least rhetorically suggest a bio-magic beyond our ken that beggars the notion of "complexity." The true magic of Life cannot be fathomed because it derives from an order far beyond what human intellect is able to attain, despite that subtle workings of the brain itself also proclaim that magic to be real And yet, while that reality transcends perforce restricted knowledge and understanding of its effects, that same limited wisdom can continue to expand towards ever-broadening horizons that shall beckon for so long as civilization may endure.

Yet in quantum physics, what the mind by means of instruments beholds or can surmise is far beyond complexity as well. The strangeness of particles that also manifest as waves, and thus transcend our everyday ideas of ordinary things, or even of mathematical objects underlying them whose ideal forms and patterns conspire to project the grand illusion of external reality, is so purely magical as to seemingly indicate their profound connection with what for want of a better word is called consciousness. To be sure, these entities and their associated fields do combine to build the very substance of our bodies and of what we perceive in accordance with unswerving laws and constants like the speed of light, but despite that empirical character they are not the sort of "things" whose spatial boundaries make them easy to identify—even though the properties of a quark or photon define them more precisely in mathematical terms than macro-objects or living organisms can be defined in words. Instead, these least of all things in actuality are One, as nodes of a collective state of singing interactions that sprang into objectivity at the dawn of Time. Hence it is perfectly appropriate to attribute to biology no less degree though different in kind of strangeness and paradox that the quantum realm so clearly displays. For by sharing fully with that realm in an ineluctable magic whose secrets are encrypted in the book of Creation itself, evolution has managed to elevate rather than cast aspersions on the worth of its ultimate human outcome, whose animal phase with its "old brain" defensive postures is waning in the light of prospects yet but dimly seen. Hence from the "bereshith" or "in the beginning" of the Bible there followed Light which led to Life and then to round out the mystery, consciousness, whose relevance as a key axiom in discussions concerning the nature of a world both objective and subjective has a long and proven history.

45. Between the Worlds

Therefore, just as mathematics has advanced from the reckoning of notched sticks or grooves in clay, through the hard abstractions of Euclid and harmonies of Pythagoras to higher algebra, calculus, and at last an endlessly elastic realm that teems with gnarly concepts like the square root of (-1), that while often commonsensically absurd are nonetheless applicable in the real world—so from "simple" atoms (that in fact are far from simple) has Life progressed to the improbable apotheosis of self-awareness that can constitute a bridge from Earth to Heaven. What wisdom, then, in declining to acknowledge that crossing or to avail oneself and society of the vital commerce it provides? Clearly, one response is that better wisdom rests in refusing to worship an imaginary God whose favor is often sought for unjust and selfish enterprises, while instead simply behaving in whatever fashion might be deemed appropriate by any Deity who did exist and would fairly dispose our fate. Yet that same disposition, which if actually from God might hopefully be tempered by Divine cognizance of human limitations, is likely in any case to include Darwinian sanctions—whose cruelty might at least be kinder than outright extinction—against a species inviting such reproof through neglecting to maintain the viability of Spaceship Earth. Nor should anyone expect providential mercy to be gained by stale, false or wrathful religiosity that has purged all semblance of the holy from a temple whose sacred fires have long been smothered under the ashes of ideology. And in science, when the vision of Truth as embodied in Creation, and of which new fragments are ever being revealed, is replaced by absolutist faith in the soundness of a paradigm co-opting concepts that, while rightly derived from Nature, have then been drafted in service of an anti-spiritual or strictly humanist ideology, then similar suppression has occurred, perhaps for reasons which could be construed as spiritual, psychological, Darwinian, or even all three, but in any case are part of the human condition where subjectivity and objectivity are inextricably intertwined.

But to distinguish between actual truth and its sincere or convincing imitations can take more than logic or reason, whose powers vis-à-vis the meta-rational worlds of science and spirit, biology and psychology or physics and philosophy are dependent on axioms which no less than in culture and society must be taken as self-evident. Yet while reason cannot prove these axioms, it can demonstrate their irreducible importance. For example, to dismiss the enterprise of science as simply a cultural phenomenon, or fashion of thinking merely of the times, perhaps on grounds that key theories like evolution or "Big Bang" cosmology cannot be absolutely confirmed, could at worst provoke resurgence of superstition and nebulous fears in contradiction to such virtual axioms as that Creation, with or without a God, must be supremely precise and logical in order to work at all, however imperfectly those workings can be grasped. And to disparage what was held by the American founding fathers as the self-evident cornerstone of democracy that "all men are created equal" can only favor those crueler and more backward societies where the political triumph of ignoble minds, as History has indeed often witnessed, is able to jeopardize both science and civilization.

In other words the axiom of underlying progressive order—whatever "slop in the system" is also needed for that pattern to remain dynamic—is essential to the core values shared by science, religion and society Science identifies and examines the nature of the physical order in exquisite degree, while religion invokes its basis as a Unity whose spiritual nature is also the source of meaning, because our lives occur in a more than material context. And society depends less on psychological or socio-biological speculations than upon an axiomatic order—itself quite hollow without the further irreducible axiom of human dignity that is crucial to religion as well—upheld by mutual interest and concerns of its members, who today are not only individuals but nations whose inter-cooperation has become increasingly vital for the sake of sheer human species survival. And that survival, which now requires victory over ancient animal portions of the brain whose nasty tendencies are abetted by modern technology, will inaugurate the phase of post-Darwinian evolution where clarity and lucid choice increasingly will help in elevating human destiny.

By similar token—namely, that of true understanding being based upon principles that can only be grasped intuitively, to what extent is the measure of human worthiness to prevail, there might be posited either of two hypothetical axioms, only one of which can be key to reality and human existence. And each can be assessed regarding whatever implications and consequences, either philosophically or scientifically, it might possess. Briefly, these are (A), there is a Deity of supernal heart and mind, or at least as in Buddhism some sort of spiritual dimension, and secondly, (B), there isn't. Clearly the relevance of (A) regarding science, and evolution in particular, would rest upon the virtually incontrovertible interdependence of spirit and science, including life science, if they share a common reality wherein their respective spheres of influence are bound to overlap or interpenetrate. That is not to say, however, that they need be conflated, as in Creationist rejection of the evidence-based idea that life has evolved from a common source over countless millennia. Nor can any Divine spark as presumably accorded to human genius in category A, under that same heading less readily be attributed to non-human Nature. Thus the latter, in a spiritual Cosmos acquires wondrous gifts that can account for strange phenomena especially apparent in biology and evolution. Yet under (B), in absence of any spiritual and thereby immeasurable parameters (the word "spiritual" amounting to a virtual axiom as well) the world might be more accessible to understanding, but at the same time a leaner and meaner place providing fewer rewards for learning on the part of those whose first priority could then become to appreciate having just one life to live, until shall flee into oblivion their moments in the sun.

Hence the philosophical significance of evolution when understood broadly and unblinkingly lies not only in appreciating how human history, including the largely unwritten tale of prehistoric homo sapiens that looms behind all events of recorded memory, is but a fragmentary part of a vaster process. That journey began long before any human minds existed and even today is intimately connected to the stars wherein may dwell the key to our future—or at worst, perhaps apocalyptic fate at the hand of a deadly messenger launched by perturbations far beyond the solar system. But said significance also lies in understanding that living phenomena insofar as they elude the grasp of intellect, show exactly how and why human minds cannot command the secrets of existence, whatever profit may derive from observing their effects. And of course that profit may assume various forms, depending on whether it is given primarily a metaphysical or scientific cast. The former sees the portrait of a Cosmos whose hidden aspects can be called supernatural because, while first appearing in the field of biology where animal psychology prefigures the human and many behaviors (as that of the bowerbird which artistically decorates its nest, even daubing pigment with a twig it uses as a paintbrush)[1] defy attempts at explanation, those aspects manifest more vividly in subjective realms of human experience, where the character of Being departs untellably from that of objective Nature.

And the more strictly scientific slant simply assumes that when unattainable horizons of complexity have been glimpsed, as for example in learning that "DNA is not the Bible of life, nor an encyclopedia of precise instruction, but is itself a flexible and dynamic system,"[2] then with the outer limits of knowledge thus defined, there still remain immense uncharted regions from the atom to the depths of interstellar space. And regardless of how we construe apparent factual truths, the contemplation of non-objective regions like the 'mindscapes" of language and mathematics, not to mention the psychology of dreaming or emotions, can help to liberate understanding from constraints whose rule of iron is assumed by those who urge reductionist views of consciousness. Reductionism cannot strip away from consciousness its existential connotations as in "the politics of experience," or the deeper psychology of science and of thought itself. For to do so is to compromise human self-knowledge, just as monochrome reason with regard to living things whose hides are nailed to a laboratory wall. The Book of Life is inscribed in waters of a flowing stream with greater eloquence than human commentaries on that Book, written on parchment that along with our mortal bio-computers is ever poised to crumble into dust whose destiny is only to return amongst the stars from whence it came. Nonetheless, it remains an axiom that biology is the bridge between mind and Nature, but whether the former is but natural or also metaphysical, with all the extra parameters and possibilities or "many mansions" thereby implied, is an issue whose determination dwells on the very frontiers of freedom.

Accordingly, the laws of life and evolution, which compel many creatures of land and sea to repeat the same routines again and again through countless generations, are mirrored by laws of psychology. And the latter often compel whoever may trust in intellect and its productions including religious doctrine as being endowed with rational virtue, to nonetheless cling to linear thinking and rigid beliefs which they no more wish to alter than to recognize that such beliefs provide but an illusion of security in an unpredictably ever-changing world. Of course, an illusion may be just as good as the real thing, if that reality is only found in hopes that given the abiding certainty of change itself, perhaps the greatest change we face, namely Death, may not really be the end. In any event, the human thirst for "explanation" whether religious or scientific can be attributed to quasi-Darwinian roots, because it derives from a quest for survival that in the psychological sphere has turned into hunger for the haven of either knowledge or salvation. And of course there's nothing wrong with that, except that apparent security of having reached the journey's end for mind or spirit can be deceptive since the journey of Life itself must unavoidably continue and shall drag us in its wake. For even the human species is still evolving, both organically and socially, whereas any eternal portion of being from whence proceed ephemeral phenomena of mind and body, may constitute the light of which all cherished phantoms of the mind are but reflections that shall fall away.

Of course, belief in the soul or God, or however designated mystical entity—especially when based merely on theology and scriptural authority without personal witness of the paranormal or metaphysical as evidence for a dimension that was more a given in ancient than in modern sophisticated philosophy—can be easily attributed to the psychology of survival inscribed in primitive parts of the brain and later translated in a social context into deluded religious notions elaborated in the same cerebral folds wherein are generated works of secular art and science. And such dismissal of religious faith also has the virtue of simplicity, as compared to any broader view wherein those aspects of the world explored by science are merely the intriguing surface of "The Divine Milieu."[3] But reduction of human nature to the strictures of a rational framework derived from evolutionary biology also tends to trivialize whatever significance that view presumes to claim. For when human individuals becomes merely glorified animals (although "glorified animals" under any religious paradigm are what our mortal part remains, while ordinary animals are themselves quite remarkable) with no reference to any supernal destiny, then rational explanations lose any inspirational value beyond their affirming of faith in reason per se, and thus can matter only in the tricky context of consensus reality. And in that context science can in fact become a substitute for religion. For theoretical abstractions can resemble religious ideas in being immune to temporal corruption along with all conceptual entities of the "mindscape" from triangles to the Holy Trinity, even though theories themselves may shift to stay in tune with expanding knowledge. Thus, should a strictly scientific consensus seem to yield the only certainty worthy to uphold, any criticism of the ruling paradigm may well be regarded as no less dangerous a heresy than were challenges to prevailing religious dogma in mediaeval times. In other words, neither adding nor subtracting any Divine dimension to or from human concepts of the Cosmos can alter the psychological fact of inclination towards belief that will ineluctably find some ideal object to elevate in however uncertain light of either faith or reason. Yet beyond psychology and reason, the so-called mechanisms of biology—the ineffable magic of Life—remain a sure indication of the commerce between mind and matter that are thus enabled to reify each other, and whereby consciousness can be translated between the strict material and more liberal mental worlds.

46. The Snails' Tale

Hence the psychology of evolutionary dogma obstructs any honest examination of what is actually meant by its basic principles and what they can or cannot explain, or may imply towards any larger understanding of existence. Clearly, for example, while natural selection may in some sense amount to merely a tautology—"survivors survive"—its absence would obviate evolution ever occurring at all. Yet on a higher level of abstraction, natural selection is deeply connected to the idea of order itself which has a key existential significance. For both in mathematics and in reality, form arises from the blank or relatively formless of the null set or the "Earth without form and void,"[1] and is then preserved and enhanced, as the order of truth or truth of order advances towards greater beauty and higher degrees of freedom. And not all of the selection that enables that advancement is blindly mechanical, for living cells can deliberately eliminate bad mutations just as the human body is able to expunge the relative chaos of infectious disease or even in some cases cancer itself. But so long as the evolutionary paradigm is viewed as needing protection from a threat of being burdened by the albatross of metaphysics, any progress towards extending that paradigm (as opposed to gains of literal knowledge in fields like genetics and astronomy) to reach the sunny side of a philosophical mountain remains difficult. Yet, despite the ingrained obstinacy of pro and anti-religious ideology that revolves around what Darwin parsed from the Book of Nature, that subject continues to present a supreme challenge for both reason and faith that demands to be unflinchingly addressed. For dreams of the scientific method having sufficient explanatory power to eventually unravel the deepest mysteries of Creation are confronted by Life and evolution to a degree less recognized today than by Darwin himself, who freely acknowledged those cases where the virtual miracles of biology most vividly appear to transgress the boundaries of what is called complexity—or the idea that blind, insensate elements can combine and recombine in a mathematical manner that finally renders all things possible.

For example, it is easier to explain chemical reactions in the soil or the composition of distant stars, than to account for the appearance of Opisthobranchia, a group of marine snails that lost all but a vestige of their shells millions of years ago and now present on the notum or dorsal surface of the exposed skin, a "profusion of forms" and often "highly complicated ornamental structures" that are, moreover, so remarkably colored that "a whole chapter could be written on the colors which appear in the notum, though little is known of their chemical structure. The entire spectral range is represented, from pure red to violet, as well as a variety of mixtures. Apart from pigments, there are a host of structural colors—white, for instance—and also many shades of blue."[2] Thus in the mere appearance, gratuitous insofar as serving no urgent survival needs such as camouflage or attracting a mate, of these obscure animals Nature both flaunts and celebrates a secret simultaneously lesser and greater than those which science is striving to extract from the heart of matter-energy and of space-time (itself perhaps imbedded in the "warped passages" of an hyper-dimensional continuum)* so as to ascertain some rationally conceivable beginning for the physical Universe and

*"We could be living in a three-dimensional pocket of space, even though the rest of the universe behaves as though it is higher-dimensional...living in an isolated neighborhood with three spatial dimensions that's part of a higher-dimensional cosmos."[4]

its likely fate. And meanwhile faith is likewise challenged by evolution to consider—even as Job was enjoined to consider the Leviathan—how the nature of soul and consciousness are affected by our unshakable bond with all flesh, whether human or non-human.

Yet Life also presents two further challenges to reason and to faith, respectively. First of all, if evolution combined with neuroscience can resolve the riddle of consciousness so fully as to vitiate any explanatory role for the purported supernatural along with any other reason for crediting the possibility of its existence, then along with the human soul must be discarded all but rhetorical argument for why any theory beyond what applies to purely practical science should merit respect from a human animal, who if divested by reason of all spiritual hopes, might simply wish to savor passing hours of a life that never stops ticking down towards oblivion. And secondly, if our nature does in fact share biological roots with creatures innocent of abstract thinking and philosophy, then religion must confront the hard truth that "the mortal mind cannot know the things of God,"[3] whereby the function of religion should be more to fully bring those things into our lives, rather than try to conform them into a conceptual framework whose felt necessity is more human than divine. However, there may always be tension between the open-ended character of spiritual, or for that matter scientific truth, and the more static and rigid form in which it has to be presented to obtain any status in the world.

Therefore, insofar as a great deal of religious discourse and controversy is culturally biased and ego-driven and in such regard more Darwinian than spiritual, an honest faith should try to distinguish between the natural, cultural and social and what could be called authentically supernatural. Yet that distinction is also futile without recognition of values that are both natural and spiritual, such as the kind of compassion or altruism sometimes found even in animals, values whose practice is vital for a global society increasingly gnawed by the festering sores of destitution, ignorance, and injustice.

Thus, the super-complexity of biology and evolution has profound philosophical resonance, because beyond even the most recondite theories of physics it indicates that the boundaries of knowledge are found not so much upon some far yet superhumanly attainable horizon as in a twilight zone where the truth is camouflaged in flickering lights and shadows. Concepts like string theory or "loop quantum gravity" for example, can at least attempt some tentative steps towards the hidden core of matter-energy and space-time. But no theories have tried to account for biological phenomena whose functional basis and evolutionary origins elude all conceivable logic. For while the neo-Darwinian premise of natural selection sifting through the pool of genetic mutations—including those whose potential may await favorable circumstance as when, for example, demise of the dinosaurs permitted the kaleidoscopic expansion of formerly humble, shrew-like (as formerly imagined, although fossils of larger Cretaceous mammals have been recently discovered) mammals into a cornucopia of creatures from bats to whales and lemurs to lions—may be foolish to question, there is no telling how all the separate adaptations and genetic changes required for complex structures or behaviors like the insulating coat of polar bears or decorative artistry of the bower bird were coordinated smoothly enough to produce a new species prepared to be woven into the fluid tapestry of Life. Surely, natural selection favored the bears' adapting to the onset of Arctic cold in formerly temperate regions, but that can hardly explain how all of the new anatomical features that enabled their endurance could arise together from a multiplicity of genetic factors whose harmonious response to the challenge of climate change can only be described as serendipity, by whomsoever might wish by such a fig leaf term to conceal those glaringly naked unknowns that Nature keeps parading outside the sober encampment of reason.

And that is because reason itself, whose debasement through what is called "scientism" suggests a vision of material knowledge as the grail of progress—as opposed to being simply one of the rewards attendant on implementing social justice or tempering the rule of law with human rights—is not the defining value of human nature, but instead simply a faculty whose proper use can go so far as to examine its own character and purpose. (Why ask why?) In fact, just as species-transforming adaptations to a shifting environment that are effected by multiple coordinated mutations, could be seen as an holistic response that is virtually immune to reductive analysis, rational science itself can be regarded as an integral part of humanity's overall response to the broad existential challenge that accompanies our own peculiar status. Hence, to rightly weigh ourselves according to the Darwinian paradigm cannot fail to highlight the limitations of a bio-computer whose development, according to that paradigm, has been driven by demands of survival and security more than by any flightier needs to decorate our nest with the accouterments of ideas and culture. Yet because the latter's intrinsically psychological meaning reflects our supra-biological nature, it can hardly be missed that while evolution has brought some higher animals like the gifted bower bird or playful otter to a threshold of mind entailing self-expression, it has borne the human race across a further threshold where liberty and not security has now become the leading theme of History. And again, while human history can be assessed by quasi-Darwinian principles as in sociobiology, to exercise that very mode of thinking first requires environmental pressures to be alleviated by technology, so that psychological survival and the struggle of ideas can replace the brutish Hobbesian regime where lacks much opportunity to muse upon what grander framework may encompass it. Nor is there any guarantee that such ideas, although conceived in ivied liberty, have rightfully assessed either Nature or human nature. For the truest measure of ourselves as rational beings speaks not only to what the limits of reason are, but how distantly "the boundaries of the soul" may be removed from what can even be conceived. For in fact it is from uncharted lands along those boundaries that the deepest conceptions and imaginings may come. Meanwhile the tale of Opistobranchia and other strange aspects of biology reveal that the soul of Nature, whose "wise blood" informs every fiber of our being, is of a measure no less profound than what Heraclitus, in the dawn of Western civilization when elemental truths were often more starkly apparent than today, attributed to the human soul.

47. The Timeless Paradigm

Of course, one could argue that some portion of those boundaries may be identified through scientific probing ever more deeply into the heart of matter or rather of matter-energy, that itself is merged with space-time in a continuum whose intrinsic fields of force, or "quantum fields," are reified as hyper-dimensional bits of mass and energy that interact among themselves according to unswerving laws. And yet those laws conform to an order that proclaims the mathematical foundations of a universe that, were its rules even slightly different, should be profoundly altered. Hence the deepest reality that physics ultimately attains is not one of substance but of idea. And the luminous shadow of an idea whose ultimate source may dwell at some untellably subtle and abstruse remove, is what examination of the physical world finally presents to the consciousness of observers. But that idea is not one of causal contingencies interwoven in a network as sometimes envisioned by theories of consciousness being emergent from the vast multiplicity of interactive processes in the brain, which are of course required for thinking and perception to occur. Instead, beneath the fabric of shape-shifting sub-atomic particles, appears the vision of a harmony whose irreducibly tiniest and thereby hardest elements may consist in vibratory nodes of dynamic Ur-substance that remain immune to the cosmic fatigue of entropy that inexorably undoes more visible and composite entities like molecules, ecosystems and stars.

In other words, vibratory "strings" or something virtually equivalent such as the knots of space-time posited by "loop quantum gravity," are at the nearly incorruptible foundation of physical existence that shall not fail unless or until space-time itself were dissolved. And that underlying, adamantine uniformity conforms to a universal order that binds together all entities at every level on the cosmic scale of magnitude in a pulsating flux of mutual interrelationships that finally engendered the seed of Life, imbued with a freer dynamic all its own. Hence the necessity of order also implies an hierarchy of seemingly autonomous yet irrevocably entangled entities or nodes of Being at every level not only of duration and size, but of measures like that of awareness whose own parameters cannot be traced beyond the interface of a rationally knowable world with whatever indescribably enfolds it.

Of course it is also true that "things" like sub-atomic particles constitute definitively separate objects only in the "mindscape" of an idealized reality, because they lack any clear boundary to divide them from surrounding space as sharply as the spatial separation that helps to distinguish people and objects in the context of daily experience. However, the truest definition of anything as recognizably individual is the identity it acquires by virtue of being a node or intersection in whatever networks of force and influence, whether cultural, ecological, or simply physical as in the case of atoms and their constituents, helps to reify its existence. And when, as in the case of subatomic things the elemental essence of their being consists in a dynamic obedience to laws that cannot be bent or broken—because strictly physical reality, as the platform for all higher types of existence, can have no tolerance for error—then those entities are stripped of all but the pure idea of an identity which is therefore no longer merely physical in the ordinary sense of that term, but instead hovers in a hyper-dimensional wonderland from whence, for example, they can manifest as either a particle or a wave.

Yet like them, our own identity is most firmly established in an ideal realm whereby, for example, we can claim to be the "captain of our soul" although in fact the latter may resonate more strongly with principles beyond our control than with any proud assertions from what may be the servant or container more than owner of that soul. Hence any spiritual substance of our being that essentially is anchored outside of time and thus immune to entropy, could also be conceived as providing a trans-rational faculty or "meta-principle" deriving from a realm in whose larger perspective the key truth of many ideas can be more clearly perceived. And from that region may emanate those principles that in turn are manifest and subsequently recognizable as incorruptible natural laws endowed by mathematical truth substanding the physical Cosmos, whose exquisite detail and sweeping grandeur have their origin and sustenance in some deathless ground of Being that abides within ourselves no less than in every atom and every cell.

Yet while the above can be dismissed as venturing far from reality and into similarly futile ground as mediaeval theology it also indicates a "meta-principle" implied by the ultra-complexity of biology and evolution, whose rhyme and reason are untellably other from that of physics, whose deepest rational framework, as suggested by ooncepts like string theory and quantum gravity, continues to elude the highest ambitions of intellect. A flock of birds, for example seagulls that suddenly quit their feeding ground on a bed of mussels exposed by the tide and fly a short distance away while a smaller and more scattered group begins to arrive and feed, may act as it does for no apparent reason. Yet these flocks also seem guided by an evident intelligence and purpose as if reflecting a virtual mind of Nature projected through subsidiary collectives of the species and its individual communities. And while whatever agency may work behind the scenes to choreograph an holistic ecology just as it does the whole array of bodily functions beyond our conscious control (including those neural functions that underlie willful actions) appears to manifest in varied degrees of freedom as in the case of a flock of birds versus the more blindly instinctual behavior of an ant or termite colony, its role seems especially obscure regarding the subtlety and scope of processes at work in evolution.

Moreover, to claim that agency does not exist despite any appearance of its doing so, is logically equivalent to saying that human consciousness per se does not exist but instead simply constitutes the integral sum of brain activity—a proposition that not only depends upon its apprehension by an observer who is presumed to not be conscious in the sense that such theories may seek to explain away, but would be rendered quite dubious by any demonstrable instance of psychic phenomena. The hope of "explaining" consciousness, in other words, depends upon first being able to prove that those phenomena do not occur. Otherwise, without that sort of proof, the gaps in putative understanding of Nature and of human nature will remain not less multifarious than Life itself—whose wonders can easily astound whomsoever may refrain from attempting to bind their concepts concerning biological phenomena with any "mind-forged manacles" whose iron, after all, is naught but electrical patterns racing through the delicate neuronal web that Nature herself can boast as her finest accomplishment..

Hence in biology more than physics may be hidden the outline of the "new paradigm" whose transformation of the current scientific worldview is longingly awaited as an existential yardstick that can better take the measure of the known in terms of evident and yet invisible dimensions which we cannot enter even though they enter into our own awareness and its driving motivations. But if in fact the case is that such dimensions lie not only beneath the surface of things—including those mental states that are also things—but beyond the bounds of scientific theory as well, then the "new paradigm" may be unattainable in words except for those reflecting an ancient version sometimes called the "perennial philosophy." For the latter declines to try and explain the holistic phenomenon of consciousness that is bonded with a metaphysical Gestalt wherein both Nature and human awareness are simply irreducible aspects of the living Cosmos that accordingly projects a multiplicity of patterns which embody physical and biological existence and are imbued with psycho-spiritual depths of subjectivity therein, objectively speaking, reflected or contained. And this entire Cosmic spectrum of being-ness and consciousness is manifested in a manner whose strata of subtlety are more magically interwoven than human knowledge, taking finite steps on an infinite road, can ever hope to encompass. And in that case neither substance, mind, nor any other presumptive existential attribute can hold explanatory pride of place, for all are subsumed to That from whence they came and whence shall finally return.

And yet if the black hole of Unity is what threatens to engulf any thinking and philosophy that pursues a path where every revelation turns out to be the mask of a deeper riddle—so that, for example, the bedrock of atoms was found to be floating upon the quicksand of quantum paradox—nonetheless Unity itself can be a touchstone where reason reaffirms its own intrinsic value for interpreting the world and its vicissitudes. Hence if employing a word like "unity" is criticized as merely an evasion of the requirements for rational discourse—a cloud of ink squirted by an obfuscating octopus—we can ask what is meant by "reason," since the same touchstone affords not only the security of confidence in addressing such questions, but the liberty of doing so in a variety of ways. For if, under the rubric of "unity," the core principles of Nature and of the brain are either closely allied or one and the same, the response to questions as to what actual meaning, if any, might be nesting in our verbiage need be no more logical than Nature herself. And while Unity may constitute the final destination of human thought whose parallel lines are fated to dissolve when they meet at Infinity, it also affords a temple for refreshment in the quest for understanding whose progressive refinement is reflected in those faculties that help to enhance our lives. For, just as the mystery of language supports our necessary illusion of knowledge, it is the unknown that ever reifies the known.

48. Power in the Blood

Hence a profound enigma that is scarcely apparent in cryptic language of the genetic code swims beneath the complicated surface of a story whose Darwinian description is surely "a good general approximation"[1] yet does not fully account for the incremental transformation of species whose successive forms have clambered up a myriad intersecting trails on the ascent from molecules to minds. For to chart the inter and intracellular choreography, for example, involved in changing a frog to a lizard and the kind of signals directing that transformation, not to mention environmental factors responsible for promoting and channeling every required step of change along the way, even further exceeds the powers of intellect than to imagine possible scenarios for the birth of the universe from a state of pre-existence utterly alien to everyday reality. Thus a hint of what subtleties are hidden in the language of DNA is shown by the fact that a single genetic sequence can contain more than one set of instructions depending on how it is punctuated, as if the same string of letters could yield two different poems or documents according to where the spaces bracketing each subgroup of letters were inserted. That accomplishment far surpasses what any intellect could devise in human language, as shown by what crude examples can be devised—re-spacing "Romancement to get her now here" turns it into "Roman cement together nowhere,"[2] a pair of phrases whose inventor may or may not have intended their implicit comparison between the tender subjectivity of love and ruthless objectivity of conquest In any event, no lesser magic must be involved in evolution, whose modus operandi accordingly cannot be captured by anything more precise than the so-called "holistic" paradigm suggested by an ancient Greek saying that "the fox knows many things but the hedgehog knows one big thing." That "one big thing" is equivalent to a Gestalt enfolding the many things that science is able to discover, but that in the case of evolution are exceptionally resistant to theoretical regimentation. And that is because the meta-logic of living Nature, like that of poetry, art and music, transcends the sheer logical necessity of those physical laws whose workings can and have been discovered, and thus defies formal understanding to the same extent as the pattern of a painting, sonata or poem shaped by the psychology of genius, whose inspirational sources are equally unlikely to ever be unveiled.

Yet of course the major evolutionary factors which can be identified have been rightly described as the process of genetic mutations and their preservation or casting out by natural selection. The former is an "effective cause," of which an example could be the human agency that finances and causes to be built a chain of department stores or restaurants, while the latter is a "formal cause" such as the economic forces that create a favorable climate that constitutes a condition favoring that those establishments appear and are patronized. But the difficulty in trying to understand how the "effective cause" of mutations (whose own formal cause is ultimately that things never stop changing) needed to turn one or more ancient amphibian species into modern reptiles like turtles, geckos and iguanas actually brought about the array of coordinated and simultaneous adaptations required is even more profound than in trying to conceive what sequence of transformations forged the delicate machinery of feathers and wings. For instance, the "amniotic egg" of a reptile in which the embryo and the yolk on whose nutrients the embryo feeds during its development is contained in the amniotic sac, is quite different from the egg of an amphibian which lacks the amniotic vessel for the embryo[3] More than just a single mutation was required to effect the change from the amphibian to the reptile egg, yet all of them had to occur at once because no partial adaptation could be viable. Just one feature which unborn reptile young must have, for example, is a horny protuberance on their snout which they use to break out of the hard shell, whereas in order to emerge from their softer, gelatinous eggs the young amphibians—which typically first appear in a fully aquatic larval form like a tadpole that still needs further radical change to become an air-breathing adult whereas young reptiles, like puppies and kittens, are simply miniatures of their parents—dissolve it by secreting a chemical substance[4]. And in so conforming to their need for simultaneous occurrence, rather than randomly and uselessly appearing piecemeal, the entire suite of mutations which refashioned the amphibian into a reptile egg while eliminating the tadpole stage, clearly had to follow a program of instructions no more accidental or haphazardly arrived at than the genetic blueprint for development of the original tadpole embryo and its way of emerging from the shell. There is strange and wondrous "power in the blood" whose tide has borne these kinds of changes onward from abyssal Time to shores of the present day—seemingly solid ground that even now is dissolving into a soon to be all but forgotten past.

Hence the concept of "intelligent design" is not very meaningful, because all it really says is that some agency we can neither understand nor identify must have played a role in shaping evolution. Certainly, but hardly more helpfully, that agency could also be called "information," which in addition to the data encoded in successfully coordinated mutations that represent the smallest conceivable increments of evolutionary change must also include the broader template corresponding to how the specific body plans of creatures are written in the language of DNA and how the deployment of those instructions is choreographed in the process of individual growth or long term evolutionary development. For each step of either process, whether characterized by the buzzwords of mechanistic, vitalist, or religious faith has its informational equivalent, albeit only under the first of those headings could that same information even hypothetically embrace all aspects of organic Nature, insofar as either vitalism or religion posit the involvement of some agent whose workings are not about to be understood, if guided by some type of intelligence presumably smarter than human science can follow. In other words, unstinting scrutiny of living phenomena unveils a stupendous hyper-complexity that beggars human understanding to at least as great and probably greater extent, for example, as the problem in mathematics of finding any regular pattern for the distribution of primes. And to realize that fact, whereby it becomes less foolish to surmise a virtual mind of Nature "that through the green fuse drives the flower"[5] —for to say that what dwarfs human intelligence is not itself intelligent is somewhat disingenuous—is to be humbled as deeply as in gazing in the night towards distant stellar engines of a physical Creation that proclaims "the awful power of non-human things."[5]

It is also true, of course, that humans themselves are made of non-human things and that "the self is made of non-self elements"[6]—and yet all these things must share in some common existential properties, which become more and more general the more finely a human is reductively divided into smaller and smaller categories of biological and finally inorganic constituents, until we reach the subatomic quantum basis of matter, whose overriding existential property is that of raw existence itself, ever trembling violently upon the brink of an indescribable void that while seemingly insubstantial is the wellspring of Creation. But if instead the non-self elements are viewed as qualitative properties of mind and consciousness, which for example could include those aspects of character or psyche sometimes attributed to astrological influences, then the "non-self" elements of what we self-referentially take to be the personal self with its ideas and opinions or perceptions and feelings, are no longer the cellular and atomic building blocks of the body but instead the blended colors of the mind. And in turn the latter could be traced to an origin in the white light of Cosmic consciousness or clear light of Divine Reality, whose single element then becomes the ground or essence of a spiritual self whose appearance of being personal to ourselves is conferred by its biological framework, including the brain, that is constructed from the many "non-self" elements—each one a tiny atomic, molecular or cellular self all its own—that constitute the physical mind and body.

And if that is not so, and the spiritual element must therefore be deleted from any valid picture of reality, then the world may become either easier or harder to understand, depending on one's point of view. But any such views have little bearing on the fact of what happens to be the case—a Reality that itself remains not only a non-human thing, but the only thing, and thus the ultimate winner emerging from the context of any argument, whether scientific or religious, concerning its nature. However, in the case of evolution, the spiritual hypothesis relieves a part of the burden of explanation, despite its lacking any specific explanatory power, because it lends the Universe a higher degree of freedom which then becomes available to facilitate living phenomena—including those that are especially awkward for whoever tries to explain them—as well as greatly enlarging the prospects of human destiny.

One such awkward example is the gray larch budmoth of Switzerland—Zeiraphera Grisiana—that displays a life-cycle, involving two subspecies, whose origin defies explaining in terms of natural selection or in any manner whatsoever. The moth larvae hatch in May and feed on the needles of the larch for about fifty days and then fall to the ground and form cocoons from which they emerge a month later as moths that live for five weeks and lay eggs under patches of lichen on the bark of the larches that host their life-cycle. However, the moth has two varieties, known as the Weak and the Strong. The latter have greater vitality and are more resistant to the parasitic larvae of a certain wasp that lays its eggs in the body of a larva of either type, but the Weak variety is more resistant to a virus that infects both species. Therefore, when the population of the Strong variety explodes as it does about every seven years, and its unchecked feeding on the larches turns them brown, population pressures undermine the moths' resistance to the virus and most of the Strong variety perish. The Weak then begin to flourish, but their population is held in check by the wasps and the Strong rebuild their numbers to the same crisis point as before.[7] Presumably, natural selection would have favored the Strong subspecies and eliminated the Weak altogether, except for a chance mutation having provided the latter with immunity to the virus. But in that case, the more vital members of the Weak moths would still have had an advantage whose preservation by selective pressures would have restored them to parity with the Strong. Hence a standard Darwinian explanation for how the two subspecies diverged into the separate roles of enacting two distinct and yet cooperative halves of the moths' life cycle, is hard to construct, let alone prove. For one must also account for how the mutation conferring immunity against the virus happened in the first place, and there are only two choices. Either it was a chance event whose usefulness was a rare stroke of fortune, or the change came about as part of an adaptive response that was just as purposeful as all other ongoing intracellular chemistry of the organism—a tendency directed by or subservient to a property or field of consciousness, wherein the processes of Life are as inherent as is the behavior of subatomic particles within their energetic quantum fields.

49. Unknown Unknowns and Valuable Values

And the latter type of explanation has of course been denounced as "vitalism," the heretical bogeyman that orthodox biology condemns for granting Life mystical properties beyond rational parameters of current science, and perhaps incompatible with any form of logical conception whatsoever. Yet of course much of human psychology, in whose arena such arguments can properly be said to occur, is also beyond the stricter versions of those parameters that determine the rules for hard theories that can be proven or falsified by repeatable experiments. But many other regions of science, for example cosmology, are equally tangential to mysterious unknowns that lurk within a no man's land whose swirling mists the light of reason is unable to penetrate. Thus it is hardly surprising that evolution—the most problematic subject in all of science—should offer difficulties that are even more compelling than those encountered in physics, in terms of their seeming to invoke the certainty of factors likely to remain forever inaccessible to human understanding. How, for example, can any known principles fully account for an Amazon riverbank insect, Laternia servillei, that resembles a miniature baby alligator closely enough to give pause to potential avian predators?[1] Surely, this clever disguise is encoded in genes that have and will be selected through countless generations, but the manner of its having come about is a question behind which the dread specter of vitalism lurks like a beast immune to the analytic blade of whomsoever happens to think that when leaving the pavement of inorganic substance to venture into the tangled thickets of biology and evolution, the path of science can easily maintain its rational compass..

But the reason for reason not being able to expose what hidden factors lurk in the fog hemming in every island of clarity that may seem securely established, (of course, that kind of clarity is somewhat different than what is sought and sometimes wildly departed from in laws and legislation, or from the "clear light of Reality" that might be described as a goal for seekers of spiritual enlightenment. Hence the tricky "light of reason" may project false clarity of an illusion that some pinnacle in the mindscape has been conquered, as in the late 19th century notion that the explanatory job of physics was all but accomplished) and that the wraiths of stranger mysteries keep haunting the frayed outskirts of knowledge, even as that boundary continues expanding into a Universe of unlimited inner and outer, or psycho-spiritual and quantum-relativistic space, is itself quite simple. For in fact human awareness of a world wherein that same awareness constitutes the major portion involves an interplay of the seemingly known and the irreducibly mysterious, just as ordinary thinking and everyday consciousness depends upon concealed neuronal processes that help to forge the physical facsimile of consciousness that echoes consciousness itself, the "res ipsa" whose coherent multiplicity pervades and upholds a Cosmos that is "a great thought more than a great machine." And the progress of reason and science is not only beset by the wild child that same advancement has created—namely, the hydra-headed throng of geometrically increasing information and theories at every level of truth or falsity that in the course of future history is bound to continue unfolding—but logic itself, in pursuing sequential cause and effect, is fated to approach a natural limit dividing causality itself from some nameless Gestalt within whose endless sky congeals "the raincloud of knowable things." Hence the study of biology, especially in its evolutionary dimension, finally reaches the mouth of an enormous cavern wherein resides the holistic dragon of Life itself, in prospect of confronting whose untellable magic reason can only quail and retreat to the manicured safety of its customary dreams.

And yet that jumbled landscape where the scientific compass starts to waver and the lodestar of truth skips erratically across the sky, is also where the biological kingdoms begin to manifest what in ourselves is more fully realized as the subjective aspect of the Cosmos. And in turn, that same aspect, in the light of ever-expanding human awareness is clearly the reservoir of those "prospective properties" that beyond any special physiology, are what make us human. Thus reason itself also belongs among those properties, insofar as its subjective aspect lends to thought a liberty that can in fact resemble the free artistry of Nature that fashions her creatures in a manner often gratuitous yet elegant as a nursery rhyme or surrealist painting. For if beauty is truth and vice-versa (as might be assented to by those elephants that paint pictures or apes who watch the sunset) that artistry is no less essential than objective natural law that assigns all creatures their proper sphere while weaving a fabric that only humankind, in corrupt misuse of its high degree of freedom, now threatens to unravel.

Hence, to the roster of whatever "values" may be held as distinguishing human civilization from the more constrained Darwinian context wherein it is firmly implanted—a context whence are derived both morally neutral values like "economic growth" and the virtually self-sustaining march of technology that is fueled by its own form of mutation and selection—must be added reverence for Life expressed through ecological concerns that are equally vital from a moral, aesthetic, or survivalist perspective. Morally, it is inhuman and even sub-animal to destroy the Creation and to continue doing so must be seen clearly as a poor choice—"I put before you this day blessing and cursing"—that completely undoes all conceivable human goals and aspirations. Aesthetically, if human works of art merit protection because, in cold-blooded terms, they have an irreplaceable informational content, then the environment deserves far greater protection because its worth, as measured in terms of information, far exceeds what can be found in libraries or museums. And in stark terms of survival, there is nothing more vital than protecting the ecological web whose integrity is required for humanity's long-term security. Putting these three together, can form a picture where the works of civilization can grow towards harmony with the natural world, but if that kind of vision is not adopted then our species will not only drift further from the moral standards increasingly enjoined on the path of post-Darwinian evolution, but from obeying the unbending requirements of natural law as well. Thus to disdain the clear morality of protecting an environmental legacy owed to coming generations, is equivalent to falling firmly into the iron grip of unforgiving natural laws, on whose stern and silent judgments human residence on Earth depends no less than did the fate of species once consigned by similar judgment to oblivion, including some of the fearsome predators by which our hominid forebears were often slain.

Accordingly to fully appreciate the wonders of bio-phenomena regardless how comprehensively they may or may not be reductively conformed to theory or the rickety abstractions of academia, is akin to helping Nature help us to endure, which will entail greater harmony of science and technology with the natural world whose own technology is ready-made and unlikely to be surpassed, for while genetic tinkering may eliminate certain diseases it will not help to make another Mozart, let alone a better version of the system represented by DNA. To revere the living miracle everywhere around and within us, in other words, is to invite greater peace and understanding to prevail and thereby dignify human nature as worthy to shine more brightly in a Cosmos rightly seen as charged by the true, inexplicable and conscious Life whose full acceptance and invitation will allow it to grace and inform humanity. And in so doing, human thinking will tend towards a higher degree of freedom that to the extent of perceiving beyond determinism shall slacken the bonds of ideological agendas or rectilinear mind sets—for these shall wither in the face of stronger belief in a sacred and living Creation—and consequently not only liberate science but magnify reason itself.

The program of scientific progress, in other words, while justifiably recommended as "lighting a candle in the dark"[2] also approaches asymptotically towards a limit on the other side of which there lies the supra-natural, concerning which no better logic can obtain than the mathematics of Infinity—which is not to say that within that limit, yet far down the road of future Time, may await what seems impossible today. And in that "otherness" the source of transformational magic behind the process of evolution and its more evident Darwinian laws may well be concealed, just as the white whale in Moby Dick was known to inhabit the oceanic depths, yet like the ultimate secrets of Life was pursued in vain. Of course, this kind of statement can be dismissed as retreating into a haze of presumptive "x-factors" whose ringleader is God, or else derided as the substitution of mere words grounded only in their own internal sense—which in calling on concepts like "infinity" departs further from reason than unproven yet more definitive theories—for painstaking analysis of whatever facts can at least be verified. However, it is also the case that infinity is a fact, or rather a meta-fact transcending the total context of events and things including not only Darwin's finches of the Galapagos, quasars at the edge of the Universe, or evidence for catastrophic extinction of the mega-fauna of North America some 10,000 years ago,[3] but also those ideal objects of the mind such as systems of faith or knowledge, that may conform less with actualities than be swayed by the psychology—whether Darwinian, Freudian, or spiritual—of either reason or faith.

Analyzing the case of the finches, for example, makes it clear that the micro- evolutionary change which divided them into several differently-adapted subspecies speaks no more to the problem of exactly how their avian ancestors evolved from fish than the artificial breeding of dogs tells us how the DNA of some distant reptilian forbear of mammals incrementally altered over millions of years into the genes of whatever wolf-like creatures became ancestral to modern dogs after being tamed in prehistoric times. Meanwhile the citing of these finches as a proof of evolutionary principles, despite their hardly demonstrating any greater degree of change than found in artificial breeding of domestic animals, appears to amount to avoidance of recognizing how theoretical approaches to Life are far more uncertain and ambivalent than in material science. That is why, for example, very few texts or reference works make any mention of the so-called "through-put" or flow-through lung of birds, which in and of itself would seem to indicate a totally separate avian lineage that could only include dinosaurs, or flightless creatures that looked like dinosaurs, if the latter also had the same kind of highly efficient respiratory system—a lately confirmed yet little noted possibility. The uniqueness of the avian lung, where tiny tubes called parabronchi take the place of the alveoli or air sacs in the lungs of mammals and reptiles, is therefore highly representative of the strange and remarkable character of biology, as befitting its intermediary rank betwixt and bridging physics and psychology. And by similar token, Life, in whose matrix we are bonded and that is grounded on imponderable unknowns is also allied with priceless values essential to human life and civilization. For those values draw their substance from unknowable unknowns that are hidden in mysteries of the Infinite, yet by manifesting in the world as realities of mind and spirit are what favor increasing hope that homo sapiens can leave behind a past where a large majority of lives were, in words from that past, "nasty, brutish and short"[4] as many remain today.

50. Filling the Void

Yet, it is also true that the relative simplicity of evolutionary explanations rests upon the major aspects of Life that they identify, namely, variation and selection, being far more obvious than the inaccessible reasons for how and why the physical Universe should possess a bio-friendly structure let alone exist at all. For insofar as probability in such wide context can be meaningful, clearly the overwhelming chances that Life, once underway, should keep evolving so far as circumstances may allow—on some planets perhaps nothing better than worms or lizards—are easier to grasp than the nature and probability of its initial appearance in the primal seas or wherever its radical chemistry first began to elevate molecular substance towards the pinnacle of human self-awareness. For the rationale of all life-forms continually striving like human society itself towards whatever enhancements of survival are possible seems obvious as compared to what hidden cause or purpose may have brought the physical universe into being from the "no-thing-ness" of pre-existence. Yet the latter question can also be seen in a perspective of even starker simplicity than that of evolution being regarded as nothing more than the sorting of mutations through a gauntlet of survival, or instead one might say selective assignment of favor to those biological advances that best enhance the entire ecosystem. For from that perspective, there clearly cannot just be nothingness, since the existence of non-existence is self-contradictory and even a vacuum or a point of zero dimensions is still something which can be identified—at least if any observer is there to do the job.

Yet whatever is accordingly bound to fill a non-sustainable void has got to be more than sheer random chaos, which itself is impossible to define in more than rhetorical terms. Therefore, whatever world or existential state by sheer logical necessity is guaranteed to occur, must also assume a shape or pattern that includes non-random elements whose character and behavior are determined by organizing principles such as the natural laws that science has discovered. And to what extent those principles and their effects may ramify and diversify can be assigned no obvious limits short of those that have channeled rather than prevented biological activity up to where it has blossomed as human self-aware intelligence with what could be seen as its vital power to reify the whole of existence. And when that level of consciousness has been attained, then curbs and restraints on the further course of intelligent human activity, such as prohibiting pornography or pork, can be partly self-imposed and if done so wisely—as in curbing pollution or genocide—will avoid the Darwinian retribution that could otherwise harshly amend or even abort all Earthly human experience.

Thus, the analysis of astronomical mega-objects like quasars can discover how and why their enormous energy may have been attained, and these explanations framed in mathematical terms.. But that is because such phenomena, while existing near the outer edge of time and space as viewed from Earth, are not beyond the boundary of reason itself but well within its ability to account for the dynamics of stellar and galactic-scale forces. Yet many biological phenomena that are more accessible in time and space—since fossils can reveal the nature of life on Earth millions of years ago more clearly than light from a quasar indicate exactly what kind of titanic process first launched that light on its journey from billions of light-years away—are also located seemingly beyond the boundaries of human explanatory power, which may be why their embarrassing presence is scarcely ever noted. Within those boundaries, of course, overall descriptions of the evolutionary process are quite possible. For whatever reason, mutations occurred in certain kinds of fish that gave them rudimentary legs and lungs that consequently allowed their venturing on shore. And their good fortune in doing so caused these mutations to be preserved and elaborated on till every terrestrial niche available had been colonized by their versatile descendants.

But why and how those fish and not others gained the capability to crawl from the shallows and then absorb sufficient oxygen from the air instead of underwater is just one part of the larger problems of evolutionary change that are unlikely to ever be solved. For, while the virtual time machine of a telescope, allowing astronomers to peer backwards in time to the first beginnings of the Universe, can yield sufficient data to form at least a general idea concerning the origin of the "particle zoo" that later coalesced into stars and galaxies, even an actual time machine permitting direct observations of successive eras of life through all the ages might, if targeted correctly, permit discovery of many more missing links and intermediate forms whose fossils have not been found. But even then, there would be little chance of coming up with any better concept of evolution, or how it has worked in particular instances such as the development of sonar in bats, silk spinnerets in spiders, or singing in sparrows than what currently obtains. Such hopes in fact seem especially distant in light of the fact that biologists are still debating general concepts such as group selection, which says that altruism is explained by natural selection favoring the genes found in groups whose members help each other—as when lions risk their individual lives protecting the group territory or in the case of penguins adhering to the social rules they must collectively obey in order to survive the harshest conditions endured by any animal[1]—an idea that would seem nearly self-evident but does not begin to explain how such behavioral traits are genetically encoded.

And that is because the rationale or modus operandi of Life is of a kind and degree transcending that of matter/energy, whose relativistic and quantum arcana already test the limits of human understanding while remaining steeped in mystery. Hence, while "many people and even some biologists find it difficult to admit that the mystery of evolution on earth is not fully solved—they cannot resist the temptation to explain the unknown whole by its known parts,"[2] there is no way to make "precise statements about processes which ensure the smooth operation by which the optical impressions received by a simple lens are transmitted to a central nervous organization ready to receive those impressions."[3] It is possible to describe how stars may have evolved from clouds of hydrogen, but "such phenomena as the combination of a large number of feathers into a single optical effect, or the appearance of rhythmical patterns across the bodies of snakes, are all formal effects that cannot be explained by prevailing mutation theories."[4] And yet the myriad unaccountable phenomena which teem throughout the realm of non-human life have a lower scientific profile than the question of human consciousness, that—compounded by some inconvenient company like emotional dogs and unexpectedly clever birds and simians—has only achieved that status by dint of certain enjoyers of that same consciousness having rather paradoxically deemed themselves privileged to obtain an answer that, in stubborn rebuttal of their quest, is certain to remain an unconquered summit towards which the "dreams of reason"[5] can only gaze from afar.

Thus while rational powers may succeed in sketching a coherent though tenuous perspective on the natural world that view will be lacking unless framed by axioms that embrace the fullness of human nature. Otherwise, the picture soon grows frayed and worn as a blanket in Bedlam, without any stronger support than the concept of a bottomless and chaotically dancing complexity, whose teasing visage keeps confronting science at every new turn in a harlequin house of mirrors where skittish reflections are hopefully labeled as knowledge—a word whose very meaning may be problematic within the weavings of Maya, by whose golden meshes all are ineluctably bound.

Accordingly quantum physics describing the behavior of particles that themselves are not solid objects with a definite location in time and space, but rather nodes of vibratory motion immersed in the fields of force that they embody or actualize, is now trying to grasp the essence of those particles as being made of "strings" that vibrate like musical notes but in many more than the four familiar space-time dimensions. And even the ten dimensions now thought to be required may not be enough, and so yet another has been added, dragging the equations and the few minds who understand them into realms of inconceivable abstraction and subtlety. "String theorists have known for decades that the equations they generally use are approximate (the exact equations are difficult to know and understand) However, most thought that the approximate equations were sufficiently accurate to determine the required number of extra dimensions." But "most recently…it is now accepted that the theory needs *seven* extra dimensions" for a total of eleven instead of ten.[6] Apparently, whatever theorists may finally determine, the "turtle" of seemingly solid existence has been found to be standing on the back of another, more shadowy creature whose substance is the evanescent play of photons, electrons and quarks—and that turtle, in turn, now appears to be supported by another more shadowy still, whose body is but the music of the "strings," a song that calls all matter into being. Nor can any say this music, which in effect we hear in every waking moment regardless how accurate or true the current theory, is not supremely rational despite whether any God composed it, since the tolerances have to be exact. Every electron, photon or quark or neutrino must be a perfect match for every other of its kind, with not the slightest deviance allowed from that identity nor from those unswerving laws that shape the flawless patterns and tireless forces of the subatomic world from whence are forged the elements and stars. Yet if consciousness is also a sort of field that fills the void along with quantum fields across the Universe, while informing the human unit on a psycho-spiritual plane just as quanta are endowed by the fields they embody, then reason will never catch up to consciousness, whether personal or Cosmic, and therefore never be able to resolve our existential enigma.

51. Infinite Reckoning

Meanwhile the evident, irreducible and endless interweaving of the non-organic fabric of reality is beggared by what in the kingdoms of Life can hardly be called complexity at all, or else is of an entirely different sort, because for example, living things possess a higher degree of freedom than atoms and molecules which also depends upon an organism's level of consciousness. Thus the complexity of Life compares to that of matter as a higher order of Infinity to that immediately below. The "countable" infinity of natural numbers, which can be tallied one by one in series, is lesser (or of lower "cardinality" in the language of mathematics) than the infinity of points on a line which cannot be tallied one by one because no matter how close together any pair of points may be, an infinite number of other points always remains between them. And by similar token, behavior of highly complex non-living entities can at least be imagined as susceptible to the reckoning of some hypothetical "final theory," even should that notion prove unattainable within the span of human existence on planet Earth or on some other world to where our descendants might have fled from the throes of a dying Sun—or perhaps, as could never be proved, not attainable period. But Evolution lies further than any aspect of physics from wishful compliance with the relative certainty of a mathematical framework. Nor is there much likelihood of similar assurance to be gained through understanding the maze of feedback loops involving hundreds of different molecular mechanisms, whose own evolutionary origins are totally obscure, that work together to produce an organism from its embryo or seed and then continue to maintain that creature's day-to-day existence that rests upon its moment-to-moment intra-cellular and biochemical foundations.

Hence, while the complexity of patterns adopted by non-living matter-energy may belong to a profounder order of Infinity than the boundless number of planets and solar systems which could inhabit what is perhaps an infinite Cosmos comprised of countless universes that could be in many cases quite different from our own, that same complexity must be reckoned as of lesser degree than that of Life. For simply considering the many-layered manifold of biochemical, neuronal and other exchanges that in our own bodies never cease, compels us yet again towards the analogy of the series of natural numbers being of a weaker version of Infinity than that of the number of points on a line—between any pair of which, no matter how close together, the quantity exceeds the limitless sum of all natural numbers. Yet even the exotic version of Infinity represented by points on a line, must bow to the still higher or more uncountable number of curves which can be drawn in space, perhaps because between any two points an endless number of curves can be given.[1]

And from the latter comparison could perhaps be taken a tentative analogy or distant echo of the relationship between biology and consciousness, a linkage that in the great chain of Being surely ranks above the connection between life and matter—dimly analogous to how comparison between an infinity of all curves and a lesser of points occupies a higher degree on the ladder of infinities, than does the relationship between the infinity of points on a line segment and the smaller cardinality of all natural numbers. Meanwhile, on entering the domain of awareness and crossing a further bridge to human self-awareness, Infinity acquires yet deeper relevance. For not only has that very concept been given shape by consciousness itself, but insofar as humans may possess a metaphysical nature of eternal provenance and purpose in addition to an animal self that is intermingled with the cellular and genetic tapestry we share in common with all living things, the real Infinite is where spiritual perception can locate our ultimate framework of Being and Destiny, that from arcane and extra-temporal dimensions keeps on unfolding.

And in such case the attribute of infinity is not merely mathematical or a matter of limitless physical extent or complexity, but instead a qualitative source of the subjective meaning from which all sense of significance is ultimately derived, including what attaches to the quest for knowledge and its longing for new horizons. And if so, then Life in having achieved the vantage of human consciousness and psychology has also opened a portal between the so-called external or objective world, that is only external in relation to subjective observers whose minds have over millennia developed the conscious ability to make such distinctions, and the inward realm concerning which Heraclitus said that "you could not find out the boundaries of the soul, no, not by following every path, so deep a measure does it have."[2] Yet that inner world is by definition largely independent of temporal causality despite that outer circumstance that often plays a part in humanity's deeply subjective drama, may affect our feelings or dreams that may also be shared with others in a "collective unconscious." Thus in having any commerce with the objective realm of causes like the chemical reactions that presumably forged the molecular building blocks of the first living cells, subjective factors indwelling the Cosmos from the very beginning could have swayed those more external causes steering evolutionary advancement towards intelligent self-awareness, whose representatives today can gaze upon the living panorama stretching back into enshrouding mists of long ago.

Nor can that commerce be denied without refusing to grant the subjective kingdoms of mind and soul any more actual reality than some figure of speech or as a peculiar enclave of the reigning objectivity akin to the weird hyper-spaces of string theory. However, the blatantly objective assertion that neuronal complexity alone provides the magic for making what some benighted brains may foolishly presume to be the metaphysically engendered property of awareness is countered by observing that a non-fanciful and thus objectively real, yet also subjectively self-aware mind and spirit linked to a body of impermanence could hardly manifest in a physical sense without the cerebral mechanism that same body contains by dint of billions of years of evolution having shaped our species into finally being able to serve as a bridge between the objective and subjective, or the ideal and the real, and thereby effecting the marriage of Earth and Heaven.

In other words if our being holds any metaphysical dimension it must then interact with the Infinite in order to claim the true reality that same dimension provides—as referred to by Jesus in having said that "heaven and earth shall pass away, but my words shall never pass away." For should the ultimate bounds of our existence be finite as would be the case were consciousness merely spun from vastly complicated machinations of the brain while also lacking any mystical parameters, then being surrounded by the vast impersonal void into which our pure illusion of selfhood was fated upon its dying to dissolve forever, should render that existence virtually infinitesimal. But if any factor that can be called spiritual—insofar as its quality and effect in physical reality derives from a source non-finite in a larger sense than that of simply an endless complexity of "feedback loops" and other operations in the brain supportive of consciousness, because allied to an order of infinity transcending that of number or extent—confers upon our consciousness the nature of a "ding an sich" as purely axiomatic and irreducible as substance, light, or space itself, that same factor then must permeate and influence the whole of reality including life and evolution. Yet as the latter has progressively seized upon greater degrees of freedom involving increasingly complex behavior and psychology, a metaphysical dimension acquires ever-growing prominence till virtually displacing brute survival as the prime determinant of human life which is expressed through language and law, art and science, religion and philosophy, romantic love, and all the attributes of society and civilization. And if those attributes are nothing more than mere concoctions of a bio-computer that formerly, in times when dinosaurs never dreamed of distant worlds nor pterodactyls ever pondered on the meaning of their destiny, was only a genetic accident waiting to happen—rather than indicating a principle more truly subjective than biological necessity and ever informing our lives—then all hope of alternate realities above and beyond analysis as constituting a more than flatly physical ground of Being has to be dismissed. But if that same hope is justified, then the scope of its mystical object cannot be formally constrained, and thus not barred from having consequence upon events such as evolutionary change, even long before those changes drew near to opening the dawn of human wonderment and wisdom.

52. The Dual Imperative

Thus in similar sense to how some yet unknown hyper-spatial attributes are vital to explain the behavior of particles that—whether akin to the entities described in "string theory" or something different—are pure motion and energy that defy description as objects having a surface boundary like a table or a car and an exact location, so are metaphysical parameters necessary to fulfill the description of human nature, that lacks any precise conceptual boundary that could define its existence in "psychic space." For even the pure biological description of human beings, for example in the austere conceptions of sociobiology (which may be accurate insofar as indicating the ongoing trend towards group consciousness and the waning of individualism as humanity becomes an increasingly socialized collective) or as manifesting genetic imperatives is highly subjective because it represents a choice taken by the mind that is essentially psychological. For that choice is to presume limits whose deeper significance lies in their forming a refuge from the Infinite and "the awful power of non-human things," whereby some semblance of understanding offers the allure of a seeming mastery of Fate. Yet similar illusion has often led nations and empires to ruin, because the forces, whether natural, psychological or economic that ultimately swayed their destiny were bigger and trickier than they could conceive or control. Thus their dominion was inferior in power and scope to the tides of History, and their goals unworthy of the moral imperative without whose admission no society can hope to long retain "the mandate of Heaven," that in today's swiftly globalizing world has become increasingly vital for civilized human survival. For while many armed conflicts and egregious excesses grow increasingly banal when measured against the moral and practical imperatives of reverence for life and social justice, it should be clear that prolonged dereliction from any nobler course for society may well be rewarded by a stark judgment whose enforcers, whether sent by Nature, God, or Fate, will be the dire horsemen of the Apocalypse.

The nature of that moral imperative, however, whose recognition is vital towards continuance and coherence of humankind, is twofold. First of all, the fact of cerebral intelligence having raised the human animal above the natural order to a place where psychological perversity and gratuitous tending to violence combined with wanton fouling of our environmental nest render homo sapiens a self-endangered species, necessitates imposing order in the form of laws. These laws have been described as part of the social contract which allows formation of governments. Yet now for the sake of preserving humanity and its ecological safety net, that legal system must achieve a global coherence and impartial scientific vision, immune to challenge by brutish parochial interests that otherwise, for example, will keep trampling on precious natural habitats or human rights. But secondly, that same imperative is to distinguish civilization as endowed with higher purpose than simply the enhancement of survival gained by organisms that are able to form societies. For that distinction can confer upon humanity the dignity of having realized a more than merely Darwinian meaning inherent in the process of evolution. And if so, then by virtue of that realization of what promise post-biological evolution may entail, the whole prior history of pre-human Life acquires a deeper meaning and more philosophic resonance as well, for living essence of the Cosmos flows in throbbing harmonies that underwrite the contrapuntal elegance of human nature, culture, and society.

To regard the whole ascending arc of Life from its beginnings in abyssal Time, should inspire no less awe and wonder than gazing upon the firmament displayed in pristine darkness of a clear nocturnal sky, that in arid regions far from urban light and haze can display a vaster multitude of tinier-appearing stars than typically visible elsewhere.

53. Lines in the Sand

Hence to rightly appreciate the teeming minutiae of biology and evolution—each of them pieces of a puzzle whose outermost perimeters are beyond our ken—both enhances and is advanced by reverence for life. What physicists like Einstein have extolled as "wonder" should be for open minds only magnified in truly considering the wonders of living phenomena. How, for example, is it that a swallow chick, introduced into a nest containing the eggs of a magpie—a bird often victimized by cuckoos that deposit their eggs to be hatched and reared by the other bird who often ousts those foreign eggs, when recognized in time, but tolerates the baby cuckoo once it has hatched—was observed to hoist on its back one of the legitimate eggs and toss it over the side, thus gaining more room and parental attention for itself? This behavior cannot have resulted from evolution—which conceivably could have provided baby cuckoos with the cunning to discard magpie eggs from the nest of an unwitting host—because swallows themselves do not parasitize the nests of other birds, nor are they ever thus exploited by cuckoos.[1] It is already amazing enough that young cuckoos are able to mimic the typical behavior of their adoptive siblings, and thereby win acceptance from a foster magpie mother, but the swallow chick's behavior—which further trials proved to be intentional—cannot be accounted for under any current understanding of how evolution works. Of course it could be explained away, perhaps by claiming that a newly-hatched swallow chick in its own proper nest might take similar action against a sibling egg of its own species. But even if that were the case, as no other report has indicated, it would be necessary to explain how the mutations supporting such a complex and arduous behavior were able to arise, even if natural selection favored those chicks whose being the first to hatch might indicate superior vitality. It is simpler to suppose that the baby swallow had some rudimentary awareness of what it was doing, and would not have thus discriminated against a swallow egg in the nest of its natural parent.

For to avoid that supposition at all costs, for fear of committing a scientific heresy akin to vitalism and the latter's invoking of mysterious influences—whose description as "life forces" or by any other name can neither augment nor diminish the chance of contingencies working from beyond whatever is or can be known—is to deny that Nature herself is endowed with a form of intelligence and of a consciousness, however alien to what humans may imagine as exclusive to themselves, that abounds in every cranny of a bio-friendly Universe and lends to Life, in a manner we cannot discern, its extraordinary powers of creative adaptation.. If that is not so, then the case for human consciousness as integral beyond all temporal vicissitude is greatly weakened, and along with it any reason for believing that our being and destiny transcends the course of a fateful juggernaut whose favored seat we, in such perspective, but fortuitously occupy. There are only two alternatives, and only one can be true. Either the Cosmos is alive and filled with magic bursting forth in every beetle, bird, and blade of grass, or else essentially dead, a scratching of senseless claws on the empty slate of endless time and space, while what might lie behind those dimensions could only be a further and unutterably more alien form of emptiness.

Thus there can be drawn a line in the sand in order to distinguish two sharply different portraits of the world. In one, an omnipresent life and consciousness that thrills in every fiber of the Cosmos, ever flows through countless channels and diversity of forms, that each and every one express a slender chord in concert with a greater symphony thematically proceeding from the Infinite, to hear whose strains may well confirm our faith. And in the other, across a division more stark than the mythic River Styx whose crossing marked final departure from sunny Earth to the gloomy Hades of departed souls, there lies an iron land of consequence and causes that the rod of Reason drives to grim conclusion where no further dreams shall come, nor music play above the fading whispers of oblivion. And should the latter constitute the case, its truth is only that of an abstraction we shall never prove. But should the former represent the real Reality in which we shall not cease to have our being though it shift into a state whereof our prior selves could scarcely dream, that truth is no figment of the mind nor simply mere idea, but wondrously alive beyond all grasp of calculation or constrained hypothesis.

Yet a different, more dynamic and vertical line can also be drawn connecting consciousness and spirit whose true extent, if any, must exceed all reckoning, with psychology that in turn is joined at its base with biology and evolution, that again are linked to matter-energy and its timeless origin—for the quantum world is innocent of Time—of the space-time Cosmos whose countless array of nuclear furnaces is where there were and are still being forged the atomic building blocks of physical existence. And of course the key juncture of strictly inorganic with living substance occurs at the molecular scale of DNA and of proteins that perform the functions of the living cell. Yet this molecular infrastructure hardly accounts for Life's total existence, because the keys of biological organization and the choreography of bodily functions at every level from the cellular to the cerebral, are held by some genius of Nature that compares to human intellect as equations involving the square root of minus one, an impossibly fantastic number that nonetheless has real applications, compare to the arithmetic of cards and dominoes. And where human biology meets the psychology of personality, emotion and dreams, of will and of reason whose workings spring from subconscious sources that themselves are rooted in a quicksand of neuronal subtlety, is in that cerebral theatre where we entertain whatever fancies may therein be bred. But the linkage of psychology and spirit is harder to identify because the entities or states involved submit to no definitive description. What they do possess instead, are qualitative properties such as the very assurance that such virtues exist and are in their subjective sphere just as real as the objectively factual realities uncovered by science. For the latter in their manifesting as knowledge are subjective also, and any trust in that knowledge as vitally worth pursuing, is no less psychological than faith in our essential nature as deriving from a state outside of Time and immune to entropy. However it is also within that state, from whence the spiritual nuclei of consciousness enter the more objective realm and assume a mortal covering, where the "mindscape" of knowledge and ideas is but one of the existential aspects of a non-objective realm, where fresh vistas keep opening before a traveler who has willfully undertaken the inward journey upon which all, howbeit unwittingly, are bound.

54. The Secret Ingredient

However, if reality itself requires the presence of an observer—because its objective aspect can only be reified through interaction with a complementary subjective polarity—then consciousness becomes an essential or perhaps primary ingredient of any Universe or condition that can be said to exist in whatever sense of that word. For the state whence Time itself began—which could be called non-objective in similar sense as that of the present, subjectively ratified objective Universe only insofar as either can be mentioned and discussed—itself is devoid of meaning and substance unless supporting or supportive of some quality of mind or awareness. And the latter if considered in dissociation from physical substance is then equivalent to a purely mental or spiritual mode of being—as for example, the Platonic realm of ideal forms or the mystical "cloud of unknowing"—that itself is more purely subjective than day-to-day consciousness through its immunity to such outward influences as noise and chemicals that can affect our minds by battering and warping the mechanisms of perception and thinking. Hence an objective meaning of "spirit" or similar words is that of subjective correspondence to the attribute of freedom whose struggles on the playing field of entropy that is often reinforced by tyranny, dogma, and the congealed oppression of social conventions like the caste system of India, constitute many of the notable events of History. And that is why the historical course of progress has been marked by actions that by advancing freedom have also furthered liberation of the psycho-spiritual aspects of human nature, towards the end that moral and aesthetic values shall someday rule over quasi-Darwinian virtues of institutional, political and economic security and survival.

Yet the long upgrading of organic forms that preceded human history is also a story of growing freedom, whose steady advancement in the timeless ages leading up to the makers of tools and fire is clearly apparent in the difference between a graceful dolphin or deer and those ungainly lungfish or primitive amphibians whose rudimentary limbs and crude auxiliary lungs—that may have evolved to help them cope with low levels of dissolved oxygen in increasingly shallow waters of their habitat[1]—enabled them as the highest form of animal Life to claim a new outpost on the shore, an even more momentous move than what carried humans to the Moon. And in that view of progressively expanding degrees of freedom, Nature can appear an outward expression of some inward and dynamic essence no less than human endeavor and aspiration may seemingly betoken an immortal soul, whose own inward essence ever seeks to colonize, as it were, the outward vales of illusion. Thus can easily be imagined how some subjective dimension that living things outwardly proclaim, has been the deepest driving source behind progressive refinement of biology, regardless what agencies or processes that science may identify as key to all the increments of Life's ongoing journey.

For, just as known mechanisms of the brain are vital to manifest the functions of consciousness despite what character of a non-temporal res ipsa it may possess, in the physical world of birth and dying knowable factors involved in biological evolution can tell us little of what meta-causes or contingencies metaphysically enfold its outwardly stupendous panorama.. For the whole of that throbbing tapestry exceeds the sum of its parts in nearly analogous sense to how the human mind is of immensely greater range and versatility than could be reckoned from a data base of all the neural hardware, feedback loops, and other workings of our sensory-cerebral theatre for all of the human illusions that keep skipping over the surface of an oceanic Magnum Mysterium. Yet if the latter also holds the very core of our being, its ultimate secret may be more accessible than much elusive trickery of the magic show behind whose tireless display that very secret lies concealed. While finding the soul, in other words—a mystic axiom whence all rhyme and reason of the world derives—may only take an instant in some timeless moment of revelation, the whole future history of science might not suffice to learn how all the ways of Life are ever interweaving, writhing and unwinding.

For true freedom can only be sourced outside of Time, in whose cycles and processes were we utterly imprisoned, our very being should then be entirely deterministic and any hope that death could prove no worse than liberation from the clutches of decay, simply a comforting conceit engendered in brains that are at birth already dying. Yet Life itself presents at every turn such wondrous creatures as the shape-shifting octopus that can mimic the appearance of a flounder and many other marine animals, changing its whole shape and coloration like some legendary beast from Greco-Roman or Native American mythology.[2] Thus while a world of rampant information and disease, of financial abstractions clashing in the clouds of cyberspace as ragged armies wage mindless conflicts far below, of chemicals that slowly kill while shiny goods keep filling the sterile halls of commerce in obedience to dehumanized economic equations, may appear as hard reality, Nature herself remains a dream—both beauteous and terrifying—that deserves to be admired far beyond the artificial fantasies that currently enthrall a large portion of humanity. And that is why the dream of reweaving civilization back into the tender web of Gaia, and of reintegrating the biosphere with human nature may well be realized in the fullness of Time, that surely before any such vital awakening shall witness many sorrows. For when and if that platform of true security for a heretofore self-endangered species shall have been attained, our ever-dreamy lives will fully harmonize with the greater dreaming of a Cosmos whose glories are both natural and Divine.

And in such case, true security depends on liberty that in turn depends on faith—faith that the deepest wellspring of our nature abides in an extra-temporal domain, whose powers can help sustain greater confidence and freedom in addressing issues ever tossed by the temporal caprice that once had been attributed to gods and spirits whose whim astrologers and hierophants might pretend to access. For that freedom in fact is bestowed by consciousness itself, if the latter is indeed the most enduring element of every human unit, and perhaps of the entire Cosmos, rather than simply legerdemain of natural law or the chef d'ouvre of physical complexity. If the foundations of the world in other words are irreducibly axiomatic—implicit poetry of "the Word that was in the beginning"[3]—then to realize as much completes a circle whereby our selfhood can return to its point of origin within the axiomatic and accordingly self-evident property of consciousness, that is at once the covert ingredient of Life and foundation for cerebral machinations of reason that vainly strive to capture that secret. But if those foundations are both mutable and impersonal so as to yield a universe of chill indifference to our accidental species, whose every path can only lead to the crumbling edges next oblivion, then even obsessive fears for an illusory and ultimately doomed security than which naught else remains, may well be advisable. Yet under that grim scenario, on realizing the sum of those fears by keeping our appointment in Samarra, they shall finally be ended. Moreover, should that narrow prospect represent the most we can expect, a negative impossible to prove, not only does its lack of promise tend to obviate any argument that such hard truth should be faced, but a great deal of poetry and philosophy can be mined from the caverns of its sobering implications.

55. Axiomatic Authenticity

On the other hand, if some version of the alternate and larger truth obtains instead, so that the linkage of consciousness and personhood is axiomatic rather than merely rhetorical or scientifically explicable at least in theory, and therefore springs—no less than "strings" or whatever quantum-mechanical magic underlies all physical manifestation—from a nameless bedrock of Being, the implications grow vaster still. For then, the poetry and aesthetics of our human circumstance that reason cannot hope to encompass or resolve, gains an axiomatic authenticity as well, whose meaning is proven through its tacit recognition. Thus, what speaks to the heart is plain and granted greater currency than what seeks to engage the mind alone, especially because the latter and the former can combine as in words or works of art whose relevance remains self-evident against all testing of time and cultural entropy. In the best or greatest classical, popular and indigenous music, for example, heart and mind are inseparably bonded, as they are to greater degree in "places of the heart" than in the "mindscape" that nonetheless retains its own inherent fascination. And yet, those works of intellect whose authenticity does not depend upon emotive apprehension but on ironclad rational truths as with theorems in mathematics, acquire a relevance that is axiomatic as well, because they express a stringent aspect of the world endowed with impersonal purity of a "hard and gem-like flame." In any universe, the ratio of a circle to its diameter, for example, would have to be the same transcendent number that we know as pi, and in any civilization lacking the concept of nothingness as codified by the number zero, the scope and scientific uses of mathematics would be greatly diminished.

Therefore, in a sense, all universes have to derive from or refer to the same ideal basis, however varied their physical modes of existing. Yet it is also striking that the equivalent logical certainty once thought proclaimed by natural laws interpreting such factual truths as that matter consists of atoms and molecules may never be completely realized, because research keeps uncovering further strata and crannies of subatomic and other subtleties that only underscore how far beyond their evanescent state abides the stranger subtlety of consciousness, whose sovereignty enfranchises those very minds who persistently are trying to unveil its secrets.

Thus it is rather ironic should those dreamers imagine human awareness to be that of automatons whose pseudo-consciousness is generated in an inter-nested stack of biological mechanisms that blindly drive and leverage themselves, rather than an irreducible property of personhood inhering within that indisputably indispensable machinery—and yet from their seat of presumptive entitlement, regard as victims of a glorious deception whomsoever happens to feel endowed with a metaphysically substantial soul or self. Yet either idea, whether of machine inside the person or of person inside the machine, both of which from analytic perspective are actually less logical than psychological, exists only in a theatre of the mind whose conceptual thespians are often enormously less versatile than the stagehands—the neurons, hormones, and various physiological functions—who make the entire production possible. And in that sense all thinking and ideas (including this very statement) are simply an illusion, and human wisdom rather feeble as compared to the wisdom of the body, by whose unflagging toil are upheld all cultural and personal fairy castles in the clouds. Thus, when a similarly superlative meta-logic of Life on grander scale is displayed in the virtual miracles of evolution, intellect can manage little more than to pick out its salient rational features, namely that "things change" and must do so in a meaningfully progressive manner in order to justify being called evolution—for if there were no rhyme or reason for change, scarcely any order could be left in the universe at all. And in that case, it is hard to imagine what might still exist, insofar as order and existence are nearly synonymous. Accordingly, the origin and evolution of Life could be seen as almost inevitable, and the identifying of its chief principles as genetic mutation and natural selection hardly subject to challenge—insofar as even a God who created Life would seem unlikely to have ignored those principles in doing so while producing a Universe that in all other respects is unquestionably organized under natural laws that are unshakable, however likely to remain ultimately unknowable as well.

And in fact, a metaphysical equation can be shown to abide behind or to substand the very existence and necessity of natural laws. That is because if God, or the Divine for those who favor an impersonal designation of the sacred, represents the highest or absolute degree of freedom then lesser degrees reciprocally imply whatever rule of laws must replace any freedom that is lacking from those layers of Being that grow increasingly subject to stricter governance the further they fall away from the most primal and unconditioned state of origin. Thus, whoever departs from their own spiritual source of freedom by rejecting all hope of its existence—not that mere verbal or intellectual denial, or for that matter affirmation, may necessarily affect the existential ground of anyone's actual inward soul or personal happiness—may reciprocally come under more stringent restraints on thinking, as when dogma, whether political, scientific, or even religious dogma whose formulas for salvation may not encourage easy access to spiritually altered states, enslaves all rational powers in its defense. In other words, Christians, Muslims and Jews who accept as holy the prophet Moses and yet ignore his injunction to abstain from killing, have placed themselves under whatever constraints that wars are bound to entail, whereas those who claim that religious hypocrisy demonstrates the falsehood of all spiritual hypotheses are also constrained through their dedicated reaction against hardened religious opinions that themselves may simply indicate a surrender of liberty in exchange for whatever security such views may provide. And indeed, that form of surrender may be wiser than vainly struggling to think when already caught in a spider web of legal, biological and metaphysical laws and limitations.

Yet paying lip-service to some higher truth may confer no superior freedom either, insofar as the psychology of personal freedom is more organic than mechanically dependent on opinion or belief—which is not to say that belief-systems, as for example in the "old-time religion" of traditional societies, cannot lend a supportive role in helping to preserve either personal or social stability. Hence the kind of faith that can both enable and be enabled by personal freedom may lend firmer assurance of the irreducible meaning, or axiomatic authenticity, of existence than rationally grounded thinking or beliefs, any number of which have been proven wrong or rendered dubious in the course of History and whose mutual opposition with regard to questions that seem fated to remain undecided may have a zero-sum result—should diversity be deemed confrontational, as need not be the case. And taking that meaning as an axiom can also lend substance to values such as reverence for Life, whose universal application would help to foster a society whose elevated modes of thought and feeling would reflexively enhance security of every kind beyond what purely defensive measures can provide. For to the extent that faith can cast out fear, the living of life assumes far greater importance than its mere preservation, an effort doomed to fail in any case on finally facing Death, "that all he chance to meet he slayeth."[1]

56. Dreaming the Dream

Yet that last statement can be translated into saying that taking risks often has Darwinian benefits, and that ignoring immediate or obvious perils, like storms that sank many of the ships that first came to America, may result in improved chances of survival or success for either oneself or the species. Accordingly "faith" has a bio-psychological (as opposed to psycho-spiritual) explanation which can displace any notion of its having mystical significance as an attribute that radiates from the soul—which in that case must also be jettisoned. But in the spiritual Universe posited by faith—where "beyond lies the great darkness of the ultimate Dreamer, who dreamed the light and the galaxies" and where "before act was, or substance existed, imagination grew in the dark"[1]—there is more conceptual room than in a lesser Cosmos where all phenomena trace back to some exclusively physical origin or network of causal machinery wherein no Gods, ghosts or gremlins are lurking. Thus in a larger, all-embracing Cosmic context—where the surreal is more apt to be or become real and vice-versa—there need be no conflict between spiritual and scientific laws, since the latter are nested within the former and remain valid in their own proper sphere. The Darwinian virtue of risk-taking that has encouraged the selection of genes that promote adventurous behavior like the first human migrations out of Africa is fully compatible with a genuinely spiritual assurance that absorption into some alternative condition more appealing than sheer oblivion will be what concludes our mortal existence. And that end will be the beginning of a larger dream for "a searcher for some transcendent realm beyond himself" who "searches as the single living cell in the beginning must have sought the ghostly creature it was to serve."[2]

Yet a spiritual Cosmos also allows for what its tamer, de-godded cousin cannot permit so easily, namely parameters able to accommodate the reasons for phenomena that lack any conceivable scientific explanation. For example, the selection and inheritance of complex life cycles like those of parasites who program the behavior of their hosts, of molecular wizardry such as repair of DNA purposefully carried out by protein molecules, or molecular mechanisms like the rotary flagella of bacteria that are said to possess "irreducible complexity," because their various components would seemingly have had to come together as a functioning unit in a single evolutionary leap, rather than to have arisen and been selected individually.[3] And even if the flagellum, for example, was once a free-swimming organism that attached itself to a larger bacterial host to form a symbiosis that was then replicated through succeeding generations, the wealth of intricate details that would have to mesh in order to accomplish the entire transformation is quite staggering. And these would have to include whatever motive or impulse initially prompted both tiny animals to form their partnership. Thus, while avian capacity for flight apparently developed through countless generations from rudimentary beginnings, as limbs that were evolving into wings could continue serving some useful purpose along the way, it is harder to imagine a mechanism more primitive than the rotary flagellum from which the latter could have gradually developed, even if it once belonged to a creature that evolved separately from the larger bacterial hosts whose propulsion the flagella now provide. The early steps of Life which led to the formation of fully functional intracellular machinery, in other words, are more difficult to conceive as having happened in incremental stages than so to envision the gradual metamorphosis of ape-like hominids into modern Homo sapiens. Yet for these initial stages to have happened all at once, as if by the hand of an intervening angel, could also appear at odds with subsequent evolutionary change having occurred in leisurely increments extended through the ages that precede all human memory.

Thus the hardest evolutionary puzzles such as how complex chemicals were transformed into living cells, in which those chemicals have somehow learned to obey the delicate choreography of a cooperative association that constitutes the cellular body, may provoke a desperate leap into speculative waters whose reality science can neither prove nor deny—and where some innate wisdom of Nature akin to the virtual intelligence that coordinates and maintains all systems of the human body, could have played a part in evolution and brought about genetic change in a manner that is hardly "random"—a term whose definition is truly open-ended—but instead no less purposeful than the behavior of human individuals and societies .

Yet living phenomena, including all those creatures whose evolutionary pathway has been broader and more winding than explanatory accounts might be able to suggest, result not only from causal contingencies far deeper than are likely to be identified, but also because certain non-physical and purely ideal principles that must govern any universe ensure that they do so. For instance, if existence implies order, and if order is subject to change, then that same process of change is compelled to represent evolutionary advance, since it could not go backwards towards lesser degrees of complexity and organization without having first reached a point from whence to retreat. And the outcome of that advance has no special reason to fall short of including living things and even conscious intelligent beings and societies. For if living cells or even simply viruses are already miraculous, then the miracle of consciousness is no less likely to appear.. Otherwise, in order to remain within whatever bounds of probability that the emergence of life and awareness might seem to have defied, the process of change would have to turn around at some arbitrary juncture and start going backwards before the magical chemistry of life could begin to take hold, and in that case there of course would never have been any form of intelligence able to say at exactly what point that reversal should occur.

Furthermore, to allow the capacity for evolutionary change as being inseparable from any conceivable cosmology is inconsistent with restrictions—other than barring egregious nonsense like talking mice or marine sponges in human attire—on what outcomes, including the neural machinery enabling awareness, are likely to be generated by a process whose logic is virtually ingrained into physical Reality. For the ultimate framework or most intrinsic laws of that reality consist not only in hidden hyper-spatial dimensions or in elusive equations being pursued by quantum or string theory, but in principles long recognized through concepts such as freedom, through whose multiple degrees both Darwinian evolution towards the expanded physical freedom of superior mobility and cognition found in higher animals, and its psycho-social successor in human societies that are still evolving towards greater liberty and away from fear and violence, have passed and are passing.

Hence, while Life having sprung from the relatively simpler though still daunting complexities of physics and chemistry may seem immutably enigmatic—although perhaps tractable to some prospective grasp of general rules that might even be able to predict its occurrence in such bleak environments as the moons of Saturn and Jupiter—biological systems have no less of a rational reason to exist than their non-living atomic substrate, in any conceivable Universe. For this or any world can only proclaim the ineluctable requirement that there has to be something, in lieu of the sheer impossibility of any actual non-existence. And by similar token, the very absence of anything, such as conscious observers, from an existential condition whose logical necessity is hard to dispute, is apt to be filled in the dynamic course of change urged ever onward by the vast potential of a Cosmos metaphysically transcendent of the physical complexity which already beggars calculation even within a single living cell. Yet the prospect of an endless variety of what can or could be known being set within a larger framework of what shall ever remain beyond our knowledge, should hardly obstruct the scientific journey nor its affiliated task of trying to cleanse the Augean stables of expanding knowledge from all the loose ends of inexplicable phenomena that journey is bound to encounter—a task more Sisyphean than Herculean. For to realize that the path of discovery shall never attain an ever-receding horizon nor its accompanying thirst for explanations ever be quenched, is surely greater cause to rejoice than any fantasy that the scientific adventure might be safely retired when the stables are thoroughly cleansed and converted into sterile ivory tower condominiums.

Thus, on the most purely abstract level where can be met such irrefutable arcana as are derived from concepts like infinity and are apt to bear tricky implications that inexorably seep through the walls sheltering our finite house of knowledge and perception from an enveloping immensity, the vying views of a spiritually-empowered Universe as versus a leaner and meaner one whose list of rules begins, "No gods allowed," are simply alternate ideas of Infinity itself. For the first conception tolerates not simply the unknown, but versions of it equally remote as the higher, non-countable ranges of mathematical infinity. But the latter view is comparable to saying that the major role for Infinity in having any rational connection to life, the universe, or human destiny is played by the endless yet "countable" permutations of complexity—countable because, unlike the non-countable number of all the points on a line segment, they could hypothetically be matched in one-to-one correspondence with the series of natural numbers. Of course, it is also true that to speak of the Infinite in a metaphysical sense transcends any mathematical analogy, whereas the "non-countable" versions of mathematical infinity also appear in physics, for example in the form of transcendental or supra-arithmetical numbers like pi or the square root of minus 1, which accordingly could be seen as loopholes between one level of logic and the next, analogous to linkages connecting life and inorganic matter. But if no further loopholes or linkages than what could, at least hypothetically, be explained by some sort of "quantum logic" are those that lead from life to psychology and spirit, then nothing may remain beyond the cold calculation of physical complexity, chaos, and the quantum flux to support our ephemeral dreams, including what then becomes the utter fantasy of having or being an immortal soul that shall awaken into larger freedom when the grinding jaws of entropy have torn its mortal frame asunder.

But in the latter, scientific materialist view, the world and all its phenomena including the consciousness of those adhering to such a philosophy becomes either deterministic or random, or possibly both, as when a sequence of mutations serendipitously happens to shape the emergence of some new and useful characteristic like the wings of a bat, after being triggered by random events such as interspecies transport by viruses of genetic material, the shuffling of genes during cell division or even cosmic rays. For example, the uncanny ability of the sonar of dolphins to distinguish between different kinds of fish, demonstrating a far superior sensitivity to that of sonar devices designed by human engineers, must be regarded as a lucky accident that came about because the ancestors of dolphins had been forced to run a harsh selective gauntlet that favored those individuals and their progeny for whom genetic mutations had provided the gift of sonar that allowed them to detect and catch more fish, and in whom that gift consequently became most fully refined. And the primitive basis of sonar that was shaped over many generations toward its final perfection by the selective process sprang from mutations that may at first have been accidental but found a purpose after entering the path of dolphin evolution. They were not put to use through some innate, instinctive wisdom of the organism itself—even though we might attribute to the wisdom of the human or other animal bodies their coordinated functions and virtually miraculous powers of recovery—because that would suggest some mysterious mentality working through Nature herself to craft the artistry of Life and to channel its evolutionary course. But if, therefore, life and evolution are, however exquisitely subtler than any possible conception of the human mind, fundamentally the blindly causal operations of a mechanistic determinism, then so are human subjective choices to believe that such must be the case. And if so, then that very belief as well as its converse are simply incidental products of one aspect of a psychology fostered in the human brain that itself arose from an ocean of causality whose depths shall never be plumbed, despite their lacking any of the metaphysical parameters, factors or elements that would inform a Universe aglow not only with stellar radiation, but more supernal and inward fires.

Therefore the Cosmos that lacks any components of a kind described as "spiritual"—meaning either they cannot be tested or examined by scientific scrutiny and rational analysis, or else that they are in fact irreducible axioms whose fundamental role is recognized by minds that are grounded in an all-pervading dimension of awareness that is equally fundamental—is an empty set, because it can include no fully autonomous observers who are not utterly subjected to its ruthlessly mechanistic objectivity. And it is also an empty set because those very limitations which would make it possible to define consciousness as being solely an "emergent property" spun from a dazzling though mindless flux of quantum and biochemical activity, also render the universe finite in all but sheer physical proportion, and accordingly infinitesimal insofar as having been, at least in such restrictive theory, divested of the true Infinity—from whence the world can only have emerged or else in which it must continue to subsist, for any explanatory boundaries science may try to impose on awareness can hardly be extended to encompass the entire Gestalt of the Magnum Mysterium.

On the other hand, to describe consciousness as an "emergent property" in a larger sense akin to how the physical Universe itself may have emerged or precipitated out of some unimaginable state of pre-existence, is nearly a tautology. For the neural mechanisms that allow awareness to manifest in the physical dimension have assuredly arisen from the background of sub-human life, concerning the varied quality and character of whose own forms of awareness we can have little conception. However, it is not far-fetched to suppose that the subjective experience of creatures who display human-like behavior, for example aggression in fruit flies, may resemble that of humans who are acting in similar fashion, despite animal behavior having a genetic basis as revealed by experiments that were able to breed increasing aggressiveness into successive generations of fruit flies.[134] For otherwise, it would be necessary to argue that the human form of such behavior did not have any genetic basis, meaning that the reasons for human aggression and its historical consequences like the Mongol conquests or the momentous failures of the Napoleonic and Nazi invasions of Russia, must have been purely metaphysical. The latter argument, however, is not required to uphold the concept of a spiritual Universe because that canvas can embrace the physical and all of its intricate levels of structure and mechanism including the genes of fruit flies and humans as part and parcel of a greater metaphysical surround whose trans-finite parameters are no less all-pervading than quantum reality itself, whose own peculiar magic could therefore be regarded as Divine..

Thus the deterministic Darwinian regime that would be fated to remain a hollow echo-chamber filled with the jabbering of idiots whose foolish dreams are doomed to fade away, if denied any mystical ingredient, need not be trivialized or rendered unworthy of attention by existence of the spiritual, but instead by connection to the latter becomes more strongly reified as a kingdom uniquely endowed with its own authorities and powers—the "Glory of God" in its most tangible form. And in fact, those same laws and powers can lend a source for poetic illumination of those starker aspects of human existence that by contrast add meaning to its moral victories, just as the affirmation embodied in a work like Chartres cathedral is greatly magnified by having arisen amidst the peril and hardship of mediaeval times. For just as physical evolution first perfected vision, and then refined the cerebral capacity whereby the subjective aspect of that sense becomes an agent of human dreams, ideas and ideals, so has a subsequent post-biological evolution introduced the concept of enlightenment and of progression towards an inner light that shall increasingly illuminate both heart and mind until it can be fully realized even in the nominally external world.

And that same realization, clearly, needs to manifest through social justice, cultural authenticity, and harmony with Nature, whose universal acceptance as major objectives of civilization would not only allow our species to claim the distinction of being human, but in a globalized society where any local infection can sicken the whole is vital towards sheer survival. For the starkly objective value of survival can no longer be detached from the more subjective virtue of possessing sufficient humanity both in mind and heart to fully focus on resolving those issues that could otherwise tip our species into a maelstrom of assorted horrors if not into the gulf of extinction. In its post-Darwinian phase, in other words, evolution has led us to a world where it is no longer true that "a living dog is better than a dead lion," because only a leonine attitude towards current global problems, rather than slinking away from them, can offer much hope of a future where survival is even worth the effort. In any case attaining such objectives as environmental sanity, economic sustainability and social justice is the only way to avoid any prospect of bitter struggle against the vicious entropy that if encouraged by all too human greed and negligence, could winnow humanity down to a ragged remnant shorn of the comforts of all but the crudest technology. That prospect, however, also provides an instructive contrast with its more promising alternative, where a sense of civilized meaning and purpose could spring from the dedicated care and protection of a lastingly sustainable existence for those coming generations who shall stand or fall according to the relative success or failure of their forefathers. Yet that meaning can only exist in a Universe where life, substance, and spirit—or biology, physics and faith—are enfolded into an all-embracing whole whose non-finite boundaries encompass the intermingled realities of space-time and matter-energy, biology and evolution, and all the various degrees and kinds of consciousness, including those avowing that their "dream will never die."

57. A Crisis of Meaning

For whether or not our cosmic habitat is in truth a spiritually expanded reality, over the course of History a vision of meaningful destiny—or for that matter of an "eternal Now" wherein ultimate personhood enjoys freedom from temporal constraints—has become not only more compelling but often more challenged as well, most lately by the concept of a strictly objective Universe that may forever attenuate and weaken towards a bland and lifeless uniformity, which is one scenario that seems to emerge from analysis of astronomical data. Yet that same concept can be countered by an alternate theory of the observed cosmic expansion that foresees its eventual slowing to a halt and then collapsing back into a ball of primordial fire and the seed of a new Cosmic cycle as told in Vedic scriptures whose authors, if right in this instance, must then have discerned a key astrophysical truth without the aid of higher mathematics or telescopes. Clearly a crisis of meaning may hinge upon which of these theories is more correct.

Yet whereas it could seem that the picture of an endless dying into a sunset that shall continue fading long past any mind being able to behold it is a stunning rebuke against any notion of human life as meaningful, from an alternate view that if valid is subjectively grounded in the metaphysical truth of our being, less definitive aspects of reality keep feeding back into the physical universe and its biological vessels of consciousness, even those who, for reasons that themselves are subjective, espouse the kind of reasoning that says all mystical views are mistaken at best, and at worst egregious folly. And in that case, even the most strictly objective face of Reality shall conform to whatever requirements any better than a fleeting and figurative meaning for human existence must demand. And if so, then modern theories that echo ancient belief in an endlessly regenerative cosmic cycle may well correspond to the truth, whereby a Universe sufficiently sensible to produce intelligent life would not then contradict itself by ending in the existential absurdity of an hopeless condition from whence no further life could be created. Yet even if not, and the impending Cosmic night shall never be re-gathered towards the dawning of a new earth and heaven, there is obviated or diminished simply the meaning and purpose of biological existence, while that of the spiritual and its own inherent, extra-temporal essence should remain, apart from a colder celestial fate than any might wish to conceive. To put it another way, if consciousness and a self made of "non-self elements" themselves not conscious is merely illusion spun from the interplay of wheels within wheels of impersonal natural laws, how can its ultimately doomed persistence, or final disappearance, possess any actual meaning? Or on the other hand, if consciousness or the soul does transcend its physical framework, how deep a crisis should the latter someday crumble, especially when in a conscious Universe incorporating many dimensions of Being, decay of the physical shell we currently inhabit can only be regarded as a mandate of Destiny?

And if thus can be resolved the existential dilemma whose grimmest reading finds that "meaning" and similarly slanted words are simply wishful effusions from the lips of an ephemeral human spark that is fated to dissolve into a senseless scurrying of particles and radiation in the ever bloating Cosmic night—and whose somewhat less gloomy interpretation finds a perpetual recurrence of self deluded and utterly mortal vanities like unto ourselves in each new Universe, reaffirming Life through sharing, along with flowers and butterflies, in its resurgence from the old—then (providing both of those readings fall short of a greater Truth) the study of matter-energy, of biology and evolution, of human psychology, and lastly of consciousness considered as connoting soul and spirit, can each afford unique perspective on a common Reality wherein all those factors conspire to produce human embodiments, whose birthright is to achieve fuller expression through bridging temporal contingencies with the ideal and eternal.

And that bridge can only maintain a rational structure insofar as it avoids veering too near to the infinite, which in the physical realm resides not only in complexity, but somewhere past those horizons where galaxies appear to be receding at close to the speed of light. But in the ideal world as represented by mathematics and the arts, the arcane varieties of infinity that soar above and beyond the endless series of natural numbers are themselves uncountable, and this meta-fact of the Platonic realm of ideas and of dreams whose "mindscape" interpenetrates the endlessly malleable terrain of human psychology, also prefigures the nature of spirit and its purely non-objective consciousness, whose hallmark is the spiritual freedom imparted from the same Divine origin that also ensources the ideal of liberty enshrined in founding documents of Western civilization. And politically speaking, of course, it is liberty that has encouraged exploration of ideas, including those whose practical applications have furthered that very pursuit by means of technologies derived from scientific ideas obtained in the quest for knowledge. But in the spiritual sense where freedom reflects the nature of consciousness itself as being no less irreducibly axiomatic than substance and energy—or even more so, given the latter can be at least provisionally reduced to properties of the interactive web that is ever being woven by "The Dancing Wu Li Masters"[1]—

liberty may encourage a mad pursuit of visions and dreams in wandering ways of the Fool, more than assist the progress of sober understanding under patient guidance of the Hierophant.

Yet in an even more basic sense than expressed through adventures of the mind, freedom is also an ultimate property of consciousness by which all worlds and universes and their creatures are able to come into being insofar as they have not done so merely through some combination of chance and determinism, or randomness and causality, but in harmony with an existential axiom that virtually requires the inward nature of consciousness itself to be objectified. Hence, the various degrees of freedom that define respective modes of being from the mineral to the Divine who "created this universe from a fragment of Myself"[2] are constrained in accordance to the character of laws demanded for every stage of the hierarchy of manifestation. At the basic level of matter-energy, for example, physical law lends an order and precision which is adamantine and inviolable, and quintessentially portrays the supremely logical aspect of reality as also demonstrated in mathematics. And because that same principle of order could not be merely approximate and still allow the world to function, it depends on rules such as that every particle of a certain class like quarks or photons must be exactly identical to all the rest, including in range of variable properties such as vibrational frequency, whose differing values in photons correspond to the various types of electromagnetic radiation. Yet just as in mathematics the most obvious arithmetical order can be transformed into other forms that are far more profound and also of broader application to external reality—as where calculus accomplishes what arithmetic cannot—so has examination revealed that the basic structure of matter-energy and of space-time is far more subtle than any mere pattern of uniform bricks of matter or packets of energy. For example, while the behavior of atoms and of subatomic particles may be predictable at least up to where quantum paradox begins to fly in the face of ordinary logic, their indefinable essence is involved with the far from obvious nature of time and space themselves. Thus the fact that space is not simply a void—for the simple reason that actual nothingness, as opposed to the "no-thing-ness" of empty space that is filled with invisible energies, would constitute a more impossible paradox than those actual ones like the wave-particle duality of light that already pervade all of space itself—drapes the Universe with an additional veil of perplexity that can only be ignored by remaining in the shallows where questions such as how even the purest emptiness, like that of interstellar space or the blanks between these very words, is also something, are not apparent. And in the depths of such mysteries as cannot be understood, there lies more hope and consequently less a crisis of meaning than implied by any rationalist claims of being able, in theory, to illuminate those lesser mysteries than which some have pretended can exist no greater.

58. The Singing Enigma

But that bafflement of what if anything constitutes space-time per se, is rivaled by the "pop-eyed insolence"(a phrase also employed to describe how tree-climbing Australian lungfish look on human passers-by)[1] of the enigma presented by the elusive and dynamic order and non or meta-order of Life itself. For while that pattern, whose interlocking stories have grown ever more elaborate through evolutionary time, is like matter-energy also based upon identities—such as the DNA molecule whose fixed chemical code has bundled together the common descent of all living things from a single cellular ancestor (unless plural ancestors had arisen independently but with the same genetic code) by endless variations built on the molecular quartet of adenine, thymine, cytosine and guanine—there is no conceptual way to establish a logical bridge between the fluid choreography of living Nature and the more readily charted though still enormously rugged terrain of the non-organic realm so as to embrace both kingdoms with one overarching theory. For the comparison of Life with the inorganic substrate whose ironclad regime undergirds its throbbing kaleidoscope, is like that of a stream to the channel constraining its flow, or flirtations and intrigues of courtiers in a palace as compared to the mutely immobile guards before its gates.

And that is why, for instance, that the explanatory ploy of random mutations being hammered into useful form on the anvil of natural selection limps awkwardly when confronted by "evidence of synchronous and meaningfully related mutations,"[2] as apparently found in cases like that of the evolution of reptiles from their amphibian ancestors. The unfathomably intricate genetic dance involved in just this one small part of evolution—though a crucial one, since the order of mammals that includes ourselves almost certainly sprang from reptilian roots—would seem to defy any conceivable explanation. That particular macro-evolutionary leap, like many others, involved a suite of adaptations involving many inter-coordinated genetic alterations. Amphibians hatch in water as aquatic, larval forms such as tadpoles which seek their food in the water until they develop into the air-breathing adult form. But reptiles hatch on land, from eggs which contain their food supply and are protected by a hard shell which resists desiccation of the albumen that holds the water supply for the embryo, and of the yolk containing its nutrients. And in order to exit the egg, the unborn reptile young require a tool which happens to be a special tooth that allows them to break the shell, whereas many fish and amphibians dissolve their gelatinous container with chemicals secreted from the snout of the larval form. Furthermore, the reptile egg is also provided with a membrane or bladder called the allantois, which holds the waste products of the embryo's metabolism, whereas in amphibians these wastes are able to filter through the soft outer membrane of the aquatic egg and into the environment. Clearly, with regard to the finely coordinated character of the many changes that were needed to effect the overall transforming of amphibians into reptiles it stretches credibility to assume not only randomness for each separate mutation, but that "the harmony of many mutations was also fortuitous."[3] No single one of all the necessary adaptations, whether the hard shell, the allantois, or the special tooth could, if having arisen independently, been able to serve any purpose while waiting for the other parts of the system to come on line through sheer happenstance.

But if not by accident, then how did all of these transitional alterations occur at once? First of all, they actually did come about by "chance" insofar as the latter term denotes a boundary dividing the facts—namely that the metamorphosis of amphibians into reptiles assuredly happened, or that a tornado may haphazardly wreck certain houses while sparing others adjacent—from what may well remain the forever hidden reasons behind them. And secondly, this and many other examples of evolutionary legerdemain, involving a technology of Nature as baffling to us as television would have been to Homo erectus, can be said to have sprung from some indefinable holistic property of Life that was able to climb the ladder of natural selection in quite similarly purposeful manner to how, on a far smaller scale, human biology manages to cope with a whole gamut of challenges including trauma, infection and poisons like alcohol, that the human body has to deal with successfully to fulfill its appointed years. Thus the issue of how the "wise blood" of an individual organism can keep protecting its viability insofar as Nature's law permits is not so different, though human vision not reach so far, from a question of what more all-encompassing wisdom might have channeled Life's ascending toward the light of consciousness from the tenebrous chasms of evolutionary Time.

And in that expanded view of how organic change has kept reaching towards more varied forms and gracile expressions for reasons no better apparent than those for a whale's singing—yet obvious as the fact that evolution is the most hopeful example of something happening simply because it can—species adapt to challenges and opportunities as purposefully as cells in the body meet the conditions of disease and stress along with all the moment to moment metabolic and other requirements that confront their parent organism. Hence, through the origin of species no less than in living processes of individual organisms is displayed the "fundamental quality of life" which has been described as that "If in a living animal, normal structural and functional relations, either external or internal, are disturbed, activities will usually be set in train that are directive towards restoring structural and functional norms, or establishing new norms which are adapted to the altered circumstances." [4] That is why, for example, while "The hormone production of many endocrine glands is remarkably independent of nervous stimuli" ..."when it is advantageous to the organism, endocrine activity is sensitive to nervous stimulation. Thus the nervous stimulation of nursing regulates the secretion of prolactin by the pituitary, adjusting the amount of milk produced to the requirements of the nursling."[5] And when emboldened fishes wished to swagger from the shallows, or a rare breed of mammals to return to the sea, their intention—though doubtless instinctive as the creeping of an infant or a vine—towards altering their circumstances brought about "new norms" established through coordinated genetic changes that incrementally built a new species from the old. And that was because we live in a universe where the truth is not merely logical but also rational in the sense that a sonnet or sonata, in obeying a higher rationality than an equation, thereby embodies a larger degree of freedom pointing towards the final liberty of consciousness, whose multifarious manifestations transcend understanding. Yet consciousness per se informs the heart of all those truths that are self-evident because their axioms or principles are no less integral than the Kabbalistic Divine qualities or Sephiroth, towards constituting the warp-threads on which the whole Cosmic tapestry and its existential meaning have been woven. And since Life is also an irreducible axiom, its pulsating "song lines" cannot help finding new and radical pathways to evolve, including human advancement towards higher modes of thought that may evoke deeper certainty than those of today, though still but birds of passage winging through an eternal sky.

59. Pocketful of Miracles

Hence to grasp the sense of how some form or aspect of what is called consciousness in humans is also at work through all of Nature, one only need consider how even the simplest of living organisms can display the character of identity, that in human beings and other higher mammals manifests as the self-awareness that is shown, for example, by the ability of certain apes to recognize their own image in a mirror. Far simpler than apes and humans are sponges, whose organization is among the least complex of all multicellular creatures—in fact, sponges are described more accurately as colonies of cells, of which there are only two basic types, "one of which forms a cuplike sac and another, with long whips or flagellae, which lines that sac." This unit pumps in water, filters out food particles, and returns the waste water to the surrounding environment.[1] Yet even sponges somehow adhere to the principle of identity that is expressed in the distinctive character of every living species, because if the entire colony is divided into its individual cellular constituents by pressing it through a fine silken mesh, those separated cells will reassemble into a new colony, though not in the same relative locations they previously occupied. "But the new arrangement is completely different from the old one, with different cells taking on each of the necessary functions." [2] And from sponges, the ladder of complexity and of more definitive identity ascends to the class of invertebrate life called coelenterates, which includes anemones, corals, and jellyfish. "In one well-known colonial form called Tubularia, the soft stem which connects the polyps undergoes a spontaneous pumping cycle produced by waves of electricity passing between the cells. The communal movements of the separate cells have been called 'concerts' and seem to be coordinated by a 'conductor' or pacemaker cell of uncertain identity."[3] Hence Tubularia possesses a rudimentary nervous system though lacking specialized nerve cells, but the same type of system appears in a yet more sophisticated colony called Nanomia cara, a "siphonophore" whose buoyancy in the open ocean is provided by an individual cell that is filled with gas, while others "specialize in protection, food collection, digestion, nutrient transportation, and reproduction." and finally, mobility of the entire colony through water-jet propulsion that can move the whole assembly in any direction "even executing stylish loops for no apparent reason."[4]. Perhaps some genetic material from this creature was transferred by viruses or otherwise found its way into genes of modern abstract artists and composers, whose loopy creative tendencies could thus be more easily explained than by attributing them to some immaterial property of mind or spirit that rational science needs to banish from the Universe once and for all, in order that the human species and society might then more freely get on with whatever its finally demystified business might then be deemed to be.

Again, such living miracles can be interpreted mechanistically, and their origins explained by a combination of chance and determinism, passing over how and why the cellular members of these colonies first acquired the ability for cooperative behavior and the mysterious means of communication that allow such activity to occur and remain consistently effective. For clearly, the cellular members of these sponge or coelenterate colonies gain advantage by a mutual association that is accordingly encoded in their genes and preserved by natural selection. But to say that is no more inspiring nor informative than to attribute the rhyme and reason of creatures like Nanomia to the wisdom of Nature having assigned them a secure and vital place in the gorgeous fabric of Earth's living raiment, upon whose supremely functional poetry all of human life, society, and culture is irreducibly dependent.

Thus, our appreciation of Nature, and by extension of human life, could continue to expand without limit, towards a fullness of realization that beggars any belief in reason and its fruits of knowledge as being the highest production of the Universe—namely of seeing "the world in a grain of sand, or heaven in a wild flower."[5] And in fact it is that same realization that scientists themselves, after gazing on microscopic marvels of the endlessly pixilated biological kingdom, might extol as "wonder" even while failing to grasp, for example, how deeply defiant of understanding are such phenomena as the ability of certain beetles and wasps to produce a pheromone, a scent that mimics the chemical recognition signal of an ant species into whose colony they accordingly gain admittance. For such a talent is one that however long a series of purely accidental trial mutations could never hit upon and then become inscribed into the genetic code of whatever species of wasp or beetle—for example, the larval form of the beetle Atemeles publicollis, that dwells in the nest of a European ant, Formica polyctena, where it steals food and sometimes eats the ants' own young, yet is not only tolerated but cared for by its host—has obtained the gift of inveigling the hospitality of ants through sheer deception.[6] Yet language itself can also represent a kind of departure from that same immediate realization, whose gift is portrayed in the Biblical tale of Adam naming the creatures[7] and whose hope of a back to Eden re-attainment simply reflects a restless dynamic of longing that suffuses all of Creation. Meanwhile Nature's pocketful of miracles—things that cannot even in theory be explained or subjected to the rules of any rational system of thought but can include, for example, the rare ability of some fortunate humans (but not, perhaps laboratory animals) to inexplicably recover from seemingly incurable cancers—remains ever capable to produce yet more astonishments for those who search among its treasures that are scattered everywhere across the Earth.

60. Matters of Mind

From consciousness that is only of or sufficient unto itself, perhaps Creation comes—"One generates two, two generates three, and three generates all things."[1] And if so, that same property (that in turn has sometimes been assigned the three separate states of waking, dreaming, and dreamless sleep) in its being synonymous with universal mind, and accordingly axiomatic rather than epiphenomenal, may continuously uphold a world whose seeming objectivity has sprung from metaphysical foundations. And understanding what those foundations are, insofar as possible, depends upon referring them again to a consciousness whose ineluctable status implies both logic—in the sense of pursuing meaningful order—and freedom. But stringent, unyielding views apply their own constraints to stubborn facts as might appear impervious to explanation—for instance, the life cycle of certain creatures such as the "tarantula hawk" and similar wasps, whose hereditary instincts would fit the category of cases of which Darwin said "no doubt many instincts of very difficult explanation could be opposed to the theory of natural selection—cases in which we cannot see how an instinct could have originated, cases in which no intermediate gradations are known to exist," and a few others.[2] He deals with these by addressing just one of them—"the neuters or sterile females in insect communities" that "often differ widely in instinct and in structure from both the males and fertile females" although "being sterile, they cannot propagate their kind." But accepting this explanation as demonstrating that human reason can account for every aspect of the deepest evolutionary riddles amounts to subscribing to the psychology of "mind-manacled" conclusions whether in astrology, biology or physics sufficing to show that a reductively deterministic basis for all that may occur or has existed is able to preclude any "qualia" or metaphysical x-factors from having any relevance in either human or biological spheres of existence. One such concept, and perhaps the weakest, was rebuffed by the Shakespearean character who remarked, "Tis not in the stars but in ourselves that we are thus or thus" although one could argue that in hyper-spatial dimensions of a Cosmos that is both visible and invisible, the stars themselves are also within us, not only as the stardust of which our bodies are made but through qualities investing them as members of a collective "ecology of mind" beyond and yet reflected in our own. Humanity's longing towards the stars may rest not only on desire to escape the binding familiarity of daily life, but also indicate a more than grossly physical connection with the extraterrestrial environment.

For such constraints as reason may seek to impose so as to better define and thus more easily defend its territory, are routinely ignored by the meta-logic of Life itself, as exemplified in a jumping spider called Portia labiata. This arachnid's tiny brain, halfway in size between that of a fly and a honeybee can solve problems involving judgment and memory, as in plotting a course of attack upon its prey where its behavior is too plastic to be purely instinctive, or in negotiating a maze to retrieve a bait whose location can only be seen at the beginning of its journey and therefore must be committed to memory. Of course, its ability might be explained as a bio-computer program with the single-minded focus of a chess-playing computer, that evolved in order to solve a limited set of problems involved in seeking prey, rather than revealing the kind of decision-making awareness found in a dog or cat whose clearly psychological motives for a variety of behaviors are transcendent of rote survival instinct.

However, the spider also exhibits "a disconcerting plasticity in its behavior" as in being able to vary its stratagem of plucking the web of another spider in order to lure the potential prey to a more vulnerable spot, whereas other spiders using a similar ploy of plucking the web of a potential victim do not, unlike Portia, alter their method of doing so according to circumstances.[3] But if such apparently deliberate planning and purposeful behavior reveals an awareness beyond hard-wired instinct that perhaps may differ from our own more in degree than in kind, that could signify the attribute of mind in both human and non-human life as having arisen from a deeper origin than simply of being an "emergent property" or function of biological complexity. And in that case, what little the spider knows may not only be untainted by knowledge, but closer to a core of living truth than humans, ensconced in their intellectually and neurotically obsessed hurrah's nests of neurons, are readily able to suppose.

An equally striking example which helps to reinforce an understanding of consciousness, in the broadest sense of that term, as an integral ingredient of the Cosmos and therefore likely to have enhanced evolutionary change—though perhaps in guises as alien to the everyday as particle physics and equally hard to describe in words—appears in the genus of bowerbirds which are native to Australia. These uniquely gifted animals have discovered how to externalize the sexual display that is used to attract mates, so that it is no longer part of their anatomy in a way that could render the male birds dangerously conspicuous to predators. Instead, they construct artistic bowers as a lure to potential mates, instead of proclaiming their fitness by means of bright and gaudy plumage. And in at least one species this production involves the use of tools and manufactured materials—a piece of plant fiber employed as a paintbrush and pigment mixed from berries and charcoal "to decorate the thousands of sticks it builds into a ten foot long avenue across a forest clearing"[4]. Some bowers are "like thatched houses nine feet high, with several rooms, standing on circular lawns which are carefully manicured and decorated daily with bright-colored feathers and berries, iridescent insect skeletons, and fresh flowers"[5] all of which is tended carefully, with each decorative item replaced if it starts to decay or deteriorate. This behavior "in its complexity and refinement is unique in the non-human part of the animal kingdom"[6] and could thereby indicate how consciousness may first appear in the course of evolution as a function of whatever level of neuronal complexity—a measure that sheer brain size may not suffice to quantify—the evolutionary process has achieved. But that kind of speculation may also mark the barrier beyond which no further understanding is accessible. For even if a certain level of brain complexity had to emerge in the course of evolution in order to facilitate such intricate behaviors as found in the bower birds, that physical requirement hardly obviates any metaphysical parameter of mind pervading both Nature and human beings, as virtually axiomatic underpinning of a Universe whose phenomenal appearance does not cloak sheer emptiness, but instead what could well be considered its opposite. Hence whatever character or level of awareness may obtain in Portia Labiata, the bower birds, or in homo sapiens—or in cruder mentalities of their arachnid, avian, or primate kin—is not simply the quasi-magical blooming of ever-burgeoning complexity but the biologically focused manifestation of a formlessly primal yet fully dynamic ground of Being.

61. Dead or Alive: Apprehending Reality

And while consciousness, insofar as that word may represent an elemental axiom whose magic bestows all power to exist and function, stands little chance of being dissected by some formula constituted of different words, nonetheless the nature of language itself is related to that of the mind and thus of consciousness. For example, if "space and time as currently conceived may be recognized as mere allusions to more subtle, more profound, and more fundamental principles underlying physical reality" or if "the properties of space and time…may also emerge from the collective behavior of some other, more fundamental constituents, which we've yet to identify,"[1] those constituents could be described as principles which can be recognized and have been identified through language—as in "Truth is Beauty, Beauty Truth"—because they lie at the heart of our own, human existence whose core of being is synonymous with that of a Universe at once objective and subjective, encompassing no less than we ourselves the properties of both mind and body. Hence, for example, the ancient Vedic trinity identifies those key principles inherent in Creation and the spirit-soul of a person or of the Universe as Life, Love, and Light.

Yet it can be claimed that the spiritual reality those three words appear to signify may not in fact exist, but only the mortal one of natural qualities wherein love, life, and light are metaphors representing optimal conditions whose attainment is the goal of individuals and societies—a healthy ecosystem, harmoniously caring relationships, and the light of perception and understanding. And in that case the ultimate basis of mind and matter and of human identity is not some greater awareness that dwarfs yet informs our own, but simply an insentient though infinitely subtle substance-energy perhaps equivalent to some hyper-spatial state whence familiar space-time and its contents have been spun, like threads of silk from the spinnerets of a cosmic spider embodying the whole arcana of impersonal laws that each upon the others in a manner that no intellect can ever grasp invisibly depends.

But if the Vedic trinity instead refers to living principles, "prospective properties" or "qualia"[2] impervious to analytical resolution, from whose supreme coherence has derived all seemingly separate things, then intellect may bow before its higher Source and be enabled to discover in the depths of mind itself those truths by which all natural and human existence have arisen. For example, if spacetime is not fundamental (as suggested by the various interchangeable geometries of string theory)[3] then what may be most fundamental to the physical universe is thought or awareness whose dimensions are not temporal or spatial—a "dharma" suffusing the entire Cosmic framework. An equation like $e=mc^2$ or an idea such as contained in this sentence does not require any particular interval of time or spatial geometry for its existence to be realized. Moreover, just as a brain with its sensory input is able to apprehend the material world and its elemental constituents—whose quantum interactions are sometimes held to contain the secret of a consciousness merely generated from rather than paranormally affecting them—by similar token some non-physical "prospective property" of or called mind, soul or self may be the true observer in the realm of ideas, that itself is also a gateway or antechamber to the homeland of our spiritual existence.

And in either case, where one or the other of these alternate cosmologies may happen to be true—or even should both obtain, with a personal God of Love concealed behind an iron mask of unswerving laws that undergird the Cosmos—human thinking and perception are less abstractly than organically inclined to favor some particular subjective view of a world, whose assignment to whatever doctrine faith or reason recommends, may be of little concern for those whose inward security does not depend on ideological support. Yet insofar as psychological freedom can further understanding or vice-versa, there should be no barrier to shifting from the realms of theory and philosophy—in whose vast arenas can be found sweeping portraits of biological and cosmic history, as well as existential pillars whereon have been inscribed the secrets of the ideal temple they uphold—to smaller and more poignant places where faith can simply be practiced in wordless prayer that helps confirm our subjective sense of truth, while reason merely enables the daily task of ordering and making some kind of sense of what ever-changing circumstance affords. In any event only a living truth can truly be known, whereas that which might appear apprehended by reason alone is no longer alive and accordingly, along with those making the arrest, must suffer from deficiency of meaningful existence.

62. A Certain Slant of Knowledge

For as personal or collective knowledge grows like moss and lichens on the walls of a castle, while finding embodiment in artifacts such as cars or computers, it also colors the psychology of whatever mind or society into which that knowledge and its language or mode of thinking has been integrated. Hence prevailing views of life and the Universe are affected by the fact of our being immersed in technology at the expense of ecology and wilderness, as much as by sharing in a collective state of mind where an often notional science along with "dreams of reason" that an ill-defined rational enlightenment might prevail, have scarcely managed to displace religious prejudice and superstitious fantasies. For that displacement is a thorny proposition insofar as no human minds are either fully rational or capable of certainty as to what degree and quality of truth either science or religion may contain whereas prejudice itself, as in faiths that denigrate women or philosophies that scoff at the soul, shall scarcely be overturned in a prejudicial manner. Yet every new experience but leads on a path unwinding from within ourselves, who are primary nodes of a hyper-dimensional Cosmos as well as, perhaps, reflections of a Being who created that Cosmos from a fragment of His/Herself, including every "spark of My eternal Spirit" that "becomes in this world a living soul." [1] Thus every aspect of the mind or limb of awareness whether biological, psychological, or ideally analytical, must cooperate with the others to rightly assimilate and interpret, or perhaps discard, what is received or discovered. And whatever mental rebirth can thus be acquired each and every day is a resultant of that digestive process, combined with the struggle of consciousness or of spirit itself to become more fully realized in a world often steeped in ignorance. Thus, the climate of knowledge, science and culture have a virtually biological effect on daily experience, by warping our very brains and nervous systems in a manner that in turn helps to shape the psychological; determinants behind whatever forms of knowledge, "seemings in the mind" or styles of living may dominate. But from a less temporally tainted perspective, the key concepts and values of a "perennial philosophy" that has buttressed all of human knowledge and experience throughout the ages, have remained steadfast and been carried forward from generation to generation while ever preserving the clarity and depth of a valid portal to Eternity.

And knowledge itself, of course, is one of those values because insofar as scientific thinking (whose proper practice itself is a kind of knowledge) and truth can help to lance the boil of bizarre or stubbornly narrow beliefs, they can also reduce the danger that superstition might serve as excuse for violation of human rights, as occurred in ancient societies that sought to appease their capricious gods through human sacrifice. And today, the virtual superstition that says we cannot be descended from a primate ancestor of apes and man, but must have been specially created, can be warped towards tolerating current environmental abuse and social injustice because, according to the same brand of dogma, God will soon destroy the world anyway, long before the plastic gods of commerce and finance might have succeeded in doing the job. However, another key value was expressed by Socrates in saying that "the unexamined life is not worth living." Thus, the goal of knowledge for its own sake is one which cannot escape the scrutiny of self-examination, because self-knowledge can be a higher good than that of apprehending such external truths as may concern the nature of space-time, black holes, nuclear energy and DNA. Of course, introspective examination may prove ultimately futile insofar as the "self," whether regarded as spiritual or psychological, is apt to remain mysterious—in which case the pursuit of outward and factual truths could seem more promising.

Yet this kind of psychological examination can indicate, for example, that it happens to be human nature to want such civilized endeavors as scientific research to "mean" something and to grant our existence the dignity of a purpose less futile than the task of Sisyphus, providing that the achievements of progress are permanent and that History does not simply keep repeating itself through a long series of ultimately doomed civilizations But haste in trying to fulfill that desire has led scientists over and over again to imagine that physics, and even biology, have neared the end of their quest, without even pausing to consider what purpose some Grail of a "final theory" could serve if and when it fell within their grasp. And the answer is simple: that theory and its interpretive commentaries would be filed away or shelved and life would go on, mainly oblivious to whatever slender, shimmering truths concerning its tiniest constituents or most elemental patterns had at last been coaxed into the spotlight of intellect. Nonetheless, the quest may well continue so long as humanity itself or equally inquisitive extraterrestrials, with every new shard of knowledge of equally finite moment as its predecessors, compared to the boundless regions of uncharted lands and seas. For however voluminous the data banks become, or deep the understanding as to what may thus be signified, that whole of human wisdom however preferable to whatever came before, shall scarcely make a dent in the Magnum Mysterium that all attempts to penetrate are vain as "a wasp dashing itself against a window pane" while "God, less merciful than man, never opens the window."[2] Yet even such perspective on the true situation constitutes an irrefutable kind of knowledge, that we are in fact infinitely tiny sparks of life and awareness—though paradoxically retaining the Infinite within ourselves—who are adrift upon the bosom of an Immensity of which only the most evident and physical proportions have begun to be sounded. Meanwhile, new stages of the endless journey still ahead could begin by recognizing that the riddles of physics are surpassed by those of biology to comparative extent as the latter by what further mysteries that no slant of knowledge, however insistently its aura of significant import "oppresses like the weight of cathedral tunes,"[3] is ever likely to capture.

63. Nature and Grace

The fact that stratospheric hypotheses in physics like "string theory" have even been proposed, however, only highlights how far the meta-logic of Life lies beyond the rarest arcana of inorganic science, for in the case of many living phenomena such as parasites that program the behavior of their hosts (a stellar example being the larva of a parasitic wasp that after hatching from an egg laid in the body of a spider, then somehow commands the arachnid to spin a stronger web to hold its body securely after the larva's poison shall have subsequently paralyzed it to become an immobile living meal for the larva as the latter develops into an adult wasp)[1] no explanatory theories are even proposed beyond observing that the parasite's talent and life-cycle must be encoded in genes whose generational perpetuation is ensured by natural selection. Hence with regard to larger questions as to how evolution transpired, confirmation of its having done so through fossil evidence of a starting point as bacteria dating back a few billion years, and of the long progression of living forms leading up to the current end point of homo sapiens, cannot unravel more specific questions concerning what transitions, and how effected, led from shrew-like insectivores (and according to recent evidence, somewhat larger mammals as well) that scurried around the feet of large dinosaurs and probably fled from some rather nasty smaller ones, to bats and whales in a mere ten million years. Nor does the rational assumption that birds evolved from bird-like dinosaurs or dinosaur-like creatures, either of which must have had an early version of the avian "flow-through" lung, connect to any further understanding of what progression and by what means led to modern birds from what must have been some sort of amphibian or walking fish quite different from the first air-breathing ancestor of reptiles and mammals. Nor does the fossil record offer any clue concerning why most African monkeys of the Congo jungle lack prehensile tails while nearly all South American simians and some other mammals in the analogous jungle environment of the Amazon possess this useful feature.[2] Such perplexities defy all attempts to resolve them, beyond observing that the same sweeping parameters of mutation and selection must pertain in these cases as in all other instances where evolution has occurred.

For in fact simply to realize just how far the true nature of Life, even as compared to such puzzles in physics and astronomy as ball lightning, black holes, and the "big bang" lies beyond the grasp of theory could constitute no less a leap of understanding than for example a fully validated theory of "quantum gravity" and its message regarding the nature of space and time. Should the latter's structure prove to not be fundamental[3] that would only confirm that whatever yet deeper principles or laws might then turn out to underlie space-time itself, are inseparable from matter-energy or the latter's underlying Ur-substance or ultimate field. Thus Life itself might similarly depend on cosmic principles beneath its recognizable features like the genetic code, and even beyond that code and its means of conveying information be impervious to human understanding. The anthropic principle, for example, explains Life and evolution by stating that they had to happen in order to produce conscious observers because if those beings, namely ourselves, had not emerged we would not be able to ask the reason why. But that tautology or truism can also be taken to mean that the past is just as firmly bonded with the future as the other way around. For if time is not fundamental, in the sense that the existence of anything solely depends on temporal cause and effect, then the overriding necessity for existence per se—whose condition would clearly be absurdly trivial in the absence of consciousness—becomes a paramount and formal cause superceding the importance of any temporal chains of causality including organic evolution. And in such case, human nature must also have deeper than merely biological roots, thereby granting us a place in the Universe that is far more secure than could derive solely from the impersonal forces of chance and causation so beloved by scientific materialists and rational atheists—as they surely ought to be in a spiritual universe whose every power is an appendage of the Divine. On the other hand, it is also true that when an austere portrait of human existence whose gray-scale hues are causality and chance, is colorized by adding their philosophical siblings called Fate and Necessity, that portrait becomes more grimly compelling. And insofar as those human roots can be actually examined, that analysis can only proceed according to whatever facts can be verified—although those facts must needs include not only the traces of bygone ages left in fossils or the heritage of DNA, but the far more alien and cryptic evidence broadcast from distant stars that sparkle even upon the very verge of Time and perhaps, when drawn into the bottomless gravitational well of a black hole, are effectively disappearing into Eternity.

For what happens to be the case is that the majority of scientific discoveries themselves appear only to lead towards conclusions that are open-ended. Thus biologists are at a loss to even guess by what conceivable ingenuity simple bacteria are able to enact cooperative behavior as in exchanging a packet of genes conferring drug resistance between two different species.[4] Nor can science, despite earning credit for such wondrous discoveries, more than marvel at how, for instance, Chondromyces aurantiacus moves by some unknown means in one coordinated mass that is visible to the naked eye, whose individual members having emerged from a number of spores in groups of several thousand each, then coalesce into a single company exuding a slimy film while oozing this way and that across the soil, multiplying and consuming whatever is available until a scarcity of food is encountered, whereupon the whole association suspends its motion and rises up into a tower about a millimeter in height—a thousand times that of a single bacteria—at whose tip new spores are formed and dispersed to begin the cycle anew.[5] In such cases and many others, whose wonders long had dimly prefigured that of the cerebral theatre where the wonders of human psychology are routinely performed, the study of Nature has attained a threshold where the rhyme and reason of biology increasingly seem likely to keep eluding the grasp of intellect. For baffling as may often be cryptic or contradictory messages from the stars, their difficulties pale beside yet deeper obscurities cloaking how and why the poetry of Life has been written.

For just as beauty—a "prospective property" reflective of truth that only human and perhaps some other higher mammals may be gifted on this planet to perceive—becomes more elegant and expressive in the blooming, buzzing biosphere, than in the starker geo-sphere of jagged strata and ragged seas, so does Life sing more lyrically yet speak less plainly than the more straightforward prose of physical law which at its highest level, still allows some hope of understanding the intricate dance of quivering elementals that we shall never see. But the more deviously convoluted riddles of biology and evolution offer little hope of resolution beyond having extracted from them the vision of abyssal Time and the broad Darwinian outline whose twin pillars of variation and selection, or change and survival, are indispensable to any formal structure of existence. Yet in that very hopelessness is greater hope than that "the dreams of reason" might be someday satisfied. For that hope equals prospective promise that the irreducible enigma underlying biology and its "immense journey" is shared at the core of our being in common with all of Life, partaking of a timeless Magnum Mysterium that is both of Nature and of Grace.

64. The Meeting Ground

The gravitational power of the Unknown can lift above distant horizons a star of realization that our limited understanding, however useful in its proper sphere where many of those uses are of plainly Darwinian relevance, shall never attain the Empyrean view at times envisioned for intellect. Yet there isn't necessarily any more of a "there" there, in some hypothetical region where squishy mysterian semblances might dissolve to reveal their hard theoretical skeleton and where human intellect may be ill-suited to venture, than there is here, where cloudy imponderables collide to form the interference patterns of illusion. For both locations may be overseen by a Deity not disposed to favor one above the other, and if "God hath created all things for Himself, yea, even the wicked for the day of evil"[1] that Being might regard an angelic wisdom able to perceive in a flash the whole history of Time, as inherently no better than the ephemeral and often hard-won happiness of human beings. And even failure to appreciate that the gift of mind surpasses any treasure that mind may be able to create or discover, gives no cause for the ongoing adventure of which it has been said that "knowledge is our destiny"[2] to not advance so far as possible. For if and when that possibility becomes exhausted before a wall of thunder that proclaims, "thou shalt proceed no further," that barrier could simply indicate new dimensions wherein by abandoning all former means it still might be possible to enter, though doing so require a transformation of human awareness involving the finding and cultivation of those dimensions—new modes of awareness rather than knowledge per se—within the mind itself. And finally, that sort of discovery could constitute an opening towards self-knowledge and the "truth of certainty"[3] on the part of the knower who cannot be known yet holds the final key to the meaning of existence.

For the quintessential subtlety of the "real" Reality—which of course includes whatever explanatory schemes may be espoused by intellect, along with the minds that invest a biological infrastructure and roam the "mindscape" (whose true nature can hardly be framed in terms of language and logic, since it is the very source of those properties) in search of new formulas on which the hope of expanding current hypotheses depends—will either clog or slip through whatever kind of sieve may be employed to try and capture fundamentals from its ceaseless flow. Thus, for example, there is no agreed-upon account for how gravitons, particles thought to carry gravitational force at the speed of light in similar fashion as to how photons carry light itself and other electromagnetic forces, can escape from a black hole to exert that body's gravitational pull when photons themselves, unable to surpass the escape velocity which is that of light itself, cannot shine out of the hole and obviate its blackness, but are trapped within the hole's event horizon.

But aside from such questions—any tentative answers to which are not easy to elicit from authorities who may bridle at the sheer effrontery of anyone daring to ask them—spiritual truths are equally more cryptic and elusive than the formulas of rational faith, on which a host of often mutually contradictory beliefs are held by their various adherents to be unshakably established. Of course there must be, clearly, some connection between Scripture and spiritual truth if the latter does exist, even if that same relationship is one of Divine deception intended to ensure that the real Truth shall remain hidden from the unworthy even as its existence is being reaffirmed for the sake of whomsoever longs to flee from what they perceive as a Gomorrah of atheistic materialism and its secular humanist or epicurean philosophies. Otherwise, an even grander deception has been perpetrated, no doubt unwittingly, through such highly poetic works as the Bible or Koran, while whosoever may have thus been deceived shall suffer for it little in their lives, and even less in the form of dust that in such perspective they must become when those lives are ended.

Nonetheless, the broad parameters of physics, matter-energy and space-time and "the dancing Wu Li masters" may yet become enfolded by some all-inclusive theory that could, for example, delineate a sphere of vibratory resonance with whose crisply impeccable melodies the entire range of subatomic entities could be shown to correspond, perhaps with the aid of such wizardry as the six-dimensional geometry of "Calabi-Yau spaces."[4] And a clear and simple faith divested of dogma and moralistic stultification may eventually emerge from the crowded religious arena, as the iron grip of tradition is weakened by a growing sense of freedom that could seep into every corner of a global society that endeavored to apply everywhere the religious ethic of "do as you would be done by," which from a policy standpoint could simply mean prioritizing human resources and welfare above corporate and financial interests.

But neither of these broad advancements could even begin to show the way towards grasping the nature of the living ground of our being and of all science and faith, whose pretensions of wisdom are most sharply rebuked not by any human dissenters, but by Life itself as in examples such as the following. The female of a species of lightning-bug named Photuris pennsylvanica, which like other members of the genus Photuris flashes a coded message—specific to the individual species of lightning-bug—to attract its future mate, has also stolen the different code of flashes employed by females of the Pyralis lightning bug species, so as to broadcast an illicit signal serving to lure Pyralis males to a sorrier fate than what the hapless suitor had anticipated, namely that of being devoured by the deadly female deciever.[5] This behavior may of course be purely instinctive rather than intentional, having been written in the "selfish genes" to whose own survival needs the Photuris females' wickedness has, in some views, been attributed. But just how that behavior was first acquired and subsequently engraved in the beetles' DNA, and how and why thence summoned forth upon occasions where it can successfully displace the message more commonly sent by Pyralis pennsylvanica females to attract their legitimate mates, are questions whose unflinching analysis reveals the microscopic roots of biology—a wonderland where one might nearly expect to hear a haunting faery melody or glimpse a smirking elf—as more remote from comprehension than a quasar that outshines a million suns.

Thus the philosophical resonance of the study of living Nature, is that there is no "dead zone" of finality that can be reached by dissecting living systems down to their tiniest constituents, which are then presumptively revealed to be faceless and meaningless in and of themselves—the molecular building blocks of a glorious illusion that crumbles into dust in the wind no sooner than whatever brains were entertaining it have perished. That is but partially true, because the substance of intention and of consciousness, the very same that humans typically attribute only to themselves or to cherished pets whose owning of willful minds cannot be mistaken, is a part of the continuum from which all seemingly separate things are made and wherein they all consist. And in that continuum—in the Magnum Mysterium—there dwells not only all things and systems of life and matter, but the pattern of them as well. For the abstract or ideal basis of matter-energy and of Life, represented in but slender degree by human knowledge, both exists and does not exist as an entity outside of Time, and if that entity cannot be fully detached from the physical facts of which it constitutes the rational essence, as it were, then science must confront those limits that are set by the impossibility of fully separating the ideal from the real by extracting a comprehensive explanatory scheme or model of natural workings in any particular department of the Cosmos, from the throbbing pulsations of Nature herself.

And yet those same limits are also boundaries that shall be crossed or transcended in the course of human psycho-spiritual evolution toward a certainty of more abiding truth than could ever be unveiled by research or confirmed by reason, though intimacy with truth may empower intellect as shown by the conviction of its most enduring accomplishments. The extreme complexity and subtlety of Nature's genius that is revealed in biology to far greater degree than any other science thus marks the outermost extent where rational understanding can but grasp the what and not the how and why. How did an asparagus beetle, Crioceris asparagi, without some integral genius or "wise blood" that courses through all living things—a metaphor merely meaning to suggest what reason cannot fathom—evolve a chemical that binds with the asparagus plant's waxy coating to produce a glue that enables the insect to attach itself securely to a needle-like branch of the plant?[6] How do the various proteins in the smallest known bacteria, Mycoplasma pneumoniae, whose complex organization shows that "there is no such thing as a 'simple' bacterium," or in any other living cell, recognize each other in order to perform and coordinate their respective tasks as, for example, chaperon molecules that guide new protein folding, and how do they know their assignment and how to perform it,[7] without some "power in the blood" that imbues the biosphere, including human bodies and their bio-computers that may stubbornly believe themselves to be supreme? For that marker also indicates a meeting place for Nature and philosophy that also adjoins the supernal Infinite and meta-rational depths of Divine reality.

65. Reasons for Being

Hence, in being framed and upheld by an Infinite of greater kind than that of space-time extent and duration alone, it is just as natural and inevitable for Life to unfold and burgeon along countless pathways, as for the least particle of energy or matter, which are of course alternate states of the same underlying substance or condition, to even exist at all. The conceptually ideal basis for the existence of Life—which ineluctably includes evolution—is in other words equivalent to and not weaker than the abstract or ideal underpinnings of the space-time physical Universe. For in either case that foundation consists in the logical necessity of Being, in conjunction with Becoming whose potential flows from the Infinite Yet while the inherent laws and logic maintaining and effecting the whole process of Creation may be unspeakably elusive—but as Einstein suggested in saying that "the Lord is subtle but he is not malicious," not deliberately contrived to shame any seekers of understanding—the rationale behind the logic at work in procedures like the biochemical minuet that ceaselessly transpires within each living cell, is quite simple. Life, whether human or otherwise, is its own reason for being, whence the striving towards attainment of whatever state improves upon what may have gone before. For just as Being was implicit in the virtual non-being wherein, as related in Genesis, "darkness was on the face of the deep," so too are Life and consciousness irreducibly implicit in the sheer actuality of concrete existence. Thus no sooner than having emerged like a squirming hydra from the inorganic chemical flux where its potential was ever lurking, living Nature is bound to progress along a changing path whereon the more exalted and ideal states are constantly descending to meet and merge with those that from abyssal depths of Cosmic time have kept arising.

For in fact this meeting which also occurs in the theatre of human consciousness, has done so in a sense outside of Time and therefore introduced into the causal dimension of the Cosmos an effectively extra-temporal element. Human brains develop, rewire themselves adaptively and finally perish, but language and ideas dwell in a region unaffected by entropy or temporal vicissitudes and whose "mindscape" is accessed differently in each historical age and anew by every human generation. Yet the same conjunction of the ideal and the real, where the true metaphysical proportions of the Cosmos first start to be revealed, can also be envisioned as a window on the realm of unknowable reasons for those factual realities of the Cosmos, both living and non-living, that have so far resisted all attempts to master them by such explanatory powers as instead, may simply declare victory (as by invoking the "formal cause" called natural selection to serve as "mechanism" or effective cause of evolution) and abandon the field. Yet that same field also includes and is not separate from any observer who may venture into it in search of knowledge. And in fact those boundaries wherein understanding is possible and explanations seem dependable, and beyond which all hope of understanding seems remote, are more clearly defined in biology than in physics, where the most counter-intuitive observations can often be conformed to theoretical models whose "fuzziness," however, may or may not ever be erased by experimental disproof or verification. Hence there are alternative explanations for why many galaxies appears to be revolving faster than Newton's laws should allow, namely "dark matter" as hidden source of the missing gravity that compliance with those laws would require, versus MOND, or "modified Newtonian dynamics" which says that gravity at sufficiently large distances may diminish by less than the standard Newtonian formula of direct proportion to the square of that distance. But which of these is true may never be any more possible to prove by experiment than to know the dreams of a fox that dens by an urban stream.

However, in the field of biology, where obstacles to understanding are more daunting by orders of magnitude, there occur many cases where no conceivable theory can be found, even those which sound plausible but could never be verified. For example, the "irreducible complexity" of a phenomenon like the rotary flagellum of a bacterium that drives its motion like a tiny propeller, might actually be explained by the concept of a smaller bacterial cell that features the flagellar mechanism having attached itself to the surface of a larger one, although that likely unprovable hypothesis leaves a host of further questions still unanswered, such as how the smaller cell could itself have evolved incrementally the same "irreducibly complex" rotary mechanism, and why and how symbiosis of the two organisms occurred. The descent into impossibly intricate and tiny detail, in other words, becomes in biochemistry and cellular biology an even more dizzying plunge than in nuclear and quantum physics. And of course, well within the aforementioned boundary, beyond which lies the forever unknowable, are found many phenomena easily handled by natural selection, for example that of bacteria developing resistance to drugs like penicillin by means of genetically latent capacities clearly being favored by selection However, the question remains as to whether those mutations conferring immunity to medicine did so purely by chance, having previously occurred for some unconnected reason, or instead represent a deliberate biochemical response to changes in the environment. In the latter case, a species such as drug-resistance acquiring bacteria or the bears that became polar bears rather than migrate south from increasing Arctic cold have shown their "wise blood" as more versatile than commonly supposed, in its capacity to pilot a lineage through the gauntlet of natural selection.

But well outside the bounds of even non-testable hypotheses occurs, for example, the curious talent of certain bacteria that can pass to others of a different species, a packet of genetic material affording the recipient the same drug resistance as the donor. Moreover, the donation is clearly deliberate, as shown in photographs of the exchange being accomplished by a tube of protoplasm extending between the two cells.[1] In such instances and many others, the genius of Gaia, that also facilitates the neural and biochemical machinery whereby our fancies whether cultural, personal, or scientific are bred, so far surpasses human understanding as to leave little to say. What can be said is that, if that genius is merely figurative or mythical rather than mystical then we do not inhabit a living Universe and all knowledge is consequently nothing more than scribbling in shifting sands on the shores of oblivion. But if we are dwellers in a Universe pervaded by living spirit both natural and divine, then Nature and its workings including ourselves can only be mystical, for that its boundaries then cannot be smaller than the "boundaries of the soul" that in a world of true meaning should enfold human existence. Nonetheless an endless host of talking points and verbal constellations they engender shall surely keep emerging within the flickering circle of illumination cast by rational awareness, while in the midst of what remains uncharted wilderness, the poetry, philosophy and science of the human and Cosmic story will continue being told, perhaps to the end of Time.

66. Coda

And yet that ending, however far away is quite immediate as well. For it also corresponds to a boundary where temporal shores are in every moment lapped by the ocean of Eternity that beyond all mortal questions and vicissitudes remains, even for those whose mortally shackled minds may fail of liberty to so conceive, the place of our securely everlasting home. Meanwhile, life and human life are composed of an infinite flow of myriad factors that are mutually and incalculably combined and interwoven. And in contemplating all of evidence, theory and wonder regarding the stream congruent with that flow that is called evolution, its most sweeping significance may dawn and finally eclipse all reasoning why and all attempts to understand. And then can be heard a Symphony by whose harmonies all troubling discord is resolved and in whose mighty current every sticking-point of sorrow and contention washed away.

"There is a whole world, a real world that exists beyond space and time as we presently know it" that is "the mythic world of archetypes or ideals" that some have called the "imaginal realm."[1] For in fact, at the cutting edge of modern theoretical physics is indicated that perhaps "familiar spacetime is but a large scale manifestation of some more fundamental entity."[2] And while that world may seem real for many in their subjective experience, the best objective signs of its existing are miracles of living Nature whose supreme subtlety and covert beginnings beggar all powers of reason. Yet these miracles also include the magical transformations performed millions of times per second by the intracellular biochemistry of human bodies, in support of whose larger needs those molecular minuets are seamlessly choreographed. For all of Life and evolution manifest the "power in the blood" whose deeper dynamic forever informs and courses through them, and that springs from some placeless place in the Magnum Mysterium that ever enfolds and dwells within our mind and heart as well.

67. Conclusion

The nature of reality or of Being is most clearly explained by the Book of Life that is written throughout Nature herself, yet that nature is ultimately mysterious. For were it not so, and all of the hidden powers and reasons behind Life, evolution and the Cosmos were in some distant future time revealed—including how and why a slime mold, a colony of single-celled organisms, can organize itself into a food distribution network as complex and efficient as the Tokyo subway system[1]—then deeper secrets behind the secret thus unveiled would remain. Indeed, the very character of knowledge itself and of minds that entertain it would continue lurking, as it does today, as a further mystery whose roots are buried in the Infinite. "The goddess of Infinity who comes as Life-power and Nature, who was born from the elements and rests, having entered the heart: this in truth is That."[2] Yet from that Infinite is where salvation arrives, not on some given day or hour but every moment wherein the world is being continually created and renewed. And not just on the path that every individual soul shall follow, in the wilderness of Divine Reality, forever and ever, but for every civilization that accepts a visionary view of the Cosmos and a correspondingly generous estimate of human nature transcending scientific explanations while based in values like reverence for life and social justice, that are vital for true security that in this temporal realm can only be attained upon the plateau of post-Darwinian evolution. Yet even a morally strengthened security has its expiration date, while every civilization, however enlightened or humane, that provides temporary shelter for spirits passing through the world shall someday be recycled by the mighty engines of the Universe. And whenever the moment draws near for the gates of Eternity to open, those who occupy a vantage transcending fear, shall freely release the past and embrace what is to come, aware that Time itself is enfolded in the everlasting and supernal.

Notes

Chapter 1

1. This quote was recalled as having been read in Brian Greene's "Fabric of the Cosmos," but in lieu of being able to verify the source, other words from that book convey a similar idea—"after more than seven decades, no one knows how or even whether the collapse of a probability wave" (when a quantum particle impact manifesting out of the wave is detected at a given location) "really happens." (F of C p.119) , "implications of these features of quantum mechanics for our picture of reality are a subject of ongoing research" (ibid p. 11) or, "when it comes to the interpretation of quantum mechanics, the standard of argument suddenly drops to zero." (Deutsch, "The Fabric of Reality" p.335). Also, from Greene's "The Elegant Universe," p.108 "The debate about what quantum reality means continues unabated."

2. Andrew Harvey, "Hidden Journey."

3. This account may have appeared in "Lifetide" by Lyall Watson, but a diligent search in that non-indexed work and various other sources failed to obtain full confirmation, although clearly this author could not have dreamed it up. However, Grzimek's Encyclopedia of Animal Life provides a partial verification—after the cub is born and climbs on the mother anteater's back, the stripes on the fur of mother and baby do at least initially present the appearance of one continuous band. Having accomplished this feat, Nature may well maintain a camouflage effect, whose purpose appears to be that of deceiving predators such as eagles into seeing the two creatures as one and thus not trying to snatch the cub, by moving forward the stripe on the mother's fur to

stay aligned with that of the growing infant as it shifts its riding position, preserving the illusion of continuity.

4. This phenomenon was described in the NY Times "Science Times" section and can also be found in Dennett's "Breaking the Spell" (p.63) where Toxoplasma Gondii is referenced as "Zimmer 2000.".

5. Gordon Rattray Taylor, "The Great Evolution Mystery" pp.95-98. Also, on page 99 is related how the visual system of shrimps utilizes "a form of mirror optics, the mathematics of which were only worked out in 1956 as a consequence of interest in optical fibres"..."instead of using transparent lenses to refract the light, the shrimps bounced it off mirrors set radially." In other words, in creatures as humble as shrimps and trilobites have been manifested feats of Nature's magic, the rhyme and reason of whose accomplishment is well beyond all explanatory powers of human intellect that itself, of course, is an equally miraculous production.

6. The so-called Cambrian Explosion, that has been explained in various ways (most recently in New Scientist, 12 9-14 07 p. 18) and is discussed or mentioned in a wide variety of sources

Chapter 2

1. A famous quote attributed to the late J.B.S. Haldane

2. The lancet fluke's life cycle is described in Sagan's "Dragons of Eden." Curiously enough it is also cited by atheist philosopher Daniel Dennet in "Breaking the Spell" (pg.1), using the ant victim's hapless behavior of climbing up and down a blade of grass as a metaphor of religious ritual futility. To not see how profound a problem for science such parasites present and how

strongly their inexplicable capabilities suggest hidden parameters of Nature—a "twilight zone" beyond which anything is possible including sources of paranormal and religious phenomena—itself constitutes a stunning example of the blindness of reductive reason when applied to existential questions such as those attending the postulates of faith.

Chapter 3

1. Spoken by novelist William Faulkner in his Nobel Prize address of 1946.

Chapter 4

1. Charles Darwin as quoted in "Evolution—a Theory in Crisis" by Michael Denton.

2. For example, "who could live and who could breathe if the joy of Brahman filled not the universe?" Taittiriya Upanishad, 2.7., Trans. by Juan Mascaro

Chapter 5

1. The actual statement that virtual photons, not real ones, are the particle associated with magnetic/electrostatic force appeared in a college physics text viewed while browsing in a library, but this book could not be relocated nor its title recalled However, the nature of virtual particles as described in a number of sources would seem to identify them as the primary mediators of magnetism in similar fashion as how photons themselves carry electromagnetic forces such as light and heat (although presumably virtual photons play a role in these as well). For

example, "There are things called virtual particles for which the mass (or more correctly, energy) can be negative. But a virtual particle does not have an individual existence as a real particle." (Roger Penrose, "The Road to Reality," p. 67). Then again, "According to quantum field theory, an electromagnetic force is the mutual exchange of virtual photons." (Gary Zukav, "The Dancing Wu Li Masters," p.251) Or, virtual particles are "allowed only by quantum mechanics (and) carry the same charge as the corresponding true physical particles but have the wrong energy." (Lisa Randall, "Warped Passages," glossary. Further explanations occur elsewhere in the text).

2. Brian Greene, Fabric of the Cosmos p. 314, various other sources such as Martin Rees, Our Cosmic Habitat p. 76

Chapter 8

1. Same as for chapter 2, note 2.

2. A good source for comprehensive explanation of cellular biology is "Life Itself" by Boyce Rensberger. For example, "cells have the equivalent of a containerized cargo transportation system" in which the containers are called vesicles, but researchers have no idea "how a vesicle signals which way it 'wants'…" to travel on the microtubule network inside the cell, wherein all the various forms of motion may be provided by as many as a hundred different kinds of molecular motors." (pp. 40-41).

4. "Journey to the Ants" by E.O. Wilson and B.. Holdobler

5. One source would be Benveniste and Todaro, "Evolution of C-type viral genes…" from Nature magazine 252, p. 456-458, as quoted in Lifetide, p.68

6. Michael Behe, "Darwin's Black Box."

7. New Scientist, 2/16-22/2008 "Engines of Evolution" pp. 40-43. An evolutionary origin of the flagellum may exist in the form of "type III secretion systems," "a class of molecular machine used by disease-carrying bacteria such as Salmonella." This machine is used to inject toxins into a victim, and includes 15-20 proteins, several variants of which are found in "a subsystem called the protein export system" that "funnels replacement flagellin" (the protein from which the whip-like flagellar filaments are built)"subunits to the filament, using a mechanism remarkably similar to" the poison-delivery syringe of Salmonella and its kin. That concept clearly does not diminish the sum total of complexities involved in the evolution of both mechanisms or unveil the magic behind how either came about in the first place.

Chapter 9

1. Wilson and Holdobler, ibid.

2. Taylor, ibid.

3. Adolph Portmann, New Paths in Biology, pp. 77-79. But "if instead we look at the comma butterfly...we shall find that though the upper surface is again vividly colored, the whole underside is particularly 'cryptic'—small white commas on a dark background simulate the appearance of bark. This cryptic coloration is associated with a characteristic form of behavior: instead of tucking its front wing away while at rest, the comma butterfly pushes it frontwards; instead of hiding part of the wing pattern" (as in Oudemans' phenomenon, where folding the wings at rest forms a new pattern whose purpose is not concealment) "it exposes the entire underside—the underside as a whole become optically 'effective' and dissolves the butterfly in

its environment...in both cases pattern and behavior have been subordinated to a total effect."

Chapter 10

1. One of the various articles on this phenomenon is found in the Journal of Clinical Microbiology, September 2005, "Widespread transfer of resistance genes between bacteria." Another source is Wikipedia, "Horizontal gene transfer-transfer of antibiotic resistance between different species of bacteria" or, "Bacterial conjugation" which is transfer of genetic material through cell-to-cell contact, an operation that might seem to indicate that these organisms know what they are doing and could thus be considered intelligent.

2. Taylor, ibid.

Chapter 11

1. Lisa Randall. Warped Passages p. 380, Rees, ibid. p.115

2. Watson, Lifetide p. 165, quoting from Darwin's chapter on instinct in his "Origin." However, in this chapter Darwin actually lists several kinds of seemingly intractable difficulty confronting natural selection, and attempts to deal with them by addressing the single instance "of neuters of sterile females in insect communities" of which he then attempts to explain "only a single case, that of working or sterile ants.". The wasps, whose behavior pattern and requisite anatomical features would need to have arisen simultaneously to serve selectable purpose, are not mentioned

3. Watson, ibid. pp. 166-7. with reference to Petrunkevich, "Tarantula vs. Tarantula Hawk," Journal of Experimental Zoology 45: 367-397, 1926.

4. Discover magazine, June 1995 "Coming Onto the Land."

Chapter 13

1. Bhagavad Gita. A similar quote would be "Know that with one single fraction of my Being I pervade and support the Universe, and know that I AM." (Bhagavad Gita, 10/42, J. Mascaro trans.).

2. Scientific American, Oct. 1992

Chapter 15

1. Greene, ibid. pp. 294-96 also, some recent articles describe what is called MOND. or modified Newtonian dynamics, for example, Sanders and McGough, Annual Review of Astronomy and Astrophysics 2002.

2. Robert Wesson, "Beyond Natural Selection"

3. These words of Darwin were quoted in a Scientific American article, "Science and Religion in America"

Chapter 16

1. Denton, "Evolution—a Theory in Crisis."

2.. E.O. Wilson, "Consilience."

Chapter 17

1. One source among many is www.Themimicoctopus.com. This creature is unique in being able to change shape as well as color, allowing it not merely to blend into a background but also resemble other marine animals like flounders and sea snakes. But by virtue of their color (despite being colorblind themselves) and pattern changing abilities cephalopods in general—squids, cuttlefish and octopi—are called the camouflage champions of the animal kingdom. NY Times, 2/19/2008, D1, 4.

2. Sagan, ibid. and Dennet, ibid.

Chapter 19

1. Watson, ibid. p.136 from Pugh, G.E. "The Biological Origin of Human Values."

Chapter 20

1. This famous remark originated from physicist Steven Weinberg.

2. "The heavens wearing out like a garment" is a paraphrase of some verses from the Bible, including Isaiah 51:6 and Hebrews 1, 10-12, as also referenced by notes 74 and 87. Clearly, these ancient authors were broadly cognizant of the concept of entropy as an ironclad law of the physical universe.

3. Bhagavad Gita, chapter 9 verse 10, as quoted in "The Biology of Freedom" by Krishna Chaitanya (a.k.a. K.K. Nair), an Indian intellectual whose broad resume extended also to art and literature. "The Biology of Freedom" and its companion works, "The Physics and Chemistry of Freedom " and "The Psychology

of Freedom" make a strong and well supported case connecting science and spirit but are virtually impossible to obtain in the United States and are now out of print in their homeland of India as well.

Chapter 21

1. Description of the avian lung can be found in Denton, ibid. or in Grzimek, ibid. An Internet article claims that the airflow is unidirectional, in other words exhaled breath does not return through the lungs.

2. This term was gleaned in a bookstore from a dictionary of biology that is not widely available, cannot be relocated and whose exact title and publisher escape my recollection. Nonetheless, the "parabronchi" do exist.

3. Ernst Mayr, "What Evolution Is" p.68. His reasons for why the dinosaur-bird connection is not plausible are: 1. Those dinosaurs most strongly similar to birds are very recent (80-110 million years ago) whereas Archaeopteryx, the earliest avian fossil, dates back further, to 145 MY. Moreover, those dinosaurs of the early Jurassic and late Triassic, before the first known birds, are not good avian ancestor candidates either. 2. The three digits of the hand of dinosaurs are 1,2,3 whereas those of birds are 2,3,4 (what this means is not explained) which makes it impossible for the avian digits to have evolved from those of dinosaurs. 3. The teeth of theropods are recurved, flattened and serrated while those of early birds like Archaeopteryx are simple, peg-like, waisted, and non-serrated. 4. The pectoral girdle and anterior extremities of late theropod dinosaurs are much too small and weak to have served as the foundation of a powerful wing. No factors known could have caused the sudden growth of the anterior extremities

in dinosaurs need for them to evolve into birds. 5. Leading aerodynamic experts claim that origin of flight from the ground up is nearly impossible.

4. Watson, ibid. p. 167 The account presented by Watson differs from what is shown on Internet videos because the latter are from the American Southwest whereas LIFETIDE apparently refers to the Caribbean Pepsis Marginata. Thus many details are unclear such as, for example, whether each species of Pepsis, or of other genera, must and will always choose its own particular species of prey.

5. Attributed to T.S. Eliot, whose own take on reality is presented in "The Wasteland."

6. David Deutsch in "The Fabric of Reality" says that patterns produced in the double-slit experiment are caused by the interference of photons in a parallel universe(s).

Chapter 23

1. NY Times Science Times, 1/10/2006.

Chapter 24

1. Attributed to the late astronomer Sir James Jeans.

2.. New York Times, January 1st 2006, Olivia Judson, "Why I'm Happy I Evolved" and numerous other sources. When Elysia eats algae, it extracts the chloroplasts that plants and algae use to make energy from sunlight and shifts them into special cells beneath the skin where they continue to function and thus provide the sea slug with the ability, unique in the animal kingdom, to live on solar energy

3.. Behe, ibid.

4.. This expression was coined by eco-feminist Charlene Spretnak (as heard on KPFK radio, Los Angeles)

5.. NY Times, 1/1/2006, by Olivia Judson.

Chapter 25

1. From philosopher Matthew van Orman Quine.

2. Shakespeare, Sonnets.

3. Watson, ibid. p.132 citing Marshall, A.J., "Bowerbirds, their displays and breeding cycles." Oxford University press, 1954.

4. Bertrand Russell.

Chapter 26

1. This quote is recalled by the author as having appeared in an essay by former editor of Nature magazine John Maddox in the NY Times "Science Times."

2. Thich Nhat Hahn, "Living Buddha, Living Christ."

3. Greene, "Fabric of the Cosmos" pp.456-8 describes the concept of parallel universes whose number could be infinite although, string theory could "one day explain the fundamental particle properties and…why the universe is the way it is" which would still leave the question as to how "space and time…emerge from the more fundamental entities…that current research is still striving to comprehend." (ibid. pp.374-5)

4. Greene, ibid. or perhaps his "Elegant Universe" since the source of this quote has been lost and could not be retrieved by using the index. Also Randall, "Warped Passages" p. 297 "There

are now many possible models that can arise in string theory... (and) none of them look quite right." And, "what we have is no more than a long list of examples of solutions to the theory. What we do not yet have is the theory they are solutions of." Lee Smolin, "Three Roads to Quantum Gravity," p.150

5. Martin Rees, "Our Cosmic Habitat" pp. 44-45.

Chapter 27

1. "Viruses have under natural conditions transferred genes between species that are only remotely related" from Nature 252 and Watson, ibid. p. 68 as cited in note 16. Also, Watson, ibid. p. 69 quoting from Thomas, "Lives of a cell" who speaks of "the dancing matrix" of viruses "transplanting grafts of DNA" and "passing around heredity as though at a party."

2. For example, "many fish display a wide range of surprisingly sophisticated social behaviors, pursuing interpersonal, interfishal relationships that seem almost embarrassingly familiar" and "have some of the most complex social systems known" NY Times, pp. D1, D6, 2/19/08

3. Bhagavad Gita, or more likely the Upanishads (Mascaro trans. Penguin edition)—either way, the meaning is clear and yet complex, because for the knower to fully know himself or herself would create a self-referential tautology with endlessly debatable psychological and philosophical implications. If the nature of human consciousness is ultimately self-awareness, that very definition is as precise as it gets—knowing oneself is knowing oneself. "A rose is a rose is a rose."

Chapter 29

1. Greene, ibid. pp. 171-176 "The big bang started the universe off in a state of low entropy, and that state is the source of the order we currently see." (p.171)

2.. Greene, ibid. p.351. "If ultramicroscopic spacetime has a grid structure, there would be no such thing as a distance shorter than the Planck length (10^{-33} cm.) "or a duration shorter than the Planck time" (10^{-43} sec.). However, "on extremely small scales" (space and time) "may gradually morph into other, more fundamental concepts."

Chapter 30

1. Adolph Portmann, "New Paths in Biology" See p. 153, fig. 30--captioned

"An examination of the head feathers of the African Crowned Crane (Balearica pavonina) gives us some idea of the number of genetic factors that have to combine in the germ to coordinate the final 'appearance.'"...etc.

2. Bhagavad Gita, chapter 9 verse 10. Also, BG chapter 13 verse 20: "Nature is the source of all material things: the maker, the means of making, and the thing made."

3. Martin Rees, "Our Cosmic Habitat" p. 125

Chapter 31

1. Greene, ibid. p.156, 170-71, Rees, ibid. p.76

2. Rees, ibid. p. 127

3. Tennyson, "Locksley Hall"—"...saw the Vision of the world and all the wonders that would be" including airborne commerce, aerial warfare and finally an age of global peace and harmony.

4. Robin Fox, "The Unauthorized Version."

5.. Hebrews 1, 10-12 (KJV)

Chapter 32

1. New Scientist, May 27 2006 "Smarter than the Average Bug."

Chapter 33

1. Greene, ibid. p. 173—"the ultimate source of order, of low entropy, must be the big bang itself." Or (p.174) "ever since" (the big bang) "the overall entropy of the universe has steadily been getting higher and higher" according to "the drive towards higher entropy that was initiated by the extraordinarily low entropy state with which the universe began."

Chapter 35

1. The five regular solids, the only theoretical objects with equal and identical sides, angles and edges are the four-sided tetrahedron, the six-sided cube, the eight-sided octahedron, the twelve-sided dodecahedron and the twenty-sided icosahedron. The sphere could be included as a one-sided figure with uniform curvature instead of equal angles.

Chapter 36

1. One account of a difference that emerges in comparing electromagnetic and strictly magnetic (or electrostatic) force can be found in "Three Roads to Quantum Gravity" by Lee Smolin, pp. 108-110. "If you pass a magnetic field through a superconductor, the magnetic field breaks up into discrete field lines, each of which carries a fundamental unit of magnetic flux" (the amount of which) "passing through a superconductor is always an integer multiple of this fundamental unit. This... curious phenomenon...is unlike the discreteness of the electric charge, or of matter, in that it has to do with a field that carries a force."

Chapter 37

1. Portmann, ibid. p.84
2. Portmann, ibid. p.85
3. Portmann, ibid. p. 85
4. Portmann, ibid. p. 85
5. Portmann, ibid. p. 85
6. Portmann, ibid. p.86
7. Portmann, ibid. p.86

Chapter 38

1. A comprehensive explanation can be found in "Life Itself" by Boyce Rensberger—"the repair enzyme travels along the newly made double helix within minutes of DNA synthesis and looks for errors—places where the opposing nucleotides are not

complimentary. Then it essentially takes out the bad nucleotide and puts in one that correctly complements the original strand.." (p.126)

2. A description of this bird appeared in Atlantis Rising magazine, #77, September/October 2009

3. "Crickets Warn Young Before Birth of Dangers of Wolf Spiders," N.Y. Times, 2/23/2010, p. D3.

4. Similar in meaning to the Biblical quotation referenced by note 5, chapter 31, these words are a paraphrase of Isaiah 51.6 (KJV)

Chapter 39

1. Grzimek, "Encyclopedia of Animal Life." Another source would be Michael Denton's "Evolution—a Theory in Crisis" which claims, erroneously, that the unique avian lung casts doubt upon evolutionary theory although the only valid question raised is whether birds could have arisen from an ancestral lineage with lungs similar to those occurring in reptiles, mammals and perhaps dinosaurs. The latter, however—or instead some other avian ancestor that outwardly resembled a small dinosaur but was actually very different—could have had the same "through-put" lung (as Denton calls it) as found in birds.

2. Denton, ibid.

3. E.O. Wilson and Holdobler, "Journey to the Ants."

Chapter 40

1. One explanation is found in "Infinity and the Mind" by Rudy Rucker, pp.221-265 "The Transfinite Cardinals.".

2. NY Times, 8/15/2006. "To metastasize, a cell must break cellular bonds to dislodge itself, break down the mortar of connective tissue, and sprout 'legs' to pull it through the densely packed tissue" after which it faces assorted dangers in its journey through the bloodstream to a new location.

Chapter 41

1. William Blake, "Songs of Innocence."

Chapter 42

1. David Foster Wallace, "Everything and More," p. 5

2 Wallace, ibid., p.10-11. Cantor's theories are presented by Wallace in this work, an alternative reference on the subject to Rucker's "Infinity" book.

Chapter 43

1. Portmann, ibid. pp.109-119

2. G.R. Taylor, "The Great Evolution Mystery." The same phrase could apply to many other scientific theories like the "big bang" which are still works in progress.

3. Darwin identified the two pillars of evolution as variation and selection, which are equivalent to a pair of incontrovertible principles that must be true of any universe—firstly, that "things change" and second, that whatever changes take place are unlikely to head back to square one and undo whatever progress has occurred, not only because they are constantly being sorted by natural selection to preserve maximum economy of the organism or system, but because any such reversal would be contradictory

to the fact of progress having already proceeded to whatever existential point that evolution had already achieved, whether algae, iguanas or actors.

4. Dennett, "Breaking the Spell." The author may have reason in perceiving religious ritual as often nothing more than superstition (even Jesus said "pray not as the heathen do" with many repetitions), but phenomena as far from comprehension as the lancet fluke have no less bearing on our understanding of Nature or lack thereof, and worldviews based thereupon, than $e=mc^2$.

Chapter 44

1. Thomas a Kempis, "The Imitation of Christ."

Chapter 45

1. Watson, "Lifetide" p.132 from Gilliard, E.T. "The Evolution of Bowerbirds," Scientific American 209; 38-46, 1963.

2. Lifetide, p.135 from Crow, L.T. et al, Cell 12; 1-8, 1977.

3. The title of a book by Teilhard de Chardin, suggesting that the spiritual element cannot be separated from Nature but is interwoven with all that is.

Chapter 46

1. Holy Bible, KJV, Genesis.

2. Portmann, ibid. p.129

3. St. Paul, Epistles

4. Lisa Randall, "Warped Passages."

Chapter 48

1. Taylor, ibid. One could ask how any verbal explanation of a system or process incalculably more complex than those described in physics could be any less approximate or more logically rigorous.

2. Carl Sagan, "Shadows of Forgotten Ancestors."

3. Grzimek, "Encyclopedia of Animal Life."

4. Grzimek, ibid.

5. Dylan Thomas

6. Bertrand Russell. It is, of course, those awful powers within the Earth whose relative dormancy currently allows our species a degree of freedom that could be sharply curtailed were those powers to bestir themselves with equal violence as happened long ago..

7. Thich Nhat Hahn, "Living Buddha, Living Christ."

8. Watson, ibid. pp. 55-56 from Baltensweller, W., "Zeirapheira griseana in the European Alps…" Canadian Entomologist 96: 792-800.

Chapter 49

1 Watson, ibid. p.174 from Poulton, E.B. "The terrifying appearance of Laternaria…" Proceedings of the Royal Entomological Society of London 43: 43, 1924.

2. Carl Sagan, "The Demon Haunted World."

3.. Washington Post, November 12 2001 p. A9, "Mammoth Extinction Mystery Draws 3 Theories." 70 species had disappeared from North America by about 10,000 years ago including large mammals such as mammoths, mastodons, horses and camels, cow-sized ground sloths, giant beavers, American lions, cheetahs, sabertooth tigers and enormous bears. The theories mentioned are: hunting, climate change, or a pathogen perhaps introduced by newly arriving humans, their pets, or hitch-hiking insects.

4. 17th century philosopher Thomas Hobbes, "Leviathan," on origins of the social contract as an important step in human progress from competition towards cooperation.

Chapter 50

1. "Survival of the Selfless" by D.S. Wilson and E.O. Wilson, New Scientist Nov. 3-9 2007.

2. Portmann, ibid. p.148

3. Portmann, ibid. p. 147

4. Portmann, ibid. p.145

5. Title of a book by the late physicist Heinz Pagels.

6. Greene, ibid. p.18, 366ff. The actual words quoted must be, however, from Greene's "The Elegant Universe."

Chapter 51

1. Further account of Cantor's theory can also be found in Bell, "Men of Mathematics" pp. 555-79.

2. Words of the pre-Christian philosopher Heraclitus, as quoted by J. Singer in "Boundaries of the Soul."

Chapter 53

1. Watson, ibid. pp.171-73, Alvarez, F., et al, "Experimental brood parasitism of the magpie," Animal Behavior 24, 907-916, 1976.

Chapter 54

1. Acanthostega, whose fossils were first found in Greenland, dates back to 300MYr ago and is the most primitive tetrapod known. Its four limbs evolved underwater rather than on land (Discover magazine, June 1995, Britannia online and other sources)

2. A video of the mimic octopus in action can be seen on "You tube" and print sources include Smithsonian magazine. Clearly, its advance in camouflage technique from simply matching the color and pattern of a stable background as accomplished by other cephalopods, to that of imitating the form and appearance of other marine animals, represents a quantum leap having no obvious explanation.

3 John 1:1, New Testament KJV

Chapter 55

1. The original phrase as found in Chaucer's "The pardoner's tale" is, "ther cam a privee theef men clepeth Deeth, that in this countree al the peple sleeth." This tale may derive from an Italian version in the Decameron of Boccaccio.

Chapter 56

1 Loren Eiseley, "The Star Thrower" p.120

2.. Eiseley, ibid. p.121

3...Michael Behe, "Darwin's Black Box."

4. NY Times 10/10 2006.

Chapter 57

1. The title of a book by Greg Zukav. Wu Li means "patterns of organic energy."

2. Bhagavad Gita.

Chapter 58

1. From Loren Eiseley, "the Immense Journey."

2. Krishna Chaitanya (aka K.K. Nair) "The Biology of Freedom" p.163 citing Arthur Koestler, The Ghost in the Machine, Hutchinson, 1967, pp.128-9.

3. Chaitanya, ibid. p. 163 (The account of the evolutionary problem involving the amphibian-reptile transition that accompanies these quotes from Chaitanya does not appear in his book, but derives from memory of an article that appeared many years ago in an obscure Catholic magazine called "Fidelity."

4. Chaitanya, ibid. p. 251, from E.S. Russell, The Directiveness of Organic Activities, Cambridge University Press, 1945, p.44

5. Chaitanya, ibid. p. 251, from Selye, Textbook of Endocrinology, Montreal, 1947, p. 24

Chapter 59

1. Watson, ibid. p. 97

2. Watson, ibid. p. 97. From Hartman, W.D. & Reisweg, H.M., "The individuality of sponges" in Boardman et al. (62).

3. Watson, ibid. p. 97-98. From Josephson, R.K.& Mackie, G.O. "Multiple pacemakers and the behavior of the hydroid Tubularia," Journal of Experimental Biology 43: 293-332, 1965.

4. Watson, ibid. p. 98. Mackie, G.O. "Analysis of locomotion in a siphonophore colony," Proceedings of the Royal Society B 159: 366-391, 1964.

5. William Blake, "Songs of Innocence."

6. Watson, ibid. p. 114. Holldobler, B. "Communication between ants and their guests," Scientific American 224: 86-93, 1971.

7. The Bible, Genesis 2:19

Chapter 60

1. Fang Li Zhi and Xie Xian, "Creation of the Universe."

2.. Watson, ibid. p.166 quotes from Darwin's Origin of Species. "We cannot see how an instinct could possibly have originated" and "in which no intermediate gradations are known to exist," while neglecting to mention that Darwin did attempt to deal with what he saw as a challenge to his theory though perhaps only in part, since as at least a "formal cause" natural selection cannot be disputed. Yet the puzzle of hereditary instinct in wasps like the tarantula hawk was raised by French entomologist Jean Henri Fabre in "The Hunting Wasps" (Dodd, Mead, 1915) as noted by Loren Eiseley in "Coming of the Giant Wasps," chapter 23 in his autobiography, adding that the whole issue was soon interred in the dusty file of inconvenient scientific truths. Eiseley concludes by saying "I know these creatures have been shaped in the cellars of time. It is the method that troubles me." (quoted in Lifetide p.169).

3. New Scientist, 5/27-6/2 '06 pp. 37-39

4. Watson, ibid. p.132

5. ibid. p. 132

6. ibid. p. 132. Gilliard, E.T. "The evolution of bowerbirds," Scientific American 209:38-46, 1963.

Chapter 61

1. Greene, ibid. p. 471.

2. .These two terms appear, respectively, in John Barrow's "Theories of Everything" and Daniel Dennett's "Consciousness Explained."

3. Greene, ibid. p. 477

Chapter 62

1. Bhagavad Gita, chap.15 v. 7

2. Watson, ibid. p. 187 Renard, J. The journal of Jules Renard, (1906) New York: Braziller, 1964.

3. From a poem by Emily Dickinson

Chapter 63

1. NY Times, 7/26/2000. The Orb spider, so-called because of its perfectly round web—a delicate structure typically rebuilt for each new day—is victimized by a wasp that first paralyzes it and then lays an egg on the arachnid's body on a spot from where it

cannot be dislodged. The spider then recovers and lives normally for two weeks, while the larva feeds on its juices and develops. But then, the larva somehow induces the spider to build a stronger, more permanent web consisting of two stout cables and cross braces between them, to serve as a secure platform above the ground for the larva's cocoon in which its development will be completed. The larva then kills the spider to ensure a tranquil metamorphosis into adulthood. Clearly, the question is not only how, or by what presumably chemical means the spider's web-building routine is reprogrammed, and how that chemical might convey its intended message more consistently than any human prescription drug, but also how evolution could have arrived at such a complicated interrelationship.

2. As discussed by Loren Eiseley in "The Ghostly Guardian," an essay from "The Star Thrower." Besides monkeys, of which the spider monkey has the most versatile tail, other Amazon animals with prehensile tails include a porcupine and a pygmy anteater. Only one of six genera of South American monkeys "lacks a grasping tail." Meanwhile, no African monkey has this feature, and of other "African animals only an obscure lizard and a peculiar scaled anteater, the pangolin" are endowed with prehensile tails.

3. Greene, ibid. pp.471-85

4 Among the many sources listed on the Internet, could be cited "Bugs Fighting Back" (http://www.chemheritage.org/educationalservices/pharm/antibiot/readings/resist.htm)

"Bacterial resistance to antibiotics can be acquired" in four ways, including "3. Plasmid exchange: antibiotic resistance can be coded for in the DNA found in a small circle known as a plasmid in a bacterium. The plasmids can randomly pass between bacteria (usually touching)." A photograph which cannot be located but may have appeared in a popular science article in the mid 1990's showed the transfer occurring in what seems a deliberate manner, through a tube of protoplasm extending from the donor to recipient. This suggests not only a purposeful behavior, but also the heretical bogeyman of adaptive rather than random mutation, since there would seem little reason for exchanging a plasmid of what was most likely to be meaningless or not immediately useful genetic information had the mutation occurred randomly and then been randomly selected for transfer. However, the fourth method of acquiring resistance mentioned is about the same—"4. Sharing of mutations, some of which confer resistance to antibiotics. Two examples are: Plasmid transfer between different kinds of bacteria" both similar and very dissimilar species. Or, "gene cassettes…can be added to a bacterium's chromosomes… that give the bacterium resistance to a variety of antibiotics… (and) "against disinfectants and pollutants."

5. Watson, ibid. p. 86. Bonner, J.T."How slime molds communicate," Scientific American 209: 84-93, 1963.

Chapter 64

1 Bible, Proverbs 16:4 (KJV). The sense of other translations may be somewhat different, i.e. "God works out all things toward their proper end, even the day of disaster for the wicked" (NIV) etc..

2. Carl Sagan, recalled as appearing in either his "The Demon-Haunted World" or "Shadows of Forgotten Ancestors."

3. "The Book of Certainty," Abu Bakr Siraj ed-Din (the Islamic name of Martin Lings, a former curator of the British Museum) a volume that deals with Islamic mysticism.

4. Randall, ibid. p.42, 451-2

5. Watson, ibid p. 229 (sourced from Dawkins, "The Selfish Gene").

6. NY Times, 12/1/2009 p. D3

7. NY Times, 12/1/2009 p.D3

Chapter 65

1 As a final note on this subject, it bears repeating that if the transfer of genes for antibiotic resistance between different species of bacteria is in any way a deliberate act (even if perhaps not more so than that of a sleepwalker unconsciously gorging on ice cream) then the gene packet being transferred would be likely to represent an equally non-random mutation, an event that some scientists believe can and does occur. An article by Galitski and Roth in Science magazine, April 21 1995, concludes: "Organisms sense their environment and make directed changes in many aspects of their metabolism. It would seem to be advantageous to direct mutability. We expect that organisms have exploited this possibility." An additional reference appears in "Alien Nation," NYT April 1st 2003. "One or two strains" of drug resistant staphylococcus "had virtually certainly gained resistance genes from an enterococcus," a normally benign intestinal bacterium that can become dangerous. Apparent cooperative behavior among the bacterial community in our bodies is referred to in the article saying that "cross talk between bacteria may be elucidated in further genomic studies."

66. Coda

1. Fred Alan Wolf, "The Eagle's Quest" p. 286

2. Greene, ibid. p. 477

67. Conclusion

1. NY Times, Science Times p.3, Jan. 26, 2010

2. Katha Upanishad, The Upanishads, translated by Juan Mascaro, p.62.

Bibliography

One of the key sources for this book was "The Biology of Freedom" by Krishna Chaitanya (pen name of K.K. Nair, a well-known scholar and critic in the field of humanities with a degree in biology as well), the middle volume of a series that includes "The Physics and Chemistry of Freedom" and "The Psychology of Freedom." It was published by Somaiya Publications Pvt. Ltd. of Bombay and New Delhi, and was printed in India and copyrighted 1975. This book would be very difficult to obtain in the U.S. but contains hundreds of references from the archives of biological research

Another important source was LIFETIDE by Lyall Watson, ISBN 0-553-13470-1, originally published by Simon and Schuster in 1979 and reprinted in a Bantam edition. Watson's book also contains hundreds of references gleaned from the scientific literature as part of a scholarly effort that like Chaitanya's work may now be difficult to obtain since both of these books are now out of print and the significance of the story they tell therefore in peril of a fate similar to what befell the ancient library of Alexandria, burned to the ground by ignorant invading armies.

A third source was "New Paths in Biology" by Adolph Portmann, a Swiss biology professor. Further details concerning its publication may be obtained from the Internet, but are missing from the text that was used, made from an original of which, again, few copies may exist in the United States or anywhere else. Portmann's examples, however, are different from those described by Watson and Chaitanya (whose respective sets of facts, in turn, entirely differ from each other)

Finally, one source cited by Portmann is still in print—"Darwin's Century." by Loren Eiseley, who also presents some further evolutionary riddles in "All the Strange Hours" and "The Star Thrower" with similar wonderment at biological mysteries as that more commonly addressed towards deep unknowns of physics and astronomy. Yet because Life's inexplicata cannot be totally ignored, the list of them keeps growing, along with the size of the "leviathan" that most have not as yet fully considered in terms of what the story first uncovered and explored by Darwin could actually mean.

Part of the purpose of "Power in the Blood" is to revive and recharge that story by reframing the kind of data that Watson, Portmann, Eiseley and Chaitanya's works describe, and that keep surfacing in the media, in a broader context of associations that are pertinent to more open-ended understanding of Nature and human nature with reference not to science alone but also philosophy and faith.